Routledge Revivals

Development and Social Change in the Pacific Islands

First published in 1989. The Pacific Islands are amongst the poorest countries of the developing world. The special problems of their small size, immense distance from major centres and, for many, very poor agricultural possibilities make development extremely difficult. However, recent new advances in maritime technology in a wide range of different areas present substantial new opportunities. This book surveys the new developments — including extended maritime boundaries; giant clam farming; increased exploitation of ocean minerals and new fisheries techniques — and demonstrates the potential for far-reaching economic and social development.

Routledge Revivals

Development and Social Change in the Pacific Islands

First published in 1989. The Pacific Islands are amongst the poorest countries of the developing world. The special problems of their small size, immense distance from major centres and, for many, very poor agricultural possibilities make development extremely difficult. However, recent new advances in maritime technology in a wide range of different areas present substantial new opportunities. This book surveys the new developments — including extended maritime boundaries; giant clam farming; increased exploitation of ocean minerals and new fisheries techniques — and demonstrates the potential for far-reaching economic and social development.

Development and Social Change in the Pacific Islands

Edited by
A.D. Couper

Routledge
Taylor & Francis Group
Routledge Revivals

First published in 1989
by Routledge

This edition first published in 2017 by Routledge
2 Park Square, Milton Park, Abingdon, Oxon, OX14 4RN
and by Routledge
711 Third Avenue, New York, NY 10017

Routledge is an imprint of the Taylor & Francis Group, an informa business

A Library of Congress record exists under LC control number: 8826494

ISBN 13: 978-1-138-24510-5 (hbk)
ISBN 13: 978-1-315-27639-7 (ebk)

DEVELOPMENT AND SOCIAL CHANGE IN THE PACIFIC ISLANDS

Edited by
A.D. COUPER

ROUTLEDGE
London and New York

First published 1989
by Routledge
11 New Fetter Lane, London EC4P 4EE
29 West 35th Street, New York, NY 10001

Printed and bound in Great Britain by
Biddles Ltd, Guildford and King's Lynn

British Library Cataloguing in Publication Data

Development and social change in the Pacific
islands. — (Ocean management and policy
series).
1. Pacific islands. Economic development.
Role of marine industries
I. Title II. Series
330.99

ISBN 0-415-00917-0

Library of Congress Cataloging in Publication Data

Development and social change in the Pacific islands / edited by A.D.
Couper.
p. cm. — (Ocean management and policy series)
Bibliography: p.
Includes index.
ISBN 0-415-00917-0
1. Fish trade—Government policy—Oceania. 2. Fisheries—Government policy—Oceania. 3. Fisheries—Oceania. 4. Fishery technology—Oceania. I. Couper, A.D. II. Series.
HD9468.032D48 1989
338.3'727099—dc19 88-26494
CIP

CONTENTS

		Page No
List of Figures		
List of Tables		
Acknowledgements		
A D Couper	Introduction	1
V Prescott	Maritime boundaries in the Southwest Pacific region	4
A D Couper	Fishery developments and social change in the Pacific	22
W M Sutherland	Policy, law and management in Pacific island fisheries	33
M King I Cartwright A Carver	Fisheries development in Pacific islands: some problems in paradise	47
P Alexander	Lessons for the Pacific technology transfer and fishing communities: the Sri Lankan experience	63
C Tisdell	Giant clams in the Pacific - the socio-economic potential of a developing technology for their mariculture	74
C Ifeka	Women in fisheries. Why women count: Prospects for self-reliant fisheries development in the South Pacific compared to the Indian Ocean	89

C A Matos J Kotobalavu	Ocean minerals - Prospects for Pacific island nations	115
M Ellis	Ocean energy developments - Prospects for Pacific island nations	127
A D Couper	Changes in port and shipping technology in the Pacific and their social impact	145
P McDonnell	Trade and shipping needs for island economies	153
N T Riley	Aid for maritime developments in the Pacific	160
H W Dick	Alternative technology - Small commercial sailing vessels. A lost cause?	168
D M Waters	Improved education and training for new marine technology and social change in the Pacific island nations	179
Bibliography		188
Index		197

LIST OF FIGURES

Figure No			Page No
1		Maritime boundaries in S.W. Pacific region	6
2		Events leading to a requirement for an increase in seafood productivity and alternatives available for achieving this increase	48
3	A	A traditional fish hook from Palau (from Johannes, 1981)	
	B	A similar modern circle hook (Mustad 39960ST), and	
	C	A pearl-shell tuna lure with an aluminium hook (made from downed World-War II aircraft and a synthetic fibre tail (from Carver, 1981).	50
4		A simple wooden handreel used in deep-water snapper fishing projects in Pacific islands	57
5		Generalised distribution of *Hippopus hippopus*, *Tridacna gigas* and *T. derasa* in historic times after Rosewater (1965) and Munro and Heslinga (1982).	76
6		Traditional method of 'smoking'; Butaritari Island	100
7		Smoke house, South Tarawa	103
8		Design for small-scale brick-frame solar drier	104
9		Design for small-scale polythene tent solar drier	105

LIST OF TABLES

Table No		Page No
1	Marine power dissipation rates	128
2	Decline in port labour at Suva	147
3	Levels of fundamental knowledge required	185

ACKNOWLEDGMENTS

The Editor of this volume is grateful to the contributors and participants of the Workshop conducted at the Research School of Pacific Studies in 1986. For the support of the Workshop he thanks Professor R Gerard Ward, Director, Research School of Pacific Studies, Australian National University, Canberra: Professor H C Brookfield, Head of Department of Human Geography, Research School of Pacific Studies; and Dr Chris Kissling of that Department. The Editor expresses appreciation to the Australian Development Aid Bureau which helped finance the Workshop and personally to the Nuffield Foundation which provided the travel grant for his own fieldwork in the Pacific region, and to the Australian National Univesity for providing a visiting fellowship in Canberra. He is particularly grateful to Joyce Suthers for preparing the manuscript for publication.

A D Couper
World Maritime University
Malmo
Sweden

1988

INTRODUCTION

A D Couper

The papers in this volume were read and discussed at a Workshop held by the Department of Human Geography, Research School of Pacific Studies, Australian National University, Canberra. The Workshop was inter-disciplinary, the main objective was to share research findings and views on the development and social impact of new marine technology on Pacific island communities.

All of the Pacific island states to the east of Papua New Guinea are small by world standards. Their populations (mid 1980s) vary from about 702,000 in the bigger Fiji Group, which has a growth rate of 2 per cent; to 97,000 in Tonga with 1.3 per cent growth; 63,800 in Kiribati with 1.6 per cent growth, and 8,300 in Tuvalu, one of the smallest states in the world but with 3 per cent population growth. Almost half of the populations of these, and the other developing island states in the Southwest Pacific, are under the age of fifteen. There are now few opportunities for migration, consequently the development of island resources for the future is of vital concern to all the governments.

The agricultural resource potential as a basis for future development is limited to a few 'high' islands. This is true also of on-shore mineral prospects which are confined to some of the islands south of the Equator, west of 180°. On most of the atolls and reef islands, which are spread widely over the Southwest Pacific, there are few development opportunities in these respects. There is no surface water on the low coral islands, soils are poor and these islands are particularly vulnerable to droughts, hurricanes and tsunamis. They lie at great distances from sources of consumer goods and markets. Consequently when unsubsidised the freight bills borne by the people are, comparatively, amongst the highest in the world.

Sources of income beyond the island economies have included remittances from labourers working away in mining and plantation employment - the phosphate sector of which has virtually ended. Remittances from relatives overseas remain important; but with fewer migration opportunities and possible erosion of family contacts in the course of time this source of income will decline. Income from seamen employed on foreign flag ships is still a source with some potential, although this is under pressure due to fleet decline in countries which have employed islanders in the past.

Over many decades attempts have been made through various aid projects to improve island transport, and alleviate the contact problem of the smaller remoter islands, including research into sail technology.

More recently the entitlements by island states to vast areas of sea and seabed, and the new developments in extractive marine technology, have focused the attention of aid donors and island governments on the marine resource opportunities. Many of the small island states have EEZs and other national designated zones of the sea which are vastly greater than those of most of the developed industrial countries. The possibilities of utilisation of these zones include increasing food supplies by artisanal fishing, commercial fishing, recreational fishing, aquaculture, mariculture, chemical, mineral and energy extraction, the licensing of foreign states for commercial fishing, new port developments, ship repairs, processing and marketing.

Some of the postulated uses of national sea areas are possible and are discussed in several of the papers in this volume. Such development schemes are essential, although some projects pose problems for small societies which wish to retain valued social and cultural mores which have many important functions. Some development projects also generate conflicts between men and women, accumulation and distribution of income, urban and rural societies, and subsistence and artisanal fishing sectors. Sometimes aid projects actually impoverish people engaged in small scale traditional activities, lead to a rapid depletion of resources, deterioration of environment, and consequent deeper economic and social problems for specific regions in the course of time.

Introduction

The papers in this volume consider some of the economic and social opportunities and problems which the new marine technology and extended maritime/national jurisdiction present to the island societies in the Southwest Pacific, and several comparisons are made with other regions. The papers were produced with the awareness that the new maritime geography of the Pacific imposes planning, management and educational tasks on Pacific Island governments of considerable complexity, which require clear objectives with respect to existing patterns of sea uses, ways of life, and the future economic and social costs and benefits on coastal communities.

Chapter One

MARITIME BOUNDARIES IN THE SOUTHWEST PACIFIC REGION

Victor Prescott

PHYSICAL BOUNDARIES

Broadly speaking, the Southwest Pacific region proper can be said to extend in the north from around the equator (but in the case of this paper 30°N) to around 55°S, close to the limit of the operation of the Antarctic Treaty where an array of special considerations apply. The eastern coastline of Australia to around 140°E sets the western limit. The eastern limit of the region is set at 120°W, hence excluding considerations involving the north, central and south Americas.

Based on the configuration of the seabed, the Southwest Pacific may be divided into three zones. First, in the west lie the continental masses of Australia and Papua New Guinea, linked by a common continental shelf overlain by shallow seas.

Second, between this continental shelf and the Kermadec - Tonga Trench, in the vicinity of 175°W, there is a complex zone comprised of a series of ridges radiating from New Zealand. Southwards there is the Macquarie - Balleny Ridge, linking New Zealand and Antarctica. Northwards there are three ridges. The Lord Howe Rise passes through the island of that name and continues into the Coral Sea and towards the tip of Papua New Guinea. The Norfolk Island Ridge links New Zealand with New Caledonia and the Solomon Islands. Finally, the Kermadec Ridge trends due north, passing through Tonga and Fiji, and further north to Wallis and Futuna and Tuvalu. Its fragmented continuation can be discerned in the alignment of the islands of Kiribati. Between these ridges and sometimes enclosed by them lies a series of deeper troughs and basins of which the largest is the South Fiji basin.

A third zone lies east of the Kermadec-Tonga Trench. It consists of isolated islands rising steeply from the seabed until, in eastern French Polynesia, spurs associated with the East Pacific Ridge are encountered, such as the Tuamotu Ridge which lies northwest of Pitcairn Island.

It is a striking feature that the size of islands generally declines eastwards through the region. Hence the continental extent of Australia and the major island of New Guinea are succeeded eastwards by New Caledonia, the Solomon Islands and then Fiji, and finally the tiny atolls of most of French Polynesia.

MARITIME POLITICAL BOUNDARIES (Figure 1)

Maritime boundaries are of economic importance to all political entities in the region in terms of exploitation of the living resources of the sea, a vital source of food and income for many of the island states, and in terms of the future potential for the exploitation of mineral resources of the seabed.

Apart from the narrow waters separating Australia and Papua New Guinea in Torres Strait, and Papua New Guinea and the Solomon Islands south of Bougainville Island, all territories can draw the outer limits of their territorial seas without reference to other countries.

Only American Samoa and Western Samoa are unable to draw any segment of the outer boundary of their fishing or exclusive economic zones without reference to any neighbour. The extent to which states and territories can fix the outer edge of their 200 nautical miles zone without reference to other countries varies widely. At one end of the scale there is Wallis and Futuna from which only a very short segment of boundary can be drawn without reference to the neighbours of Western Samoa, Tokelau, Tuvalu, Fiji and Tonga. At the other end of the scale lies New Zealand, which is only prevented from making a unilateral determination of the outer boundary of its exclusive economic zone in two short segments which adjoin the detached Australian territories of Norfolk and Macquarie Islands.

The final type of unilateral boundary concerns the outer edge of the continental margin, where the continental shelf margin is wider than 200 nautical miles. This occurs in the southwest of the region, south of Fiji and New Caledonia, and in the vicinity of Australia and New Zealand. The main areas are the Tasman Plateau south of Tasmania, and the

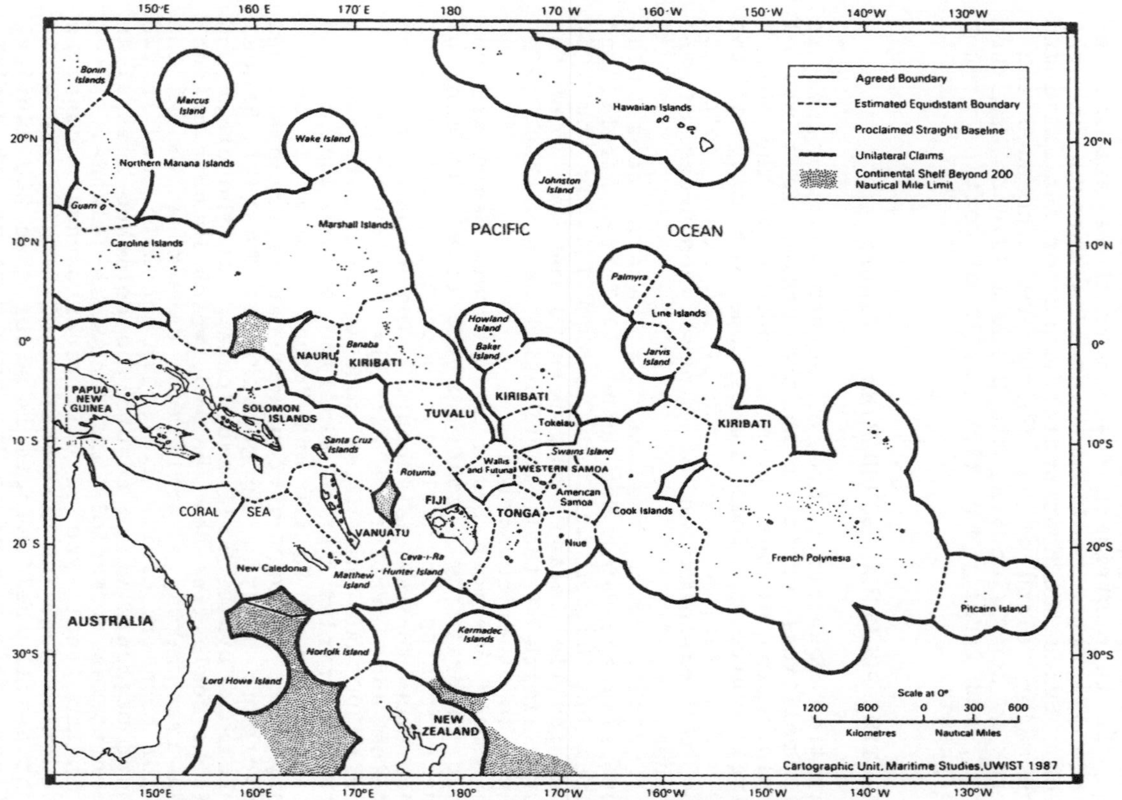

Figure 1 Maritime political boundaries

Campbell Plateau and Chatham Rise south and east of New Zealand. These areas can be claimed unilaterally by Australia and New Zealand respectively. Other wide shelves will have to be divided by bilateral negotiations, such as those which produced the division of the continental shelf between Australia and the French territory of New Caledonia.

PROCLAIMED BASELINES AND THE PARTICULAR SIGNIFICANCE OF ARCHIPELAGIC REGIMES IN THE REGION

Proclaimed baselines in the Southwest Pacific fall into three groups:

1 Those of Australia, which has proclaimed straight baselines around parts of its mainland and islands coasts.

2 Archipelagic claims of Papua New Guinea, Fiji, Vanuatu and the Solomon Islands, which are of special relevance in a region that contains the greatest number of archipelagic states and territories of any in the world.

3 Most of the remaining states and territories have made some general statement about baselines without defining exact locations.

Australia's Baselines:

These were proclaimed and came into force in February 1983 as the finale to a complex set of constitutional arrangements by which the federal authorities transferred to the States and Territories of Australia control, for specified purposes, over the territorial seas and seabed, extending at present to 3 nautical miles. As a prelude to this move, matching legislation dealing with fisheries and mining was enacted by all States and Territories. If, in the future, Australia's territorial sea is extended to 12 nautical miles, the area vested in the States and Territories will not be increased beyond the present 3 nautical miles.

The proclamation is a complex document. It does not specify legal bays enclosed by straight baselines, but states the rules by which such bays may be closed. Hence an individual navigator would need to determine whether a particular bay contained internal waters. The 'preliminary' definitions also note that the outermost parts of permanent harbour works constitute part of the coast and that low tide elevations have only been used in drawing straight baselines if they are surmounted by lighthouses or similar installations.

There are three tables to the proclamation. In the first, there are 297 segments of straight baselines outlined in respect to the mainland of Australia. These have been drawn in accordance with the 1958 Convention on the Territorial Sea and Contiguous Zone but appear to conform with the proposed rules for drawing baselines in the new Convention awaiting ratification. The second table outlines 50 baselines segments in respect to Tasmania. The third table defines straight baselines in respect to Macquarie Island and around the Furneaux and Houtman Abrolhos Groups.

Around those parts of the Australian coast not enclosed by straight baselines or closing lines across legal bays and river mouths, maritime claims are measured from the lowest astronomic tide - i.e. the lowest level to which the tides will fall in a full cycle of 18.6 years under normal atmospheric conditions.

In an additional proclamation the Australian territorial sea around islands in Torres Strait is defined by boundaries marking the outer edge of those seas. These lines were established by the Torres Strait Treaty agreed between Australia and Papua New Guinea in December 1978.

Island States Archipelagic Baselines:

Article 47 of the Convention on the Law of the Sea describes the tests which archipelagic states must satisfy in order to draw archipelagic baselines. The baselines must include the main islands; they must enclose an area of water at least as large as the area of land, but the area of water must not be larger than nine times the land area; no segment of baseline may exceed 125 nautical miles in length; not more than 3% of segments may exceed 100 nautical miles in length; and the baselines must not depart to any appreciable extent from the general configuration of the archipelago.

These tests are not equally rigorous. The term 'main islands' could be interpreted to mean the largest islands, the most populous islands, the islands which generate the most revenue, or the islands which occupy a primary place in the history and culture of the country. Perhaps the only consistent expectation would be that the island with the country's capital would be included.

The rule that only 3% of the segments may exceed 100 nautical miles in length can always be satisfied by simply increasing the number of segments. The requirement that the baselines must conform to the general configuration of the archipelago will never, it seems, be a critical test, since different observers would often have distinct perceptions of the configuration of the archipelago, and, in any case, states are empowered to draw baselines around the outer edge of the outermost islands.

The rule which invokes the ratio of water to land will be easy to apply if there is no uncertainty about what is land and what is water, but the Convention introduced fringing reefs to be counted as land for the purposes of this calculation, and allowed the same discretion for waters overlying steep-sided oceanic plateaux, which are enclosed, or nearly enclosed by a peripheral chain of limestone islands and drying reefs. While the first dispensation will be easy to interpret in the case of perfect atolls such as Maupiti in the Society Islands and Ontong Java in the Solomon Islands, it will be difficult to apply in the case of broken discontinuous reefs.

There should be no problem in deciding whether any segment is less that 125 nautical miles long; it provides an objective test, capable of consistent interpretation by different commentators. But there could be some difference of opinion about the correctness of using certain features as termini of baseline segments.

At the beginning of Article 47, archipelagic states are empowered to draw baselines around the outermost islands and drying reefs. In the fourth section of the same Article, countries are instructed that baselines may only be drawn to low tide elevations which lie within the normal territorial sea, or which are surmounted by a lighthouse or similar installation. A low tide elevation is described in Article 13 as a naturally formed area of land surrounded by and above water at low tide and submerged at high tide. This description exactly fits a drying reef. Thus it is hard to resist the claim of a country which wishes to draw its baseline to a low tide elevation beyond the normal territorial sea and devoid of lighthouses or similar structures if it argues that it is a drying reef. Of course, it would be open to other countries to take the more restrictive view in the fourth section.

Aside from the question of its claim to Matthew and Hunter Islands, Vanuatu is the only territory in the region that can declare an archipelagic baseline around all its territory; such baselines were in fact proclaimed, and came into effect on 11 October 1982. The baseline system consists of twenty-one straight-line segments and two stretches of low water mark. The longest segment measures 90 nautical miles and the land to water ratio within the baselines is 1:4.7. If Vanuatu were to secure Matthew and Hunter Islands, it would be unable to tie them into the existing baselines because they are more than 125 nautical miles from the nearest island of Aneityum.

Papua New Guinea, Fiji and the Solomon Islands have all drawn more than one set of archipelagic baselines, although Fiji has not formally described the baselines around the Rotuma Group as archipelagic baselines.

Papua New Guinea, by the National Seas Act 1977 (which entered into force in March 1978), made an interim delimitation of archipelagic waters. Baselines were defined by eighty-four turning points; the longest segment measures 120 nautical miles and the ratio of land to water was 1:1.3. Two island groups called Tauu and Nukumanu were left outside the baseline system, although these were defined as archipelagos, and it was noted that their internal waters might form part of the archipelagic waters of Papua New Guinea. The baselines around these two groups are defined as continuous lines between the outermost points of islands, shoals, rocks and reefs. The Tauu Islands could be incorporated into the archipelagic system but Nukumanu is more than 125 nautical miles from the Tauu Islands, so it must remain detached.

Fiji's archipelagic baselines were contained in the Marine Spaces Act 1977. The Act excluded Rotuma Island and its dependencies and Ceva-i-Ra from the system; they are respectively located 245 nautical miles to the north and 270 nautical miles to the southwest of the main group. However, the statement by which Fiji announced that it had declared an archipelagic system contained the observation that an amendment would be introduced to allow an archipelagic regime to be established for the Rotuma Island and its dependencies.

The Marine Spaces (Amendment) Act 1978 contained the change that the phrase 'seas of the Fiji archipelago and the Rotuma archipelago' should be substituted for the phrase 'sea of the Fiji archipelago'. However, there is no evidence that an archipelagic regime has been established for Rotuma Island and its dependencies. The innermost limits of the territorial waters of Rotuma Island and its dependencies were declared by the Marine Spaces (Territorial Seas) (Rotuma and its Dependencies) Order 1981, the baselines being defined by nineteen turning points located on the outermost islands and reefs.

Fiji appears to be the only archipelagic state which has created internal waters as sanctioned by Article 50 of the Convention on the Law of the Sea. However, the definition of internal waters by reference to the outer edge of fringing reefs is not permitted by Article 50, which refers only to legal bays, river mouths and harbours. Waters within the reefs can be counted as land for the purposes of calculating the ratio, and if such waters are counted as land the ratio would not fall below 1:1.

The Solomon Islands declared archipelagic waters around five groups of islands in the Delimitation of Marine Waters Act 1978. The five groups are New Georgia, Santa Cruz, Duff, Ontong Java, and Rennell Island and the Indispensable Reefs. Each set of baselines faces problems in satisfying the tests for archipelagic baselines, and they do not secure the largest possible area of archipelagic waters. For these reasons, the baselines are being revised.

Other Proclaimed Baselines

Tonga's Territorial Sea and Exclusive Economic Zone Act 1978, which came into effect in June 1979, describes the baselines from which these zones are measured. The baseline consists of the low water mark along the coast or fringing reefs, and straight lines across legal bays. It therefore appears that Tonga has decided not to claim any archipelagic baselines. Certainly the Tongan islands are too widely scattered to allow a single set of baselines to surround them all, although some groups of islands could be surrounded by archipelagic baselines.

None of the other countries or territories in the Southwest Pacific Ocean appear to have declared straight baselines along parts of their coasts. In most cases their claims to territorial waters refer to a baseline, and then stipulate that the baseline will follow the low water mark along the coast and reefs, except where bays or rivers occur, or where the coast is deeply indented or there are fringing islands. Hence these countries appear to have kept their options open to draw straight baselines in the future.

CLAIMS TO MARITIME ZONES

All states and territories in the Southwest Pacific region claim territorial seas of 12 nautical miles except Australia, Tuvalu and American Samoa which claim 3 nautical miles. Only Vanuatu claims a contiguous zone, but all states claim fishing or exclusive economic zones 200 miles wide.

This pattern of claims means that states will be able to fix the outer edge of the territorial sea unilaterally when the nearest opposite state is more than 24 nautical miles away. The outer edge of the fishing or exclusive economic zone will be capable of unilateral determination when the nearest neighbouring state is more than 400 nautical miles distant.

Claims to maritime zones exceeding 200 nautical miles only arise where there are extended continental margins, but even so there is an absolute requirement in the LOS Convention that the outer boundary must not lie more than 350 nautical miles from the baseline from which the territorial sea is measured, or more than 100 nautical miles seaward of the 2,500 metre isobath. Within the region, margins wider than 200 nautical miles only occur south of Fiji and New Caledonia and in the vicinity of Australia and New Zealand.

INTERNATIONAL AGREEMENTS ON MARITIME BOUNDARIES

Maritime boundary agreements in this region are those concluded between Australia and Papua New Guinea; Australia and France; France and Tonga; Indonesia and Papua New Guinea; Tokelau and the United States; the United States and the Cook Islands; and France and Fiji. The last two countries have agreed to two boundaries separating Fiji from New Caledonia and Wallis and Futuna. The agreement between Australia and Indonesia in the Arafura Sea was covered in a Research Memorandum No. 1/302(80).

Australia and Papua New Guinea

Australia's agreement with Papua New Guinea is incorporated in the Torres Strait Treaty. The Treaty was signed on 18 December 1978.

The Treaty deals with issues relevant not only to the Torres Strait but to the whole area between Australia and Papua New Guinea. It sets down the agreed position of the two countries on their sovereignty over certain islands in the Torres Strait and on the delimitation of their territorial seas. Under its terms, all Australian islands in the Torres Strait will remain Australian and all Papua New Guinean islands there will remain Papua New Guinean, including the three islands of Kawa, Mata Kawa and Kussa, close to the coast of Papua New Guinea. Careful examination of original documents has revealed that, notwithstanding errors in many maps published since 1879, these islands were in fact never annexed to Queensland.

The Treaty establishes a fair and equitable division of sovereign rights over fisheries and seabed resources in the whole area between the two countries extending some 2000 kilometres from the Arafura Sea through the Torres Strait and out into the Coral Sea. A line delimiting seabed jurisdiction runs across the whole area; in the Torres Strait it lies to the south of the islands of Boigu, Dauan and Saibai but north of all other Australian inhabited islands. A line delimiting fisheries jurisdiction coincides with the seabed line except in the central Torres Strait area where it runs to the north of Boigu, Dauan and Saibai. The territorial seas of the Australian islands north of the seabed line, and of Papua New Guinea in the area between Boigu and Saibai, are to be a maximum of three nautical miles, and territorial sea boundaries are delimited between Boigu and Papua New Guinea and between Dauan and Saibai and Papua New Guinea. Neither country will in future extend its territorial sea across the seabed line.

A Protected Zone is established to safeguard the traditional way of life and livelihood of the traditional inhabitants of both countries who live in or near the Strait. The traditional inhabitants will be able to continue to carry out their traditional activities, including traditional fishing, and to move freely about the Zone for this purpose. The two countries are to co-operate in the application of their immigration, customs, quarantine and health procedures in such a way as not to prevent or hinder such free movement but each country will retain the right to implement national controls to prevent possible abuse.

The Treaty contains provisions covering agreed principles, parallel measures to be taken by, and co-operation between the two Governments for the protection and preservation of the marine environment. It provides for co-operation between the two countries in the conservation and management of commercial fisheries in the Protected Zone, and for sharing the catch of those fisheries on an equitable overall basis. The two countries are to co-operate in the issue of licences for those fisheries, and in inspection and enforcement arrangements. There is to be prohibition of mining and oil drilling of the seabed in the Protected Zone for 10 years from the date of entry into force of the Treaty.

Appropriate freedoms of navigation, overflight and passage will be provided for Australian and Papua New Guinean vessels and aircraft, as well as for the vessels and aircraft of other countries, based on principles of international law in the Strait area.

There is provision for consultation between the two countries on the Treaty's effective implementation and on any matters relating to it. An Advisory Council will be established to keep implementation of the Treaty under review.

Australia and France

In January 1982 France and Australia agreed on maritime boundaries separating the Australian mainland and New Caledonia in the Southwest Pacific and the Heard and Kerguelen Islands in the south Indian Ocean. Both boundaries separate France's economic zone from Australia's fishing zone and the continental margins of each country.

Equidistant principles appear to apply except in the case of one segment of boundary east of Fraser Island, on the coast of Queensland. In this case, as Fraser Island is more than 200 nautical miles from the nearest French territory, the segment relates to continental shelf.

France and Tonga

In January 1980, France and Tonga agreed on a

convention fixing the boundary separating the exclusive economic zones claimed from Tonga and Wallis and Futuna.

In defining the boundary line, Tonga had proposed a line of equidistance and France agreed that such a line would conform to the application of equitable principles. The convention made provision for the determination of this median line but did not specify co-ordinates.

The United States and the Cook Islands and the United States and Tokelau

In June 1980 the United States and the Cook Islands agreed on a commmon maritime boundary, under which the United States abandoned claims to the islands called Pukapuka, Manihiki, Penrhyn and Rakahanga. The boundary was defined by twenty five points, and the geodetic and computational bases for the coordinates of those points were carefully defined. The western point also appears as the eastern point in the boundary which the United States agreed with New Zealand to separate maritime claims from American Samoa and Tokelau. The agreement is dated 2 December 1980, and under it the boundary is defined by eight points. The United States has recognised that the islands called Atafu, Nukunonu, and Fakaofo form part of Tokelau pending an act of self determination in accordance with the Charter of the United Nations. Both these boundaries of American Samoa appear to be lines of equidistance.

France and Fiji

Early in 1983, France and Fiji published an agreement delimiting the boundary between the economic zone claimed by Fiji and those claimed by France from Wallis and Futuna and New Caledonia. The boundary with New Caledonia is a line, defined by two points, measuring 310 nautical miles. This line of equidistance is based on Hunter Island for New Caledonia and Ceva-i-Ra for Fiji. The dispute over the ownership of Hunter and Matthew Islands between France and Vanuatu will be discussed below. Fiji has made no judgement on this issue because the third article of this agreement specifies that the agreement is without prejudice to sovereign rights of any neighbouring state in areas to which the agreement applies.

Indonesia and Papua New Guinea

In September 1982, Indonesia and Papua New Guinea ratified a maritime boundary agreement which extended a short maritime boundary which Australia had negotiated with Indonesia before Papua New Guinea became independent. That agreement, dated 18 May 1971, drew a single segment of boundary from the northern terminus of the land boundary between Indonesia and Papua New Guinea. It terminated at 2° 8' 30" south and 141° 1' 30" east and measured 27 nautical miles.

The latest agreement extends that boundary for a further 199 nautical miles through three points, so that it terminates at 1° 1' 35" south and 140° 48' 35" east. This terminus appears to be 200 nautical miles from the nearest Indonesian and Papua New Guinean Islands. There is a reference in the agreement to the preservation of traditional and customary fishing rights of both parties in the waters which fall to the other country.

It should be noted that while the boundary is a seabed boundary, in the same manner as the original Australian-Indonesian agreement, Article 4 provides that it will also be the boundary between fishing or exclusive economic zones.

The boundary to the south in the Arafura Sea was fixed by the agreement of 18 May 1971 between Australia and Indonesia. There are two straight line segments, the first joining the coast with a point in a southerly direction and the second extending from there in a more southwesterly direction to 9° 08' 08" south, 141° 01' 10" east. As with the northern boundary, it is a seabed boundary and also the boundary between fishing or exclusive economic zones.

MARITIME BOUNDARY DISPUTES IN THE SOUTHWEST PACIFIC REGION

Specific problems which are the cause of maritime disputation in the Southwest Pacific region are considered under the following headings:-

1 Pocklington Reef and its impact on the maritime claims of Papua New Guinea and the Solomons.

2 Matthew and Hunter Islands and the competing claims of France and Vanuatu.

3 Minerva Reefs and the maritime claims of Fiji and Tonga.
4 Problems for the maritime claims of Western Samoa and American Samoa.
5 Problems of maritime enclaves and corridors in the Southwest Pacific.

Areas of dispute involved in numbers 1-4 are shown in the above sequence on map 1, and are considered in that order in the following text.

Area 1 - Pocklington Reef and its impact on the maritime claims of Papua New Guinea and the Solomons

Pocklington Reef is located in the Solomon Sea and belongs to Papua New Guinea. The problem with the Reef is that it is capped only by some rocks; in 1977 there were also two wrecks one of which was in a single piece, while the other had broken into two parts. If this reef is used as a basepoint in settling any boundary with the Solomon Islands, the boundary will be deflected in favour of Papua New Guinea. The question for the Solomon Islands is whether the rocks on Pocklington Reef could have an economic life of their own. If Papua New Guinea is unable to answer such an enquiry with positive evidence that the area is used for fishing on a regular basis, then the Solomon Islands could argue that the reef is only a rock within the meaning of the Law of the Sea Convention and can only be used to claim territorial waters.

Area 2 - Matthew and Hunter Islands and the competing claims of France and Vanuatu

The question at issue is whether Matthew and Hunter Islands belong to Vanuatu or New Caledonia. Hunter Island is a volcanic block, standing 300 metres above the sea, which is covered by patches of grass and a few trees. Matthew Island is also volcanic in origin and has two distinct cores measuring 140 and 175 metres in height. This island is arid and lacks any vegetation.

In 1944, it was asserted by the United Kingdom Admiralty Naval Intelligence Division's 'Pacific Islands' Volume III, that 'they have not been claimed by France or Britain, or by any other Power'. The 1914 Protocol establishing the Condominium of France and Britain in the New Hebrides simply refers to the Group of the New Hebrides including the Banks and Torres Islands. The two latter groups lie to the north of the main archipelago.

In 1965, there was an exchange of letters between the New Hebrides Joint Court and the British and French Resident Commissioners in which it was recorded that Britain was content with the view expressed by the French authorities that the islands formed part of New Caledonia. This was also the view of the editors of the Official Gazetteer of Place Names, published by the Survey Department of the New Hebrides in 1979.

However, Vanuatu sees no reason why it should give up its claim without testing the strength of its arguments in legal and diplomatic exchanges. Possession of these islands is important, since they entitle the owner to claim economic rights over an area of 59,400 square nautical miles of sea and seabed.

The apparent determination of Vanuatu to press its claim was revealed when a party from that country landed on Hunter Island on 9 March 1983 with the express purpose of claiming the island for Vanuatu and raising the national flag. The landing party included customs chiefs from Aneityum, Tana and Futuna, the three most southerly islands of Vanuatu.

Area 3 - Minerva Reefs and the Maritime Claims of Fiji and Tonga

It is possible that Tonga's claim to North and South Minerva Reefs may pose difficulties in respect of the maritime boundary between Tonga and Fiji. In Fiji Marine Spaces Chart 81/3, Fiji revealed the extent of its exclusive economic zone and it encompasses the Minerva Reefs; the limit in this area follows the median line which lies east of the reefs. A note on the chart states that 'North Minerva Reef and South Minerva Reef are claimed by Tonga'.

These reefs are called Tele Ki Tokelau and Tele Ki Tonga respectively by the Tongan authorities. Tonga claims an historical association with them and there is some evidence of traditional fishing in the area. In 1972, after an organisation known as the Ocean Life Research Foundation proposed to set up a Republic of Minerva, the King of Tonga sailed to the reefs and supervised the erection of small artificial islands on them. That year the members of the

South Pacific Forum recognised Tonga's historical association with the Minerva Reefs, welcomed the Tongan government's continuing interest in the area, and agreed that other claims would not be recognised. This means that the South Pacific Forum stopped short of recognising Tonga's claim to sovereignty.

The reefs are about 18 nautical miles apart. The northern reef is circular, with a radius of about 1.6 nautical miles. The southern reef has an hour glass shape, measuring 4.7 nautical miles on its long axis and 1.8 nautical miles across at its widest section. There are a number of boulders which have been thrown up onto the reef by storm surges which have broken off parts of the outer reef.

These features are impermanent; for example, the conspicuous boulder shown on charts dated 1979 had disappeared by June 1980. On each reef the Tongan government erected an artificial island and a navigation beacon. The artificial islands consist of walls of coral boulders filled in with debris and measure 3 metres by 2 metres with a height of 1 metre. On the southern reef there is also a refuge tower with three levels.

North Minerva Reef is 168 nautical miles from Ata Island, which belongs to Tonga. It is 154 nautical miles from Tuvana-i-ra, which belongs to Fiji, and which marks Point 14 in the Fijian archipelagic baselines. When a line of equidistance is drawn with these two points as the basepoints, it is found that North Minerva Reef lies 11 nautical miles west of the line, and South Minerva Reef lies 15 nautical miles west of the line.

According to Article 60 of the LOS Convention, only the sovereign power can construct artificial islands within its exclusive economic zone. So the problem for Tonga is to persuade Fiji that Minerva Reefs are in Tonga's exclusive economic zone. According to the Territorial Sea and Exclusive Economic Zone Act 1978, which Tonga enacted on 25 June 1979, the outer boundary of the exclusive economic zone will be the median line when Tonga's claim overlaps that of a neighbour. Once artificial islands are constructed, the coastal state has exclusive jurisdiction over such islands for purposes of immigration, health, finance and safety.

The Article makes it quite clear that the only zone which can be claimed about an artificial island is a safety zone 500 metres wide. It is specifically noted that artificial islands have no territorial sea of their own, nor do they affect the delimitation of claims to territorial seas, exclusive economic zones or continental shelves.

If Tonga were to claim an exclusive economic zone from Minerva Reefs it would overlap with New Zealand's claim from the Kermadec Islands.

Area 4 - Problems for the maritime boundary claims of Western Samoa and American Samoa

Problems arise because Western Samoa is zone-locked by its neighbours, and because Swains Island, which belongs to American Samoa, plays a key role in restricting the maritime boundary claims that can be made from Western Samoa.

Swains Island is 194 nautical miles north of Tutuila; it has an area of 1.5 square nautical miles and was approved by the United States of America in 1925. Ownership of this island accounts for about one third of the total maritime claim for American Samoa.

If the authorities in Western Samoa seek any improvement in their situation they will need to rely on the goodwill of the American authorities for relief. There is no doubt that the entire suite of maritime claims can be properly made from Swains Island, and its status as an island has already been recognised by the Treaty with Tokelau.

Area 5 - Problems of maritime enclaves and corridors in the Southwest Pacific

The archipelagic and scattered nature of states and territories in the Southwest Pacific Ocean results in enclaves of high seas surrounded by national claims to exclusive economic or fishing zones. Some of the areas, such as the three located along parallel 14° south, are comparatively small, but others, such as that separating the claims of Indonesia, Papua New Guinea and the Trust Territory of the Pacific Islands, are extensive.

Such zones of high seas complicate the enforcement of regulations applying in exclusive economic and fishing zones. It might be possible to make out a case for allowing bordering states to annex small enclaves of high seas, and for permitting states bordering long corridors of high seas to bound them with a series of straight lines. That would make it easier for navigators to know when they were inside or outside areas subject to national claims. This is not a novel suggestion - it was made by S.W. Boggs at the 1930 Hague Conference on the Law of the Sea.

Chapter Two

FISHERY DEVELOPMENTS AND SOCIAL CHANGE IN THE PACIFIC

A D Couper

This paper considers in a general way the social dimension of technological change in Pacific island communities. This is recognised as a difficult and often neglected area in the development process.

All major technological changes are likely to be accompanied by environmental, economic and social consequences. In many projects involving the introduction of new technology it is possible to apply objective criteria which may predict and evaluate some of the probable physical and biological impacts. It is also possible to determine likely industrial multiplier effects and to measure the general contribution of the project to economic growth. It is more difficult for researchers and decision-makers to predict and objectively assess social impacts, since these may involve changes in the ways of life of communities, the perceptions and values of which are partly products of history and group culture.

There is a considerable body of literature dealing with the concepts and methodologies for measuring social impacts (Finsterbusch, et al, 1983), although most of this relates to Social Impact Assessment (SIA) techniques derived from advanced market economy conditions. For developing countries there are fewer validated models and simulation methodologies for the application of SIA. On the other hand, there is a range of field studies relating to technological change. These deal primarily with the socio-economic consequences of such aspects as new roads, infrastructural changes, land uses in rural areas and urban developments.

THE LACK OF MARITIME COMMUNITY INTEREST IN DEVELOPING COUNTRIES

For maritime communities in developing countries there are neither adequate theoretical models on the social impact of technology nor, until recently, has there been much interest by administrators or researchers in maritime areas compared with the vast amount of work in the agricultural sector. In the case of administrators, there are several reasons for the low levels of maritime awareness. There is the traditional 'landmindedness' of the administrator, even in archipelagic regions. Emmerson, in his work in south-east Asia, points out that although he could obtain figures on land area, road and rail length and size of truck, data on sea areas, coastal length and seagoing vessels were rare (Emmerson, 1979:2). Fishing activities generally come under Departments of Agriculture, and even Forestry, in some administrations; and fishermen, when they are identified as a separate occupational group, are seldom disaggregated in statistics into their various functional components and areal distributions.

In the case of academic researchers, the reasons for the paucity of maritime field research in the developing world is due partly to the difficulties of observing the activities of fishermen at sea, and the minimal data usually available on the marine resource base. In fishing communities there can be complex relationships in and between the socio-economic system and the marine ecological system. It is necessary, in order to understand the raison d'etre of the community and its stages of development to consider the village, the market, the gear, the boats, the sea and the fish stock. The linkages between these components are often economic, cultural, legal, political, technological and biophysical.

A particular problem faced by social science researchers studying the changing human ecology of a maritime community is the nature of the resource base. As with the social system, so with the marine biological system, most of the valuable work and classical models have been derived from developed market economy countries based on research mainly in the continental shelf seas of the northern hemisphere. The physical differences between reef slopes of oceanic islands and continental shelfs, and the diversity and complexity of tropical sea fisheries reduce the value of these biological and bioeconomic models. The effects of increasing fishing effort, selectively fishing certain species, fishing the same species at different depths, the relationships between inshore and offshore stocks, and the fish population dynamics, are still less well understood in tropical than in temperate waters.

RECENT ADVANCES IN MARITIME COMMUNITY RESEARCH

In spite of the problems involved, and the lack of a wide body of field work, there are a few classical texts and some excellent recent detailed research on fishing communities. These may well add up to the emergence of clearer theories and improved practices for understanding relationships between the fishermen, the market and the resource base. This is not the place to attempt an extensive review of the state-of-the-art in this respect, but Raymond Firth's Malay Fishermen, written as far back as 1944, would surely rank as one of the first and foremost in its analysis of the subsistence sector and the role of fishermen in society, while Ed Knipe's Gamrie, published in 1984, is an excellent description, albeit for a very different environment, of the processes of marine technological adaptations in commercial fisheries. Within the forty year timespan between Firth and Knipe it is primarily in recent years that most of the well researched studies have appeared. These include Szanton (1971) and Spoehr (1984) on the Philippines; Johannes (1979 and 1981) Micronesia; Halapua (1982) Tonga; Morauta, Pernetta and Heaney (1982) Papua-New Guinea; Alexander (1975) Sri Lanka; the work of Lawson (1983 and 1985) in West Africa; and the challenging contrasts and conflicts between Western concepts and Asian experience in fisheries made by Emmerson (1983). FAO and UNESCO have sponsored several valuable approaches; and the work of Arthur Hanson (1984) on coastal community development in S E Asia contains useful pointers for an interdisciplinary approach to the study of social, economic and biological components in the developing world maritime communities.

Many of these more recent works re-emphasise both the distinctive nature, and the several common features, of fishing communities in different parts of the world. In most developing countries fishing is village-based, it is carried out daily, and women often play important roles in gathering and netting in the inshore areas. On the high islands of the

Pacific fishing is normally combined with agriculture, but on low coral islands it may predominate and can be almost the only natural source of animal protein. Villages are often located on the lee side of islands at sites with suitable access to the sea and to lagoon and reef resources. There may be integrated village activities based on the fishery, including boat building, repairing, net and trap making, processing and distributing. Many fishing villages are isolated and remote from formal land transport links.

Fishermen can spend a large part of their time away from villages. Fishing communities, even in many parts of the developed world, are often characterised by a preponderance of women, children and old men during most days, and where deep sea fishing has been adopted most men are absent for several days and weeks at a time. Fishing families are, consequently, different in many respects from agricultural households. They are exposed to greater economic risks, and the fishermen to greater physical risks than agriculturalists. Fishermen tend to have more variable incomes, incur higher debts and have less political influence than agriculturalists.

The impacts of technological changes on fishing communities show some parallels in many general ways in several parts of the world. A typical sequence of events at the early stages of the commercialisation of a fishery are described by Johannes (1978: 35b):

> the fisherman finds himself competing for money and therefore for fish. In order to compete effectively he must buy better equipment and fish harder. This process is self-reinforcing. The need to spend more money to get more efficient gear to harvest more intensively increases as the number of fish decrease. As equipment becomes more sophisticated, its price ultimately rises beyond the means of the average fisherman. A new profession, moneylending, arises. The fisherman borrows to finance his purchases, and he often falls into debt. Employment opportunities diminish as more efficient boats drive out native craft.

The adoption of bigger, more seaworthy, mechanised craft and more sophisticated gear may raise the need for better and deeper reef passages, new berthing arrangements, engineering repair facilities, slipways, ice plants, and access to land transport. Small communities cannot respond to these needs and this can lead to the centralisation of fishing activities at fewer places, the separation of vessel ownership from kinship and its transfer to urban businesses, and the shifts of boat building, repairing, fish processing and other ancillary services from vertically integrated village activities to separate functions at the bigger ports, with the consequent decline and impoverishment of many coastal fishing villages.

The process of spatial shifts in the centres of fishing activities under the impact of technology has been, historically, a common phenomenon worldwide. There are variations to this centralising scenario. In the northeast of Scotland several of the villages remain the homes of deep-sea fishermen while they commute by crew buses to and from boats based at the bigger east and west coast ports. In parts of Canada, government support has been provided to retain distant communities operating with less competitive boats and gear. These are not solutions easily available to most developing countries.

NEW MARITIME AWARENESS BY ADMINISTRATORS

It is only in recent years that there has been increased awareness by administrators of the maritime orientation of much of the Pacific and Southeast Asia. This perception has been heightened by the consciousness of new marine resource potentials, the need to increase the supplies of protein for urban areas, and by the opportunities of greater control by developing island states over archipelagic waters and vast national sea areas, as a result of the 1982 UN Convention on the Law of the Sea and the declaration of 200-mile Fishing Zones or Exclusive Economic Zones (EEZ).

In many regions the new awareness of maritime values has given rise to reappraisals of the extent of fishing and the dependence of coastal communities on marine resources. The results have come as something of a surprise to several administrations. In Southeast Asia there are 3 to 5 million small-scale fishermen with about 21 million people dependent on them (Marr, 1981:87). In the Village Agricultural Survey carried out in Vanuatu during 1983 it is reported:

In the past, fishing activity in Vanuatu has

> always been considered to be a very secondary activity, if not even a marginal activity, in relation to agriculture. The results of this study however indicate that fishing is more generally practised than was thought. Indeed about half the rural households around the archipelago are involved in fishing, corresponding to 8600 households. (David, 1985:6)

In Fiji there are at least 22,500 commercial and subsistence fishermen. Fish consumption in Fiji averages 40 kg/person/year (Ministry of Primary Products, 1985), which rates among the higher world levels, and fish exports from Fiji rank third in value after sugar and tourism.

TECHNOLOGICAL CHOICES IN THE PACIFIC

There is considerable diversity of equipment, craft and fishing methods in the Pacific. Differences exist even between neighbouring islands and adjacent coastal communities in their use of traditional methods and adoption of new technology. In Vanuatu, Malakida Island concentrates on traditional canoe fishing while Epi, Erromango, Tana and Aneityum have between them half of the boats of European design. Some 28 per cent of Vanuatu fishermen still use traditional gear (David, 1985:5). In Fiji subsistence and lagoon artisanal fishing and gathering are often women's activities, while commercial fishing from boats, especially beyond the reef edge, is carried out by men.

The transfer of technology in Pacific island fisheries is being stimulated by an appreciation of the availability of fish stocks at greater depths on outer reef slopes, the existence of ocean migratory fishing in EEZ areas, and the increased market potential for marine produce such as crayfish, giant clams, beche-de-mer, seaweeds, live aquarium fish, trochus shell and precious coral, and the possible developments of mariculture and aquaculture.

The motives on the part of administrations for increasing the extraction of marine resources may include securing improvements in exports, balance of payments, local food supply, employment, incomes, profits, licensing of foreign fishermen, welfare of small coastal communities, encouragement of urban fishing activities or the curtailment of rural-urban drift. Not all of these objectives can be pursued at once; several are mutually incompatible. The support for and choice of new technology may therefore be determined by the wider policy priorities of administrators. The extent to which social considerations enter into this depends on the degree to which small communities are consulted on their needs and values.

When it comes to the 200-mile zones the benefits for some coastal communities are as yet difficult to discern. Hanson (1984:12), commenting on South Asia and elsewhere in the developing world, says:

> There is certainly sufficient evidence to indicate a high level of distress and problems in coastal communities, which suggests that the initial years of 200-mile extended jurisdictions has not produced anticipated fishery benefits to coastal communities.

In the Pacific there are additional problems in the choice of technology and policy for the extended fishery zones. These involve highly migratory species which pass through national fishery areas. Up until recently island commercial fishing for the migratory skipjack tuna, in particular, has been carried out from small craft using the simple pole-and-line technique. These vessels are relatively cheap, they can be built locally (although few have been), the method is labour-intensive and the catch can sometimes be enhanced by fixed aggregation devices (FADs). Pole-and-line captured fish are of good quality and vessels can produce 100 tonnes per month - which at times of favourable market prices give a reasonable rate of return and income to fishermen.

During the 1980s market prices were reduced by as much as fifty per cent in some places. This has been due primarily to the enormous landing from high technology vessels used by Japanese, Korean, and especially United States companies. The US$5m to US$10m purse seiners employed by US fishermen have sophisticated bridge controlled engines and bridge controlled gear systems; electronic navigational aids; fish-finding and fish-speed monitoring equipment and sometimes helicopters. The nets are of almost two kilometres in length, fitted with sonar depth controls and are capable of catching up to 100 tonnes of fish within one day.

With the drop in prices, Pacific island countries have been forced to make certain choices, e.g. limit fishing to local needs, and possibly higher quality markets, and secure additional income from fees by foreign purse seiners fishing in national zones; restrict the volume of foreign catches in national zones; or, increase the tonnage of catches by island vessels to compensate for reduced prices per tonne. The latter policy means the move from pole-and-line and longlining to the more productive purse seining.

The problems for small island states entering purse seining are economic - including the price of vessels, gear, spares, maintenance, and crew training; and social - including longer periods at sea, and the different relationships in status, skills, workcycles and division of labour on board a purse seiner compared with the pole-and-line vessel. There are uncertainties also regarding the maximum sustainable yields with further increased fishing effort in some zones, and there is the problem of high capital investment in somewhat inflexible types of vessels for regions where there is seasonability of fish migrations.

Here is seen, at another level of fishing, the 'circular causation' type of technological pressures already referred to by Johannes for the early stage of development. This time it is not simply the individual fisherman who is being driven to acquire more technology in order to catch more fish to pay for technology - it is island national fishing enterprises. In the case of Fiji the pressures to raise the levels of technology are intensified since catches have to support a cannery employing 300 or so Ovalau women, and the cannery output has to sell in a competitive world market. There are doubts if either the quantity of landings to maintain the necessary economies of scale of the cannery, or the volumes of catches necessary to provide expected levels of incomes for Fijian fishermen at current prices, can be sustained from pole-and-line techniques.

LEARNING FROM PACIFIC FISHERMEN

For approaches to some of the problems of Pacific island fisheries it is necessary to consult Pacific island fishermen. Many of the traditions, methods and levels of technology in Pacific fishing communities have developed closely adjusted to the ecology of lagoons and reefs. Much has still to be learned from local fishermen about these environments in fish biology, catching and conservation. In agriculturally poorer reef and atoll oceanic islands, in particular, it was evident to the indigenous inhabitants that the valuable inshore marine resources on which they depended were not infinite, and they evolved conservation and management methods to prevent over fishing and improve stocks. Johannes, who has conducted most of the limited amount of field recording amongst Pacific fishermen, shows that all of the conservation methods introduced in recent times by western commercial fishing were in use in the Pacific islands for centuries.

In his work, especially within Micronesia, Johannes has described Pacific island traditional marine tenure, with spatial divisions between villages extending from beach to outer reef edge, and beyond in some islands. The conservation methods used by the Pacific island communities have included gear restrictions, limited entry to the fishery, closed seasons, and taboos on certain species. Indigenous fishermen have built up and passed on within their groups enormous funds of knowledge in oral form regarding fish behaviour, concentrations, feeding and spawning and other biological and geographical characteristics of a multi-species fishery.

Halapua, (1982) has also recorded some of the knowledge and methods of indigenous fishing groups in Tonga. He has re-emphasised also the very different modes of production and distribution in Pacific island fishing communities compared with western models. New fishing technology which is introduced from elsewhere without close reference to what local fishermen know of the marine environment may result in stock depletion. It may mean also a shift from part-time to full-time fishing with a consequent neglect of agriculture. The stronger orientation to the market may result, in turn, in a disruption of complex social relationships within small societies, not only in fish production but in their distribution between fishermen, boat owners, market and traditional networks, and between household consumption and reciprocal exchange with kin. For these reasons Halapua advocates small development projects with "slow steady change" which do not disrupt traditional lifestyles. As a basic purpose in fishery development should be improvements in the quality of life of island fishermen, the social aspects and the local knowledge and customs clearly need careful study with the introduction of new technology.

CONCLUSION

This introductory paper has focused on some of the wider social aspects of new maritime technology in fisheries, and in the process has raised more questions than it has answered. It has not touched on many of the political and legal problems, or on policies for multiple sea uses. These have vitally important implications for coastal communities in such aspects as licensing of foreign vessels in EEZs, allocation of archipelagic shipping routes, new port locations, the discharge of mining and other waste into the sea, offshore mining and hydrocarbon exploitation, offshore dumping, fish farming, recreational fishing, marine parks, and other tourist-related activities in areas which traditionally (and sometimes by indigenous tenure) are utilised by coastal fishing communities. Some of these issues are discussed in subsequent chapters.

A point of emphasis is - the more that marine technology is adopted the more it is necessary to manage a fishery and formulate coastal zone and community policies. On the administrative side this entails establishing procedures which ensure feedback from fishermen, coastal communities and other users of the sea. On the research side it means learning from fishermen and guarding against what Evans (1976:381) regards as the '... socially isolated growth of marine science institutions'.

There is, in both the above respects, a requirement for a new approach to marine affairs and marine science. This includes an output from Pacific centres of research and education of marine administrators, ocean resource managers and coastal zone managers, with relevant skills and concepts who can contribute to the development of marine resources in ways which are practical, economically sound, environmentally safe, and socially aware.

REFERENCES

Alexander P, 1975 Do fisheries experts aid fisheries development?, Maritime Studies and Management, 3(5), (London: Taylor and Francis)

David G, 1985 La Peche Villageoise a Vanuatu (Vanuatu: Mission Orstrom).

Emmerson D K, 1979 The case for a maritime perspective on Southeast Asia, unpublished paper from Singapore Seminar, United States Social Science Research Council.

Emmerson D K, 1983 Rethinking Artisanal Fisheries Development: Western Concepts Asian Experience (Washington, D.C.: World Bank).

Evans E B, 1951/6 Marine scientific and technological assistance to developing countries: science for development or technology for malintegrated growth?, Economic Development and Cultural Change, 24, 375-85.

Finsterbusch K, Llewellyn L G and Wolf C P (eds), 1983 Social Impact Assessment Methods (Beverly Hills: Sage Publications).

Firth R, 1966 (2nd ed.) Malay Fishermen: Their Peasant Economy (Hamden, Connecticut: Archon Books).

Hanson A J, 1984 Coastal comunity development: an international perspective (Halifax, Nova Scotia: D.O.S.P. Publn., Paper prepared for the 26th Annual Meeting, Canadian Commission for UNESCO).

Halapua S 1982 The Fishermen of Tonga, Institute of Pacific Studies, University of the South Pacific, Suva, Fiji

Johannes R E, 1978 Traditional marine conservation methods in Oceania and their demise, Ann. Rev. Ecol. Syst., 9, 349-64.

Johannes R E, 1981 Words of the Lagoon, Fishing and Marine Lore in the Palau District of Micronesia (California: University of California Press).

Knipe E, 1984 Gamrie: An Exploration in Cultural Ecology (Lanham: University Press of America)

Lawson R, 1985 Economics of Fisheries Development (London: Pinter).

Lawson R and Robinson M, 1983 Artisanal fisheries in West Africa, Marine Policy, October: 281.

Marr J C, 1981 Southeast Asian fishery resources and fisheries, In: Chia Lin Sien and Colin McAndrews, (eds.) South East Asian Seas - Frontiers for Development (Singapore: McGraw Hill).

Ministry of Primary Products, 1985 (Suva: Fiji Fisheries Division).

Morauta L, Pernetta J, Heaney W (eds) 1982 Traditional Conservation in Papua New Guinea, Institute of Applied Social and Economic Research, Papua New Guinea.

Spoehr A, 1984 Change in Philippine capture fisheries: an historical overview, Philippine Quarterly of Culture and Society, 12, 84.

Szanton D L, 1971 Estancia in Transition: Economic Growth in a Rural Philippine Community (Quezon City: Ateneo de Manila University Press).

Chapter Three

POLICY, LAW AND MANAGEMENT IN PACIFIC ISLAND FISHERIES

William M Sutherland

This paper surveys the policy, legal and management considerations which presently face the fisheries regimes of the Pacific island states and considers their impact on the wider societies. Following an outline of the various fisheries in the region and the broad policy objectives which have been established for their further development, some of the major legal issues associated with the management of fish resources are examined and an assessment is made of the contribution of the Forum Fisheries Agency to the management regimes of the region. The paper concludes with some pointers to possible problem areas in the future.

FISHERIES POLICY IN THE PACIFIC ISLAND STATES

Subsistence fishing is an integral part of Pacific island societies and the importance and sensitivity of the social and cultural arrangements on which it is based has meant that governments have generally been cautious in their approach to it. Typically, government policy on the administration and development of subsistence fisheries is one of caution and protectiveness. Existing programmes are therefore concentrated on the improved supply of reasonably-priced fishing gear and the improvement of processing techniques in order to minimise waste and loss (Shepard and Clark, 1984).

In the field of small-scale commercial operations, there are two main types of activity: first, the harvesting and export of products such as beche-de-mer, trochus and sharksfin to specialist Asian markets; and second, local small-scale commercial fisheries geared primarily to the local market but which are important in terms of job creation, cash income generation and reduction of imports. Much of these fisheries is concentrated in inshore areas and with the increasing demand occasioned by growing populations and urbanisation, the impact on inshore resources has been a matter of concern for governments. National policies have therefore centred on trying to effect a shift away from the more fragile and heavily fished reef and lagoon resources and more towards the comparatively underexploited resources of the outer reef slopes and the pelagic resources in deeper waters. In that effort, government policy has been greatly assisted by two regional programmes: the Deep Sea Fisheries Programme of the South Pacific Commission which is aimed at catching deep bottom fish on the outer reef slopes and which involves droplining techniques; and the UNDP/ FAO Regional Fisheries Programme which involves the deployment of fish aggregation devices in deep offshore waters. These devices encourage collections of fish such as tuna, skipjack and mahimahi and so provide high catches and thus make trawling operations around them lucrative (ibid).

Despite significant successes in these types of fisheries, various problems remain. Further improvements need to be made in respect of credit availability; supply of fishing gear; increased subsidies or reduced taxes and duties on fuel and supplies; landing and storage facilities; fish collection and distribution; and marketing arrangements both locally and abroad. Also, although the use of FADs is an attractive fishing method, it is still fairly costly; for example, materials and placement costs for a raft anchored in depths of 800 to 1,500 metres is about US$5,000. Finally, in respect of inshore fisheries particularly, the risk of overfishing continues to be a major concern and it is here that government policy is confronted with its greatest difficulties. In many cases regulatory regimes do exist but effective policing of such regimes is almost impossible, especially as all the island governments are constrained by their limited resources.

Another important fishery in the region revolves around tuna bait. The existence of bait has been a major determinant of the pole and line fishery and baitfish are generally most abundant in waters around larger land masses. In part this is due to the fact that freshwater runoff into lagoons appears to be a major factor in providing the natural conditions in which baitfish thrive. In the Pacific region, then, there are fairly well-developed tuna bait fisheries in Fiji, Papua New Guinea and Solomon Islands and these are closely tied to pole and line operations in those countries.

Several features of the tuna bait fishery have important consequences for management policy. Because baitfishing is prominent and catches are relatively large, there is a need for rigorous programmes of research, and control and efforts along those lines are already in place. Second, in Papua New Guinea and the Solomon Islands much of the catch is taken from grounds which are still under traditional ownership and local government control. Bait fee payments therefore are a source of income for bait ground owners and local governments. Often, however, negotiations are difficult and protracted. Thirdly, pole and line operations are the site of the most obvious interaction between inshore and industrial offshore fisheries and for that reason require the most rigorous research programmes and the most difficult management regimes (ibid).

The importance of small scale fisheries, then, lies in their income and employment creating potential and their use of appropriate forms of technology. Government policy has therefore been to encourage these fisheries as much as possible within the objective of minimising overexploitation. The realisation of that goal, however, continues to be complicated by persistent shortages of adequate administrative and regulatory resources and the sensitivities of traditional social practices.

Highly migratory species - tunas and billfish - are the only commercial offshore resource and throughout the region government policy in respect of the management and control of this resource is clear. Very broadly, policy objectives revolve around three major concerns: the desire to develop national tuna fishing and processing industries; the wish to control and extract the maximum benefits from foreign fishing in their waters; and the need to co-ordinate their policies on the exploitation of these species with other states in the region and also to develop co-operative relations with distant water fishing nations at a regional level. Of these, the first is accorded the highest priority for the medium term and this is indicated by the fact that the objective of increased employment, incomes, government revenues and foreign exchange earnings from industrial tuna fishing figures highly in the national development plans of all the island states (ibid: Appendix B).

The evidence from Fiji, Solomon Islands and

Papua New Guinea suggests, however, that the considerable effort expended by island states on the development of national tuna industries has not, unfortunately, been matched by the gains. The reasons for this have to do very largely with resource constraints but they are also tied more generally to the wider historical trajectory of tuna fisheries in the region.

The history of tuna fisheries in the region has been adequately described elsewhere (Bour and Galenon, 1979; Kearney, 1979; 1981; 1982) but the emergence of locally-based operations occurred in the mid-1950s when bases were opened for Japanese longliners fishing for albacore tuna. The fish, destined for United States canners, were landed in Tahiti, Pago Pago and Santo. Drawn by the more lucrative distant water sashimi fishery, however, the Japanese later abandoned albacore longlining to Korean and Taiwanese fishermen whose operations came under increasing stress as economic conditions worsened progressively. In the early 1970s, the booming demand for skipjack led to an expansion of Japanese pole and line operations. Large fleets were drawn to the good southern fishing grounds and with economic sense pointing to the desirability of having processing facilities close to those grounds, joint venture canneries involving government were set up in Fiji (with C Itoh) and Solomon Islands (with Taiyo Fishing Company). Van Camp operated a base in Palau and a major transhipping facility eventually controlled by Starkist and Mitsubishi operated in Papua New Guinea.

By the late 1970s export earnings from these operations stood at about US$70 million. Encouraged by this and the expectation of further gains, especially in the light of the establishment of 200-mile EEZs, moves were made to the establishment of national tuna industries. The Ika Corporation was formed in Fiji, the National Fisheries Development Limited in Solomon Islands, and more recently, in 1981, Te Matauri Limited in Kiribati. Tuvalu and Tonga each operate one longliner. The limited success of these operations raises doubts about their future and that uncertainty is compounded very considerably by developments in purse seining.

With recent improvements in technology, there has been a dramatic upsurge in purse seining in the region. Until recently, this fishery has been dominated by large vessels, especially the Japanese 500 gross tonne and American 1,200 to 1,500 gross tonne boats. Several factors have altered the situation somewhat. On the one hand, the drop in demand for frozen fish, changes in taste patterns and high production costs have produced a geographical shift of processing capacity away from the US mainland and also from the US Pacific territories. On the other hand, better knowledge of fishing grounds, improved designs of smaller vessels, and the greater use of FADs have all improved the competitive use of smaller vessels.

In this new situation, there now appears to be some possibility of greater national involvement in purse seining and although some island countries appear to be moving in that direction, the substantial costs involved will probably be prohibitive for most island countries. Important policy decisions will have to be made and the difficult choices confronting island governments between relatively small longliners, pole-and-line vessels and purse seiners. The former types of vessel generate more jobs and are less expensive and complex, but with low prices for tuna are less competitive than the purse seiners. The latter, however, require vastly more capital investment and generate fewer jobs.

Fiji recently purchased a purse seiner and Kiribati is contemplating one. Whether this will set a trend for other countries to follow is not clear. What is rather more certain is that with the depressed state of the international tuna industry and the enormous competitive advantage which distant water fishing nations enjoy, it is unrealistic to expect that any forays by the island states into purse seining will pose anything like a threat to established interests. Moreover, it is questionable whether purse seining really does constitute the kind of option which will advance the developmental objectives of the island states. In the longer term, therefore, it may well be that the most fruitful option might be the further development of locally-based pole and line and longline fisheries organised around the use of smaller vessels and appropriate forms of technology. As for the immediate future, it is reasonable to expect that the greatest gains will probably be derived from access agreements concluded with distant water fishing nations. And it is in that area that regional cooperation has reached an advanced level.

MANAGEMENT, CO-OPERATION AND THE FORUM FISHERIES AGENCY

Elsewhere I have described the developments leading up to the creation of the Agency and also its structure and operations (Sutherland, 1985;1986). Here I simply point in a general way to the broad regional needs which the Agency was meant to respond to, briefly assess the Agency's achievements to date and, finally, indicate some likely problem areas in the future.

Prompted largely by developments transpiring at the UNCLOS III negotiations, the island states began in the mid-1970s to turn their attention increasingly to urgent task of maximising their share of the gains which extended maritime jurisdiction would bring. Constrained by themselves from fully exploiting their marine resources there emerged the widely-proclaimed need for co-ordination and co-operation on a regional basis. Alongside that general goal was the more immediate need to evolve a co-ordinated approach to negotiations with distant water fishing nations over the exploitation of highly migratory species, especially tuna.

At its seventh meeting, held in Nauru in July 1976, the South Pacific Forum took a series of initiatives which, three years later, led to the formation of the Forum Fisheries Agency (FFA). From a very early stage in the discussions, the point was firmly made by the island states that they would not countenance any development which would bestow on it powers which they felt were intrinsically those of a sovereign state. Essentially, therefore the Agency was to play an advisory and co-ordinating role. Article 56 of the ICNT of the draft Convention on the Law of the Sea, which is repeated in the 1982 Convention, affirmed the sovereign rights of coastal states to manage the resources of their EEZs and the Pacific island states were intent on defending that right.

However with rights come duties and for the purposes of this discussion the relevant duties were those relating to the conservation of the living resources of the EEZ and also to co-operation with other states in respect of those resources. Analyses of these rights and duties have been made elsewhere (Sutherland 1985; Slatyer 1985; Clark 1984;) but the co-operative duty imposed by Article 64 in relation to highly migratory species requires special consideration. For not only do the requirements of that Article bear upon the structure and operation of the FFA, they also help to clarify the original role for the Agency, and that which it subsequently came to perform.

An examination of the traveaux preparatoires of the FFA Convention reveals that in the discussions leading to the creation of the Agency, two issues were central: the competence and the membership of the proposed organisation. On the question of competence, it is clear that Member States did not wish the organisation to have management functions. It was to be an advisory and consultative body. (Sutherland, 1985: 24,27) The question of membership proved rather more thorny but eventually it was decided that the organisation should include only the Member States of the South Pacific Forum. The exclusion of distant water fishing nations, especially important ones like the United States and Japan, provoked the criticism that the organisation was in breach of Article 64 (Kent, 1980:170; Van Dyke and Heftel, 1981:48).

In a penetrating analysis, however, Professor Burke has argued that the form of co-operation mandated by Article 64 was not confined just to a "broadly-based" organisation. Coastal states also have the option of co-operating with other states in a series of one-to-one interactions. (Burke, 1984: 291) This the island states have continued to do, but they have also encouraged co-operative arrangements between the FFA and other regional and international organisations. For the island states, therefore, the activities of the FFA must not infringe their sovereign rights of management.

Booth is therefore correct when he says that the FFA is not a fisheries management body which recommends or sets management measures such as total allowable catch, local fishing capacity, foreign fishing surplus, limitations on fishing areas and methods. This , he goes on to say, is "neither surprising nor disappointing" because "(m)any of the Pacific's new nations in 1979 lacked the experience and confidence, both in new regional bodies and with possible foreign co-members, to accept any other organisation than an intra-regional, primarily advisory body" (Booth 1984:164) Without necessarily denying validity to that explanation, it misses the main thrust of the island states' objection to a broadly-based organisation.

At issue was the highly important tuna resource and there was serious concern that effective management and control of that resource could not be guaranteed if the desired co-operation between island states were to be effected through an Article 64 organisation. Belief in the imperative need to safeguard their sovereign right of management and control produced a determination to prevent any development which threatened to undermine that right.

Theoretically that problem should not arise even in the context of an Article 64 organisation provided that the competence of such a body could be defined sufficiently clearly as to exclude management and control functions from it, and indeed that possibility was recognised. Nevertheless, there was persistent doubt as to whether such formal proscription of authority would, indeed could, effectively prevent intrusions upon sovereign rights. In practice, the line beyond which the legitimate activities of such a body might begin, however imperceptibly, to impinge upon the sovereign right of management and control was a thin and hazy one. Even the exercise of purely technical function could conceivably have that effect. Distant water fishing nations could, for example, especially with their virtual monopoly of scientific information and fisheries technology, present data in a manner which could effectively (even if unintentionally) structure decision-making options in a particular direction. Faced with such structured and perhaps limited alternatives, the island governments might then be forced into courses of action which may, in significant measure, be contrary to their national interests.

States, to be sure, have a legal obligation to discharge their duties in good faith and there is no firm evidence to suggest that the island states were necessarily suspicious that distant water fishing nations might renege on that obligation. Rather, their main concern seems to have been that there simply did not appear to be any objective basis upon which to establish with an assuring degree of certainty that the activities of distant water fishing nations within an Article 64 organisation would not prejudice either their sovereign rights or their national interests.

With that lingering apprehension, then, the view was reinforced that the proposed fisheries organisation should not be of the type envisaged, however inadequately, by Article 64. On the other hand, the island states did recognise the need for such an organisation and the Forum Fisheries Agency Convention is not silent on that issue. In part, Article III.2 of the Convention states:

> the Parties recognise that effective co-operation for the conservation and optimum utilisation of the highly migratory species or the region will require the establishment of additional international machinery to provide for co-operation between all coastal states in the region and all states involved in the harvesting of such resources.

At the Forum Meeting in Honiara in July 1979 a directive was issued that the possibility of creating such an organisation be explored and since then the idea has been the subject of periodic discussions.

The concern about safeguarding the sovereign rights of coastal states and the misgivings about distant water fishing nations, therefore, were crucial influences in determination of the role of the FFA. It was to be an advisory body concerned with facilitating the discharge of the sovereign rights of the Member States. And in that task it has, despite the constraints, given good account of itself.

Assistance has been given in the delimitation of maritime boundaries, and Agency staff now participate in almost all fisheries access negotiations as technical advisors to the governments involved. The Agency conducts workshops on access negotiations, national fisheries projects and joint ventures. It provides training programmes for national negotiators, data analysts, administrators and legal and enforcement officers. It also co-ordinates the important Regional Research and Development Programme and maintains a high degree of collaboration with regional and international organisations - the South Pacific Commission, South Pacific Bureau for Economic Co-operation, United Nations Development Programme and the Food and Agriculture Organisation.

High in the list of achievements must rank the programme of harmonisation of fisheries policy and the establishment of the regional register of foreign fishing vessels. Through the harmonisation programme, there is now a regionally-harmonised set of minimum terms and conditions with which all access agreements must comply. Included in those requirements is the regular provision of standard information on vessels, catches and fishing activities. This information is processed for scientific, negotiation, regulatory, and enforcement purposes. The operation of the Regional Register of Foreign Fishing Vessels has been described elsewhere

(Sutherland, 1986) but essentially it is a list of vessels which have been accorded "good standing". Those, however, which seriously breach the laws of any single Forum State and do not submit to the legal processes of that State are blacklisted and subsequently access to the fishing zones of the region may be permitted only after due satisfaction has been obtained.

In sum, then, the main role of the FFA is to provide information, analyses and advice to Member States and also to assist in co-ordinating the harmonisation of their laws, policies and negotiating positions in relation to distant water fishing nations. Its achievements to date point to a degree of success with which it and the Member States can be reasonably satisfied. That success probably owes much to the small size of the states and populations involved.

In practice the activities of the Agency are, largely through the interventions of the Forum Fisheries Committee, subject to fairly regular political scrutiny; but therein lies the advantage of smallness. In its daily operations, the Secretariat of the Agency enjoys access to the highest echelons of regional governments. The high level of personal contact that generates, coupled with the noticeable and apparently general desire to accommodate differences and national particularities, and also to arrive amicably at satisfactory decisions, would thus seem to account in large part for the effectiveness of the Secretariat. Finally, from a legal point of view, the activities of the FFA have been influential in the development of state practice. As I have argued elsewhere, state practice in the region points to an emergent regional custom which may well represent an important contribution to the progressive development of international law.

However, despite these commendable achievements, there remain issues which may well prove problematic in the future and will therefore require serious consideration.

SOME FUTURE CONCERNS

Although progress is being made in the area of maritime boundary delimitation, much work remains to be done and resource constraints will doubtless continue to be a problem. Also, because there are instances of overlapping maritime boundaries, there is potential for disagreement (Broder and Van Dyke,

1982; Prescott, 1980; Prescott this volume). The states concerned might therefore fruitfully consider appropriate dispute settlement regimes, in the light especially of the relevant provisions of the 1982 Law of the Sea Convention. High seas enclaves bounded by EEZs are another potential source of difficulty and the accommodation of competing interests on an equitable and amicable basis will require creativity and compromise.

The same might be said of the increasing use of an evidently appropriate form of fishing technology - FADs- and here there is a whole series of potential problems. Conflicts could arise from interactions between competing fishermen for a number of reasons: sabotage; poaching; complaints that FADs draw away fish to which there is some customary entitlement or that they draw fish from nearby fishing zones of other states or that they interrupt the normal migratory patterns. FADs could be navigational hazards and in instances of surreptitious use it may be difficult to identify the places - a problem which could be serious when there is a need to establish liability. Related to that are jurisdictional problems. Would, for example, national courts have jurisdiction to protect proprietary rights outside territorial waters? For it appears that generally national fisheries legislation in the region gives jurisdiction for fisheries offences up to the limit of the EEZ but often not for criminal or civil offences such as theft or malicious damage.

Yet another possible area of concern would be the situation where distant water fishing nations might deploy FADs in high seas enclaves in sufficient numbers that they draw large quantities of fish from surrounding fishing zones. Then there is the perennial problem of resource constraints. It would appear, then, governments will need to give further thought to strengthening their administrative and regulatory regimes so as to minimise conflict between users of FADs; but this also applies to the whole area of surveillance and enforcement generally, although it is clear that the establishment of the regional register represents a major advance especially as the evidence so far suggests that, as a regional sanction, it has contributed significantly to ensuring compliance by foreign vessels with the fisheries laws of the island governments.

All of these issues will of course bear directly on the future trajectory of national fisheries policies but in terms of national efforts being directed at maximising gains in the short and medium term, two particular objectives will doubtless engage the attention of policy makers: the further development of locally-based fishing industries and the optimality of conditions for foreign access into fishing zones. In respect of the former, one of the most crucial decisions which now confronts the island government has to do with striking the optimal balance between, on the one hand, a small-scale commercial fishery centred on a form of technology which will generate jobs and income and, on the other, a larger scale commercial tuna fishery based on more effective but expensive technology and which therefore is less likely to provide high levels of employment. In that regard, the view is now being expressed that what is needed is a (pole-and-line?) vessel of a size, cost and design which will allow sizeable numbers of people to harvest offshore pelagic fish in a cost-effective way. A tall order perhaps, but challenging none the less.

On the matter of foreign fishing, two issues ultimately shape the regime of access: market demand and the size of the resource. Apart from vigorous marketing and advertising strategies, the island states have little influence over the former. The supply side of the equation is rather more amenable to island influence for although consideration will need to be given to the impact of fishing activity on stock levels, there are good grounds for restricting access. From the broad economic proposition that scarcity creates value comes the corollary that enforced scarcity is likely to produce increased revenue. And this is the kind of thinking which now appears to be gaining wider currency in the region. The focus, in other words, is now shifting towards limiting fishing effort. This could be achieved in a variety of ways. Fishing effort might be limited by regulating the number and/or capacity of vessels, gear type, length of season, fishing area or by simply manipulating fee levels. It is reasonable to expect that measures such as these will be adopted in future access agreements, including that which was reached in principle between the US and the Member States of the South Pacific Forum in Tonga in December 1986. Certain aspects of the agreement have yet to be finalised and the general expectation is that it will be signed in the near future. At the moment, however, little is publicly known about the details of the agreement, so it is not possible to ascertain the extent to which it limits fishing effort.

In any case, there is a recognition among the island states that better control of fishing effort may well require a more coherent arrangement than the existing pattern of fishing agreements. That in turn raises questions about the possible need for a more comprehensive institutional machinery which, importantly, may have to be endowed with some management authority. To meet such a need, the role of the FFA could perhaps be widened. But not only does that have consequences for the sovereign rights of coastal states, it would also resurrect yet again the unsettled issue of involvement by distant water fishing nations.

One final observation which is pertinent to the theme of this volume can be made. State Parties to the 1982 Law of the Sea Convention have a duty under Part XIV to promote the development of fisheries technology in developing states with a view to accelerating their social and economic development. Moreover, this duty arises irrespective of whether the technology owning state is fishing in the waters of the developing state concerned. The clear and important implications of this for the island states of the region are evident. For as Slatyer (Slatyer, 1985:7) argues:

> it is fundamentally misconceived to suggest that technology transfer should ever be traded off for fisheries access. States are required, under Article 269, to establish programmes of technical co-operation for the effective transfer of all kinds of marine technology to States which may need or request technical assistance.

The Convention of course has yet to enter into force and it is unlikely that all the distant water fishing nations which have an interest in Pacific fisheries wil be Party to it when it does. But the island nations might fruitfully bear this argument in mind.

REFERENCES

Bour W and Galenon P, 1979 The Development of Tuna Fisheries in the Western Pacific. (Noumea: South Pacific Commission)

Booth I, 1984 Regional Co-operation in South Pacific Fisheries: Legal and Institutional Aspects, in Christopher C Kissling ed. Transport and Communications for Pacific Microstates: Issues in Organisation and Management. (Suva: Institute of Pacific Studies, University of the South Pacific)

Broder S and Van Dyke J, 1982 Ocean Boundaries in the South Pacific, University of Hawaii Law Review, 4(1):1-59

Clark L, 1984 Fisheries Issues in the Pacific Islands. Honiara, Forum Fisheries Agency Report 84/11

Kearney R E, 1979 Some Problems of Developing and Managing Fisheries in Small Island States. (Noumea: South Pacific Commission)

Kearney R E, 1981 A Brief Review of the State of the Stocks of Highly Migratory Species of Fish in the Central and Western Pacific. (Noumea: South Pacific Commission)

Kearney R E, 1982 The Development of Tuna Fisheries and the Future for their Management in the Tropical, Central and Western Pacific. (Noumea: South Pacific Commission)

Kent G, 1980 The Politics of Pacific Island Fisheries (Boulder, Colorado: Westview Press)

Prescott J R V, 1980 Existing and Potential Maritime Claims in the Southwest Pacific Ocean, In: E M Borgesee and N Ginsburg (eds.) Ocean Yearbook 2 (Chicago : Chicago University Press)

Shepard M P and Clark L, 1984 South Pacific Fisheries Development Assistance Needs: Opportunities for Participation by UNDP, FAO and Other Donors Interested in Supporting South Pacific Fisheries Development. FAO/UNDP Project RAS/73/025

Slatyer T, 1985 The New International Law of Fisheries as it Relates to the South Pacific. Honiara: Forum Fisheries Agency Report 85/5

Sutherland W M, 1986 Fisheries Management and Coastal State Jurisdiction in the South Pacific, International Journal of Coastal and Estuarine Law, No.1.

Sutherland W M, 1985 Regional Co-operation and Fisheries Management in the South Pacific. LLM thesis, University of Hull, UK

Van Dyke J and Heftel S, 1981 Tuna Management in the Pacific: An Analysis of the South Pacific Forum Fisheries Agency, University of Hawaii Law Review, No.3.

Chapter Four

FISHERIES DEVELOPMENT IN PACIFIC ISLANDS: SOME PROBLEMS IN PARADISE

M King

Fisheries in Pacific islands can be conveniently divided into three areas (a) reefs and lagoons (b) outer reef slopes and seamounts and (c) offshore waters. The nearshore reefs and lagoons contain species which have traditionally been fished using simple methods such as spearing, trapping, netting and hand lining. The outer reefs and offshore areas are traditionally fished by those islanders, typically the Micronesians and Polynesians, that have retained their seafaring heritage. In the offshore waters of the South Pacific annual tuna catches are around 450,000 to 500,000 tonnes (1983) with a value of US$500 million, making tuna one of its greatest resources. Most of the benefits of this catch fall to the distant water fishing nations (DWFNs), although it is hoped that with the advent of the EEZ's benefits to the islands will increase.

An increase in seafood production can be, and in some cases has been, realised in several different ways, including.

(a) increasing the efficiency of existing traditional fisheries
(b) diversifying fisheries to exploit new inshore species
(c) the farming (aquaculture) of selected species, and
(d) developing offshore fisheries.

These options are summarised schematically in Figure 2.

The above factors are discussed as well as those which may militate against the achievement of the intended results from the application of imported technology. Examples are given, from the personal experience of the authors, of projects which have been extremely successful, and of others which have fallen short of expectation. An attempt is

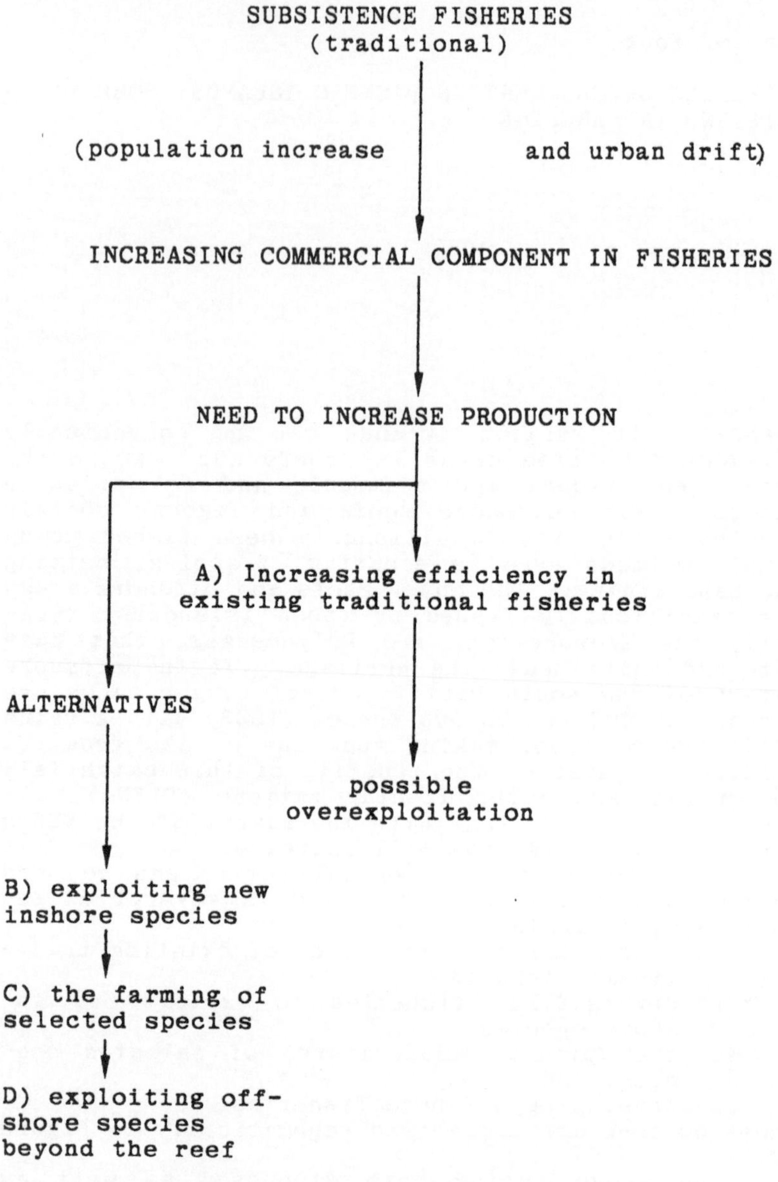

Figure 2 Events leading to a requirement for an increase in seafood productivity and alternatives available for achieving this increase.

made to identify those factors which are critical to the success or otherwise of a given project.

With the exception of the inland populations of Papua New Guinea, Fiji and the Solomon Islands, South Pacific islanders have always relied on fish and other marine organisms as a staple item of diet. While populations remained static, fish were plentiful, and comparatively easily obtained using traditional fishing methods which have evolved over many centuries.

Today, the pressure of increasing populations, and of urban drift, or the tendency of islanders to migrate towards 'capital' islands, with more and better facilities, have encouraged governments to explore ways of increasing the harvest of the sea, both to provide a source of income by way of exports, and to utilise locally-caught fish, on a cash market, as a substitute for imported canned fish.

The process of fisheries development has been assisted over recent years by a plethora of aid programmes from many sources, both bilateral and multilateral. While the total fisheries aid to the region in 1981 was less than 3% of the world total, it represented by far the highest per capita (over $1500 per 100 inhabitants) provided to the developing regions of the world (Josupeit, 1983). The nature of this assistance is varied, and includes capital aid for infrastructure requirements, provision of equipment, technical assistance and training, both within and outside the region.

INCREASING EFFICIENCY IN TRADITIONAL FISHERIES

Pacific islanders have been using tried and tested fishing methods and even practising forms of resource management for many years before Europeans invaded the Pacific.

As interesting as it would be, a review of traditional fishing methods is beyond the scope of this paper - it is necessary, however, to discuss how fishing methods used in the past have been altered with the introduction of new materials and technology.

Let us first examine the most simple and basic piece of fishing gear - the hook and line. Traditionally fishing hooks were made from bone, shell or wood and attached to lines made of sennet (coconut husk fibre). In many northwestern Pacific islands, including Kiribati where one of the authors (Carver) was stationed, World-War II brought a legacy of military junk. The high-grade aluminium from wrecked aircraft is now used to fashion barbless hooks attached to pearl-shell lures for trolling tuna (Carver, 1980). Such hooks, when attached to synthetic line, are practically indestructible and only need replacing after loss. Johannes (1981) cites a similar use of stainless steel wire from downed aircraft by natives of Palau for fashioning fish hooks. It is interesting to note that although modern materials are used, the traditional design and shape of hook are retained, the western "storebought" j-shaped hook is generally regarded as inferior for catching many tropical species (Johannes, 1981). It is no accident that those master fishermen of the developed world, the Japanese, use tuna long-line hooks which are similar to the centuries old recurved or "rotating" hooks of some Pacific islanders (Figure 3). Rotating hooks which are capable of locking over the upper jaws of fish are small technological masterpieces requiring some knowledge of the bone structure of fish.

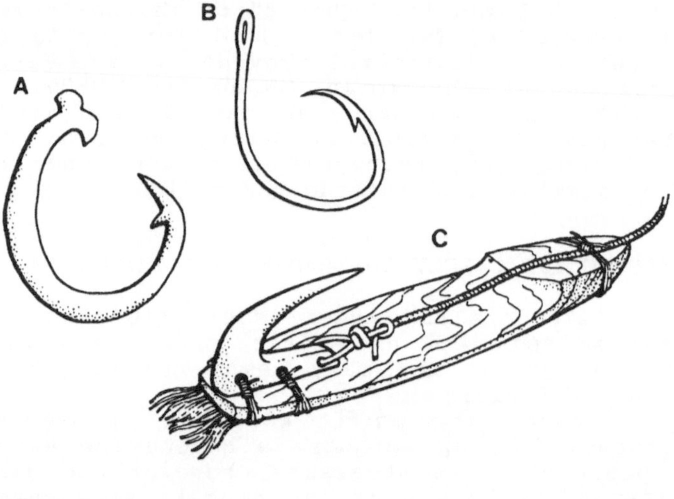

Figure 3
A a traditional fish hook from Palau (from Johannes, 1981)
B a similar modern circle hook (Mustad, 39960ST), and
C a pearl-shell tuna lure with an aluminium hook (made from downed World-War II aircraft and a synthetic fibre tail (from Carver, 1981).

There are many other cases of new materials being used in traditional fisheries. Gill nets are set vertically in the water so that when fish swim into the netting, the twine locks behind their gill covers. The efficiency of such gear increased dramatically with the introduction of the thin and almost colourless monofilament nylon netting which is now available in almost all Pacific islands.

The intricate stone fish traps of Tonga which were traditionally set at right angles from the shore to catch migrating mullet are presently made from wooden stakes and chicken wire.

One fishing method unintentionally introduced into the islands was the use of explosives for the capture of fish in shallow reef areas. The destructive practice has been outlawed in most island states, along with the similar yet traditional fishing methods employing natural vegetable toxins.

An essential part of many fisheries development plans is the availability of satisfactory boats, providing a suitable working platform for both the catching operation and safe transport to and from the fishing grounds. Gulbrandsen (1984) acknowledges that the introduction of motorised boats into the subsistence/mixed economies of the Pacific may lead to problems both from a safety and economic point of view.

During the 1981-83 period in Kiribati over seventy craft were reported missing, of which 18 were never recovered, with a loss of 45 lives. The ratio of non-powered to powered craft is 10 to 1 yet approximately 50% of those lost were small, outboard powered dinghies with no alternative means of propulsion. Major factors contributing to their loss were their light construction, mechanical failure and unsuitability for using sail power. Advising naval architects have recommended against the import of aluminium dinghies and have urged island countries to develop craft based on their own traditions. (Fyson, 1984).

In Tonga, a long running FAO/UNCDF boat-building programme made little progress in the early stages due to lack of research into traditional vessels and the type of hull that would be acceptable to local fishermen. "V" bottom plywood boats, which have been a resounding success in Fiji were built but rejected by the Tongan fishermen, who had grown used to the rounded lines of local whaling boats, of planked construction. Large catamarans and trimarans were then tried, again with similar results, until finally an FAO consultant designed a vessel constructed along the lines of the Tongan whalers. This vessel has been readily accepted, and uses an auxiliary sailing rig, having both safety and fuel economy advantages.

In all of the cases given above, the use of modern material has either increased the efficiency of the fishing gear itself, or the ease of its manufacture and repair has allowed more time for fishing (fishing effort). The same can be said, with the reservation already expressed, about the use of modern fishing craft.

Any increase in catching efficiency (without a corresponding decrease in fishing effort) will result in an increased pressure on the resource. The question that many fisheries advisers in the Pacific area have to answer is whether a particular resource can withstand any increase in fishing effort. The answer to this question relies on having basic biological and statistical data, particularly on catch and fishing effort.

Although fisheries science is a relatively modern discipline in western societies, management measures are part of village lore in some Pacific islands. It is considered tabu (taboo) in many Fijian villages to catch small sardines (Daniva) in shallow water. The belief, and not an unreasonable one, is that the sardines attract the larger carnivorous fish (mainly Salala, Indian mackerel) into shallow water where they provide a more substantial catch for villagers. This simple management measure is, in fact, quite a sophisticated one; fisheries regulations in developed countries are usually directed towards protecting the target species itself rather than its ecological relationships.

The mathematical models so beloved by temperate-water fisheries managers are difficult, if not impossible, to apply to tropical reef fisheries. In temperate-water fisheries, biologists have extensive catch and fishing effort data on fisheries based on large numbers of just a few fish species. In tropical seas there is such a large variety of fish landed, and such a paucity of catch and effort data that the single species management models developed in temperate climates simply do not work - a fact which has not always been recognised by fisheries advisers sent to the Pacific from Europe under various old schemes.

In spite of the lack of scientific data there is much anecdotal evidence that stocks of fish traditionally caught are over-exploited, or at least fully exploited, in areas of locally dense populations (King and Stone, 1979). There are, however, other ways of increasing fish production without increasing pressure on existing traditional fisheries; these are discussed in the following sections.

EXPLOITING "NEW" INSHORE SPECIES

It is the case in most countries that a small number of particular organisms has become the preferred target. There are two main reasons for this; either the species is present in large numbers and easy to catch (eg a schooling fish which is susceptible to netting), or there is a social preference for the particular species. The mullet is a highly desired fish in some Pacific islands, but is despised (for no good reason) in other countries including Australia. Small sharks (a popular seafood in Australia) are shunned in many Pacific islands; in Fiji, for example, there is a belief that if sharks are eaten, immunity from shark attack will be lost to the consumer. To develop new fisheries there may be prejudices to overcome as well as new fishing techniques to introduce. In some cases it is possible to develop fisheries for species which are not desired for local consumption but are a valuable export commodity.

Holothurians (beche-de-mer or sea cucumber), for example, are being collected in several Pacific islands where villagers are being trained in processing and market requirements (Gentle and Conan, 1979). The most valuable species, the "teatfish" (Microthele nobilis), when properly smoked and dried, has been sold for over $5.50 per kg (in Fijian dollars, 1979) for export to Southeast Asian markets.

Tropical rock lobsters (Panilurus species) have not traditionally been exploited in some island groups. Fisheries based on these species have been developed by local and overseas entrepreneurs although with the use of modern SCUBA equipment there is the possibility of over-fishing .

FARMING SELECTED SPECIES

Fish farming or aquaculture often appears to be an attractive proposition in tropical countries. Tropical aquaculture developments have two main advantages over temperate ones. These are:

(a) the faster growth rate of warm water species allows shorter holding times and lower food costs, and
(b) the juveniles of many species suitable for aquaculture may be collected from the wild, thus obviating the need for expensive hatcheries.

In spite of these advantages there are many problems associated with the introduction of aquaculture in Pacific island countries. Intensive farming systems require a degree of technology and the provision of back-up services (power, engineering and marketing facilities) as well as cheap sources of food for the farmed species. Extensive farming systems which require large areas and a high labour input have been successful in Southeast Asian countries and may be more suitable for Pacific islands. It should be remembered, however, that whereas Asians have had a long history of farming (marine as well as terrestrial) many Pacific islanders have not.

Several species occurring naturally in Pacific islands are biologically suitable for aquaculture. These include penaeid prawns (Penaeus species) and bivalve molluscs such as oysters and mussels. A number of aid agencies are presently involved in aquaculture projects in the Pacific and CNEXO (Tahiti) have been notable in their efforts to introduce simple methods of prawn farming to many island countries. Although biologically successful the economic future of prawn farming in the Pacific appears gloomy. The total production of prawns from aquaculture in the Indo-Pacific area is predicted to increase threefold to over 140,000t by the end of this decade (van Eys, 1985) and result in an over-supplied market; of this total, only 100t is likely to be produced in Pacific islands.

Giant clams (Tridacna species) are presently being farmed experimentally in a project supported by ACIAR. Although these species have an extended lifespan, initial growth rates are very high and they are unique amongst farmed animals in that they are phototrophic (they can "feed" on sunlight through a symbiotic relationship with algal cells).

This project not only opens the possibility of marketing "baby" giant clams but also reseeding reefs where the species has been depleted (see Tisdell, Chapter 6). Giant clams have been heavily fished in many areas by both local inhabitants and poachers from Southeast Asian countries. Another mollusc, the top shell (Trachus species), used in the pearl button industry, has been cultured successfully for seeding reef areas.

The coconut crab (Birgus latro) is a crustacean which spends most of its life ashore, although it is thought the larval stage spends time in the water, normally of lagoons, or within reefs. The mature animal possesses a fearsome claw, which it uses to extract sustenance from coconuts. It is a highly prized delicacy, indigenous throughout the Pacific region, but now in extremely short supply almost everywhere, to the extent that it is thought to be extinct on many islands. A research programme is underway, funded by ACIAR, to investigate the possibility of farming this species, and to attempt its re-introduction throughout the region.

Other than producing species to restock depleted areas, aquaculture development in Pacific islands may be most successful where simple methods are used to grow high value species for local hotels and tourist facilities. The cost of such aquaculture would place the product beyond the reach of most local people.

There have also been proposals and attempts to farm small baitfish in some islands (eg Kiribati and Fiji) although the economics of the operation are marginal. Obtaining baitfish may be a serious constraint to the development of local pole-and-line tuna fishing operations. The marine alga Eucheuma which is used as a source of carrageenan gel for food, pharmaceutical and cosmetic industries is being farmed commercially on Tarawa atoll, Kiribati (Why, 1985). Although farming techniques for the seaweed have been successfully developed the financial return to the growers is likely to be small because of high freight costs.

DEVELOPING OFFSHORE FISHERIES

Although Polynesians have traditionally travelled far from land to fish for species such as flying fish and tuna, very few Melanesian islanders have historically fished beyond the reefs.

Flying fish (family Exocoetidea) are common throughout the region, though little is known about the existence of various stocks. This species is commonly caught at night near reefs by using a bright light in conjunction with a surface or above surface net. Kerosene pressure lamps have replaced coconut frond flares as the source of light, and monofilament gill nets have replaced the traditional sennet (coconut fibre) nets. Both these innovations have eased the fishermen's lot considerably.

Tuna have been traditionally caught from outrigger canoes by using a pearl shell lure attached by a short line to a bamboo (or nowadays a fibreglass) pole. Alternatively, similar lures may be trolled on long lines towed behind sailing boats - an operation which has become more successful since the introduction of the outboard motor. Several aid projects have been involved in setting up small tuna fishing operations. In Western Samoa, for example, aid funds were used for the local construction of small aluminium catamarans which were sold directly to fishermen on the condition that repayments were made from the fishermen's tuna catches. The otherwise successful project was marred by the fact that money from the landed fish was paid directly to fishermen who then had to face demands from extended families; payments were often not kept up and many boats were re-possessed. The simple expedient of requiring fishermen to sell their fish through a marketing authority which handed on the remaining balance of money after extracting the vessel payments would have meant complete success for the project. A case, perhaps, of a project based on inadequate sociological background information.

Larger and more sophisticated tuna fishing operations rely on the use of live baitfish being held in seawater tanks. Baitfish are thrown into the sea to maintain tuna in a feeding frenzy in which they readily take unbaited hooks. The use of such larger vessels depends on the transfer of more sophisticated technology and on the availability of large quantities of baitfish.

Commercial tuna fishery vessels have been involved in some conflict with villagers in several areas. In Fiji, for example, tuna vessels move into coastal areas to net baitfish at night; the taking of small fish is regarded as _tabu_ by some villagers. In some of the larger islands such as Fiji, the Solomons and Papua New Guinea, villages hold riparian rights over coastal areas.

More recently, Pacific island fishermen have been encouraged to fish beyond the reef for deep-water snapper (family _Lutjanidae_). These fish, being remote from coral reef ecosystems, are less susceptible to ciguatera - the fish poisoning which affects many shallower water and reef species. The South Pacific Commission has employed three master fishermen to train Pacific islanders to catch deep-water fish species. The training programme has been extremely successful because small craft and simple fishing equipment are used, and training is actually conducted at the locations concerned. The fishing technique involves using lines and hooks set vertically in deep water - a handreel for hauling in the large amount of line was designed for local construction using wood (Figure 4).

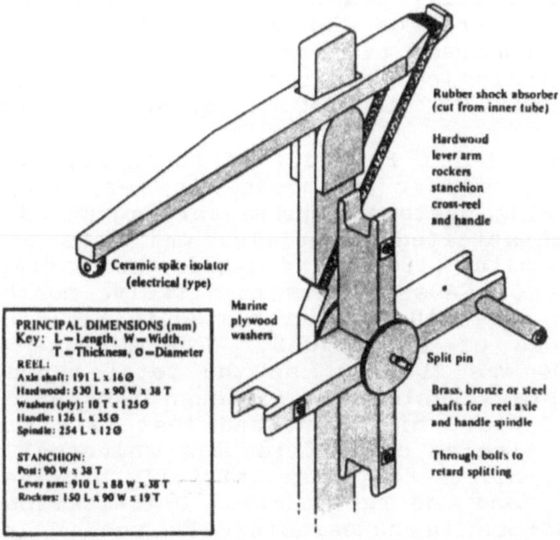

Figure 4 A simple wooden handreel used in deep-water snapper fishing projects in Pacific islands

Another group of species, deepwater shrimps or prawns (mainly <u>Heterocarpus</u> species) have been discovered in many Pacific islands (King, 1984). The magnitude of the resource is believed to be large with an estimated potential production of up to 900,000kg in Hawaiian waters alone. The species are caught by using baited traps set in depths of about 650m. The greatest commercial use of the resource has been in Hawaii, no doubt because of its large cosmopolitan population and access to more sophisticated local and overseas markets. At present, however, the economics of the fishery are marginal mainly due to the high costs of fishing in deep water (King, 1986).

It has been known for years that pelagic fish are attracted, and congregate, around debris floating in the ocean. Indeed, tuna purse seiners commonly target on floating logs and other debris, and may stay with a particular log for some time, setting the net round the log. The reasons why logs or other devices (Fish Aggregating Devices - FADs) attract fish are not fully understood, nor are the mechanics of fish behaviour in their vicinity. Floating logs clearly provide a micro environment suitable for the growth of barnacles and other marine organisms, as well as shelter, both of which will attract small fish. Larger fish will then be attracted to prey on the small fish, but it is not clear why hundreds of tonnes of fish may aggregate round a single log or other device, how they behave in the vicinity of the device, or what controls that behaviour.

Purpose-built FADs are of necessity expensive, and if they are to be moored in very deep water, their mooring systems require very advanced technology, sophisticated materials, and lots of money. Boy and Smith (1984) indicated the average life expectency of FADs is less than twelve months, with 434 out of 604 FADs around the South Pacific reported lost as of March 1983. The average cost of these FADs was $US3000, so the total represents a considerable investment. Although FADs have proved efficient, their high cost and loss rate has meant that many fishing communities are reluctant to provide replacements for those initially provided under aid. The Food and Agricultural Organisation of the United Nations is researching the social, economic and management experience with FADs, including an assessment of their effect on local communities, and the feasibility of obtaining fees from users of the devices.

At this stage it is worth mentioning the heavy dependence of many islanders on imported canned fish. Canned fish have several advantages over fresh fish, particularly in the tropics where high quality refrigeration is not readily available. Proposals to develop canneries in tropical countries often stem from the belief that tropical seas are highly productive and packed with fish waiting to be canned. This is unfortunately not so. It is a biological principle that whereas tropical seas are noted for the huge number of different species of fish, the overall abundance of any single species is usually low. This poses a problem for both the operation of canneries and factory vessels. The large trawlers which operate in the cold north Atlantic, for example, catch large numbers of dominant species which conveniently fit the filleting and processing machines on board. Such efficient mechanised operations are not viable in tropical seas where scores of different species may be caught in a single tow of the net.

Nearly all the valuable fisheries of temperate waters are based on highly-developed fishing operations targeting on a single, but abundant, species. The fact that this cannot be done in the tropics (with the notable exception of tuna) is one of the many problems of fisheries development in tropical Pacific islands.

DISCUSSION

Population changes and the availability of new materials have changed the face of traditional fisheries in Pacific islands. Some traditional methods have been lost and others have become so efficient that the resources are over-exploited.

Options, including the exploitation of new species both inshore and offshore, have been presented and discussed. All of these options involve, to a greater or lesser degree, the importance of new technologies, material and methods. The transfer of technology, as part of fisheries aid projects, has not always been successful or appropriate.

The term "appropriate technology" which is sprinkled through so many fisheries aid proposals is less than useful in that it means different things to different people. To some fisheries advisers with a missionary zeal, "appropriate" means using materials that are locally available. A fisherman using such fishing methods as sennet nets and dug out canoes, however, is condemned to several hours work on gear manufacture and repair for each hour actually spent fishing. If the object of the exercise is to catch more fish rather than provide some sort of occupational therapy, or picturesque amusement for tourists, the fisherman would be better provided with a fibreglass hull and synthetic netting. At the other end of the scale, appropriate technology may refer to a transfer of technology which is appropriate to the target species sought. It may be thought, for example, that the appropriate way to catch tuna is by using a large and sophisticated purse seiner. This would, however, require a commensurate on-shore infrastructure to provide for servicing and spare parts as well as catch-handling and marketing. Several large vessels provided as aid now lie rusting against wharves in Pacific islands. Gifts of large vessels as well as costly fisheries facilities have imposed heavy burdens in the way of continuing running costs in several Pacific islands.

The answer to technology transfer surely lies between the two extremes given above. The introduced technology should fulfil the requirements of the developing country rather than be imposed by the donor. As stated by Ben-Yami (1984) the introduced technology should not exceed the general technological level of the country involved. In addition, a crucial part of any such transfer of technology should be that personnel are trained in its use and maintenance. Many fisheries development projects have been short-lived because training and back-up facilities have been neglected. General training in fisheries studies, for personnel at all levels from fishermen to fisheries managers, is available at a few centres in the Western Pacific region including the University of the South Pacific (Fiji), Nelson Polytechnic (New Zealand) and the Australian Maritime College (Tasmania). Pacific islanders are also being trained at the Australian Maritime College in fisheries surveillance operations for patrol craft being built in Western Australia with Australian aid.

In reviewing some of the success stories in fisheries development it appears that imported technology is generally more successful in its application the less sophisticated it is. Since technology is by its nature sophisticated, this is an apparent contradiction in terms. However, technology that is capable of being handled by artisanal operators with little or no training, is frequently successful. This is particularly so where the project concerned is one of immediate and peculiar interest to the participants, and where infrastructure levels are appropriate to the maintenance of imported equipment, without imposing an unacceptable economic burden on the fishermen.

Orderly development suffers from the, perhaps inevitable, succession of 'experts' and 'advisers' imposed on the Pacific peoples for short contract periods. While these people are invariably well-intentioned, sometimes to the point of crusading, they tend to see an overriding necessity for results "by the end of the contract". More balanced development may take place as indigenous people acquire the ability to act in this capacity themselves.

In conclusion then, one may say with some confidence that aid, if it is to be successful, must be appropriate. One man's aid may be another man's poison. The Pacific islanders have millennia of myths and legends guiding their traditional practices. These practices, and indeed their traditional way of life, have been under increasing siege since the advent of European exploration. So much so that their traditional ways are fast disappearing, and many may already have been lost for ever.

As islanders of new generations, sympathetic to the ways of their fathers, become schooled also in the ways of the west, they must develop a harmonious balance between these different ways, skilfully marrying ancient principles with modern technology, and accepting what is appropriate from each.

REFERENCES

Bailey K, 1985 Logs as Fish Aggregation Devices in the Equatorial Western Pacific. Paper 13, South Pacific Commission Seventeenth Regional Technical Meeting on Fisheries. Noumea, New Caledonia. 7p.

Ben-Yami M, 1984 Technology transfer. Parts 1 and 2. World Fishing (September and October issues).

Boy, R L and Smith B R, 1984 Design improvements to Fish Aggregation Device (FAD) mooring systems in general use in Pacific Islands countries. South Pacific Commission Handbook No 24.

Carver A, 1980 Australian Fishermen could learn from islanders' tuna techniques. Australian Fisheries 39:7 p18-19.

Fyson J, 1984 Workshop - Artisanal fishing vessel in the Pacific Islands. Sixteenth Regional Technical Meeting on Fisheries. Noumea, New Caledonia.

Gentle M and Connon C, 1979 Beche-de-mer of the tropical Pacific; a handbook for fishermen. South Pacific Commission, Noumea, New Caledonia.

Gulbrandsen O, 1984 Ten years boat development in the South Pacific - what can we learn from it? Paper 14, South Pacific Commission, Sixteenth Technical meeting on Fisheries, Noumea, New Caledonia. p26.

Johannes R E, 1981 Words of the lagoon. University of California Press. 245p.

Josupeit H, 1983 External assistance to the fisheries sector of developing countries in Asia and the Pacific - A short survey INFOfish 3; pp10-12.

King M G and Stone R M, 1979 Commercial fisheries in Western Pacific islands: In: Utilization and management of inshore marine ecosystems of the tropical Pacific islands. University of the South Pacific/University of Hawaii. pp72-84.

King M G, 1984 The species and depth distribution of deep-water caridean shrimps (Decapoda, Caridea) near some Southwest Pacific islands. Crustaceana 47:2 pp174-191.

King M G, 1986 The deepwater shrimp resources of Pacific island countries. FAO Technical Paper (in press).

Van Eys S, 1985 The shrimp industry in the Asia/Pacific INFOfish Marketing Digest 1. pp27-31.

Why S, 1985 Eucheuma seaweed farming in Kiribati. Paper 19 South Pacific Commission, Seventeenth Regional, Technical Meeting on Fisheries. Noumea, New Caledonia p7.

Chapter Five

LESSONS FOR THE PACIFIC TECHNOLOGY TRANSFER AND FISHING COMMUNITIES: THE SRI LANKAN EXPERIENCE

Paul Alexander

Programmes to develop artisanal fisheries through the introduction of new technologies have usually specified twin aims. First, they seek to increase fish production, the major protein source in many of these societies, or, at least, to increase the share of the catch taken by indigenous fishermen. Second, they seek to raise the living standards of the fishermen who are usually among the poorest communities in countries which are themselves poor.

During the early period of planned fisheries development - approximately pre-1970 in most of South and Southeast Asia - it is doubtful that the second goal was taken seriously during plan implementation, despite the flowery phrases in the plans themselves. In recent years, however, as the circular for this workshop emphasises, it has been recognised that effective planning requires equal attention to biological, economic and social dimensions. While fisheries administrators are still usually drawn from marine biology or economics, they have actively sought suggestions which might enable fisheries development programmes to improve the lives of fishermen.

Unfortunately, social scientists, and particularly anthropologists, have seldom been able to provide useful suggestions, at either the planning or the implementation stage. There are probably several reasons for this, but two stand out. The first is that despite the increasing employment of anthropologists as consultants, there is a general, if somewhat flattering, misunderstanding of the possible contribution of anthropology.

Anthropologists are seen as experts on society and culture, able to draw on their training and the literature of their discipline to provide the same sort of technical advice as economists or biologists. But while anthropology aims at general theories of society and culture, such theories are empirically grounded in intensive fieldwork for at least a year in a single society. Prolonged attempts to understand another society should lead to an appreciation of the complexity and divergence of cultures; this may make anthropologists effective spokesmen for the indigenous people's view of proposed developments, although it is preferable that they should be enabled to speak for themselves. But the extent to which prolonged research in one society generates practical suggestions for planning in another, is very limited. An anthropologist who has spent two years in a Sri Lankan fishing village, for example, could make only a limited contribution to a fisheries project in Java. Anthropologists with extensive experience in Java are likely to be more effective, even if their research was in an area far removed from fishing. And, of course, the planning agency will have to wait while specific field research is carried out.

The second difficulty concerns the results of anthropological research, which now includes a considerable literature on the results of planned fisheries development (see Emmerson 1980). In my view, this literature has important implications for future planning, but the implications are seldom spelt out and they may be unpalatable for fisheries administrators. Most of the literature is concerned with the results of fisheries development plans rather than with the process of development planning and, unfortunately, most studies are attempts to account for plans which failed to meet their social objectives. All conclusions seem to point in the same direction: new technologies do not increase rural employment and often exacerbate social inequalities in rural communities.

THE SRI LANKAN EXPERIENCE

As an example of the impact of technological innovations, I want to look at the results of twenty years of fisheries development in Sri Lanka, concentrating on the extent to which the biological/economic goals of fisheries planning are compatible with the social objectives of equity and employment. The development of Sri Lankan fisheries through the provision of small mechanized craft owned and operated by village fishermen was something of an accident; the government was unable to finance the expensive industrial craft that were recommended by five successive teams of foreign consultants. Instead they adopted a 3.5 ton craft which was already being built locally and limited the expenditure of scarce foreign exchange to importing diesel engines. The boat was initially designed for the same type of fishing as the main indigenous coastal craft, line fishing and trolling, but over about ten years it was modified for driftnetting and more powerful engines were added (FAO, 1977; Pietersz, 1978). By 1977, at least 2,500 craft had been built - 7 boatyards in 1957 had become 32 in 1977 - and maybe half were still afloat at that time (Director of Fisheries, Administration Reports, 1957-77).

The craft had a rapid and immediate effect in increasing fish production. The total catch rose from 36,000 tons in 1956, to 135,000 tons by 1975. Fish imports fell from 81 to 24 million rupees, while exports rose from 1 to 75 million rupees (Director of Fisheries, Administrative Report, 1975). The unsatisfied demand for fish kept prices high so that operating a successful craft provided a substantial income. However, even at this level there are hints of some problems for the equity objectives of the scheme. Some portion of the apparent increase in the catch can be attributed to the replacement of traditional craft whose catches were not accurately recorded, and the government recovered not more, and probably far less, than half of the costs of the new boats from their owners. Furthermore, far less fish was consumed in the rural areas because of high urban prices, and better transport and icing facilities.

Lifting rural standards of living was always a professed objective of the scheme (Director of Fisheries Administration Reports, 1975, 1967, 1971). Appreciating that the high costs of the boats - about four times the annual income of the richer village households - was beyond the reach of genuine fishermen, the fisheries department issued them through local co-operatives and through a hire purchase scheme. The co-operatives were an unmitigated disaster, few boats were still operating at the end of their season, and hire purchase became the norm. Genuine fishermen selected by the MP to participate in a ballot, paid a 10 per cent deposit and were then expected to make equal monthly payments for the next five years.

Reviewing the first fifteen years of the project in the Sinhalese fishing communities of southern Sri Lanka, I argued that the human consequences of the innovation were dismal (Alexander 1975a, 1975b). Although the gross village income had risen, most of the benefits had been captured by a small elite of successful boatowners and fish traders, and the income of the majority of households had fallen. Employment in fishing had certainly not kept pace with population increases and probably declined. I concluded that the villages were increasingly polarized in both political and economic terms. In place of the large class of free peasants, a small elite, and an equally small group living in poverty, there was a large elite amounting to 15 per cent of the population with the rest sinking towards poverty.

Five years later, a Dutch anthropologist, Marteen Bavinck, examined the impact of the small craft in a Tamil village in northern Sri Lanka (Bavinck 1984; Bavinck and van Dijk 1978). His conclusions could not be more opposed to mine. The income of the village increased and its benefits were relatively equally shared: 'most households seem to have benefitted from the change in technology and the higher village income.' 'Whereas the ownership of fishing gear was formerly monopolized by a small group, and poverty and seasonal migration were common, two-thirds of the households now own nets, catamarans or boats.' 'Mobility in fishing has become ordinary: many of the present day propertyless (often young married couples) have distinct chances of acquiring the means of production in the future (Bavinck, 1984:29-30). Assuming that the empirical data are correct, and there is considerable supporting evidence for both southern and northern Sri Lanka (Stirrart, 1974, 1975), why did the craft have radically different social consequences in the two areas?

SOUTHERN SRI LANKA

In explaining the problems with the 3.5 ton craft in southern Sri Lanka, I placed most emphasis on two interrelated factors: the consequences of the new craft for traditional fishing methods, and the social relations of production (Alexander, 1982).

Prior to the mechanized craft, the major fishing technologies were beachseining and the use of a large outrigger canoe for pole and line fishing or trolling. Both types of gear were relatively expensive - about a household's annual income - but they were built and rebuilt over long periods and there was a highly developed system of share ownership. In the case of the large canoe used for offshore fishing, the seven crew members were entitled to two-thirds of the catch. The other third was divided among the owners of the boat who were usually three or four of the older crew members. The beach-seines, which provided most of the catch, were run on similar lines. The catch was sold at auction and the fish traders, whose enterprises were fairly small-scale, seldom invested in production or advanced credit.

The mechanized craft radically altered the economics of fisheries along the southern coast. Although well-intentioned, the loan scheme had several technical defects. The provisions for a deposit and the fact that the loan covered only the cost of the hull and engine, not the gear, meant that the fishermen had to have access to capital. Because the men lacked experience in the operation of mechanized craft and net fishing, breakdowns were frequent in the early operating period, and as no provision was made for financing repairs the boat operators had to have access to private capital for this purpose also. But the most important defect was that the loan repayment was not related to the value of the catch, but was to be met by a fixed monthly payment, and even the most successful fisherman was faced with months in the off-season when the loan repayment was greater than his income.

In addition fishermen were often faced with the theft or total destruction of a set of nets worth more than Rp.7,000 and engine repairs costing in excess of Rp.4,000. As both the labour and the materials for repairs came from outside the village, repair costs had to be met immediately upon completion and were too high to be paid out of current income. The management problems were exacerbated because crew members were drawn from the canoe crews and shares were allocated in the traditional manner. The four-man crew were entitled to half the catch after fuel and bait costs were deducted. The sum remaining to the owner was not sufficient to meet repair, hire purchase and depreciation, even in months of high catches (Alexander, 1975:337-41).

The mechanized craft were an asset with a high capital cost and a short operating life; approximately five years for the engine, eight years for the hull, and three years for the nets. Although the ratio of the operating costs to the value of the catch was similar to that of the traditional craft, the amount of money that was involved was very much greater and there was little flexibility in making payments. Fuel costs and repayment of the government loans had to be met each month, irrespective of the size of the catch.

The major economic advantage of the new craft to their owners was the large annual catch of high value fish and this led to a system of 'tied' boats, between owners and fish traders. In return for the right to buy all the catch at ruling prices, the fish trader provided both short and long term credit for capital, operating and subsistence costs. The procedure for loan repayments was very flexible: during poor months there were no repayments; in good months as much as 40 per cent of the catch was retained by the fish trader.

Consequently, the history of most boats fell into a repetitive pattern. If the owner was unlucky, he was faced with heavy repair and gear replacement costs during the first two or three years' operation, and consequently became indebted to a fish trader for one to one-and-a-half years' income. Despite the debt, the owner's income during these years was likely to be high (Rs.3,000), because the debt was repayable at a rate of only 40 per cent of the 'boat's' share of the catch and the owner was not repaying the government loan. In many cases the owner responded to this apparently high income by ceasing to fish and by giving the craft to a close relative to skipper. But once the fish trader decided that the owner was unlikely to ever repay the loan, he refused to advance further credit and the boat had to be sold to pay some of the debt. Due to the uncertainty of title and the outstanding loan, prices for second hand boats were very low. A three-year-old craft in reasonable condition but needing repairs would be unlikely to fetch 10 per cent of the initial cost, the craft being bought by other fishermen, not fish traders, although the latter might advance the money (Alexander, 1982:105-114).

The sequence for a skilful, or lucky, owner was rather different. If the repair and gear replacement costs were low during the early life of a boat, the owner could limit his debt. Consequently, when boats from less successful owners were marketed, he was in a good position to buy them, either from his current income or with the aid of a loan from a fish trader. The new boat was given to a close relative to operate, but the 'boat's' share went to the owner. Once the owner had acquired two or three boats he could manage them in a manner derived from the traditional system. In some cases the craft were operated under this system from the beginning as when two or three brothers were allocated boats. With the income and credit facilities of all three boats at the owner's disposal, repair and gear replacement costs could be met immediately they fell due, and as less time was lost through repairs, the income from the craft was higher than average. When one of the boats was beyond repair, the owner could easily purchase, repair and re-equip a second-hand craft to replace it, or in a few cases, finance the purchase of a new craft.

The mechanized craft had radical effects on other fishing methods. The outrigger canoes rapidly disappeared because of the diversion of crew members and capital to the mechanized craft; beachseining was affected as their sites were taken over for anchorage. Because employment on the mechanized boats gave much higher income than other fishing, jobs were eagerly sought, but boat owners limited employment to their relatives, thus reducing the extent to which benefits might 'trickle down' to other members of the community. In the later stages, however, as the boats became clustered in the hands of non-fishermen and based in fewer villages, wage labour was introduced.

NORTHERN SRI LANKA

Fishing methods in northern Sri Lanka prior to the introduction of the 3.5 ton boats differed in several significant respects from those of the South. Beachseining was important, but the nets had a single owner and were operated by wage labour. The main form of offshore fishing employed the catamaran - essentially a raft of 6-7 logs - using nets. Nylon nets had replaced cotton nets in the late fifties, so that the Tamil fishermen, unlike the Sinhalese fishermen, were familiar with their use when mechanization began (Stirrart 1975).

Perhaps the most important difference, however, was that the catamaran, unlike the Sinhalese canoe, proved adaptable to outboard motors. These motors were much cheaper than mechanized craft, and the records suggest that about 5,000 had been bought between 1964 and 1975. The combination of a catamaran, outboard motors, and nylon nets was an effective, if very tiring and wet, fishing method which produced around four times the catch of an unpowered craft. Not only was the capital cost low - less than two years' income - but there were well-developed share systems which treated each unit of the gear as a separate item. Shares in the nets and the engine, for example, might be held by non-fishing members of the fishing community.

When the 3.5 ton boats entered the area in large numbers after 1965, they caused little dislocation to existing fishing relationships. All of the boats were in a strict sense illegal, having been bought from fishermen in the South, and thus were probably acquired below the usual cost. Some were initially hired from owners in urban centres, but by 1977, 70 per cent of the craft were owned by men who fished in them and all were owned within the village.

Bavinck (1984) traces their success to two factors: compatibility with existing fishing techniques, and a share system which reduced the 'lumpiness' of capital. To take the second point first. On the modern northern boat, the initial charge on the boat is the operating expenses plus a fixed sum for the boatowner. The catch is then divided into two parts: one for the labour and one for the nets. The labour share is divided equally among the crew; the net share is allocated in ratio to the ownership of net segments. A mechanized craft can carry up to 50 net segments and the catch is seen by the fishermen as a function of the number of net segments. It is possible, therefore, for both fishermen and non-fishermen to contribute capital in relatively small amounts and to draw a return on it. Crew members slowly accumulate investment in nets: beginning with a couple of segments (often transferred from the catamaran) and adding others when replacements are needed. Not only did this provide an avenue of social mobility, and a source of income for retired fishermen and women, but it reduced dependence on capital sources outside the village.

The outboard-powered catamarans were, and remain, important for the success of the 3.5 ton boats. Initially they were the source of fishermen who were skilled in the use of nets and engines, and they are still the training ground for newcomers. Most of the additional labour for offshore fishing has become owners of mechanized boats within ten years, investing their earnings in shares in engines and nets. The possibility of the crew returning to the more disagreeable work on the catamaran keep the crew's shares on mechanized boats at reasonable levels - at least three times the wage of the beach seines - and the beachseine owners can only obtain labour outside the village. By the time Bavinck left in 1979, the fishermen were beginning to replace the catamaran with a 17-foot fibreglass boat, rather than buying the bigger craft. Tied boat arrangements have not developed in northern Sri Lankan fish marketing and the level of investment by fish traders in the means of production has decreased. One reason is that the Tamil fishing communities are far less reliant on the fish traders for capital. The fact that the fish traders are mainly Sinhalese may have had some effect. Another reason is that women are more directly involved in fishing in the north. The former cotton nets needed constant mending and this was often women's work. With the introduction of nylon nets, women freed from this task took charge of marketing the catch. Whereas Sinhalese fishermen must sell their catch quickly so that they can sleep, northern women often take the catch to local markets and retail it themselves.

CONCLUSION

It may not be unduly cynical to suggest that one reason for the success of the craft in the north was that Tamil fishermen were not the subjects of planned development. It was the fishermen themselves who sought the boats, developed methods to finance them and integrated them with other methods of fishing. The fact that the benefits were relatively equally distributed within the village, however, was less an objective of this process than a consequence: it followed from the lack of access to extra village capital and the ability to break capital requirements down into small segments. Although the southern fishermen also developed strategies of finance and employment which made the new craft profitable, it took them much longer and destroyed the equity provisions of the programme in the process.

To some extent the reasons for the differing consequences of a single innovation were historical and contingent and they would not have been predicted in advance by the most perceptive anthropologist. Among those mentioned, were the nature of existing technologies, the social relations of production, and the extent of prior capitalist development. Critical factors which have not been discussed include the position of the Tamils in the Sri Lankan state and the lower population pressures in the more isolated of the northern villages.

Nevertheless, a comparison of the two cases does suggest some lessons for effective economic planning. An important problem, for example, is that new technologies are usually too expensive for capital costs to be met from village resources, in either the short or intermediate term. Fixing repayments to cover capital costs, will impoverish unlucky operators, increase social tension, and inhibit the development of mechanisms to finance the replacement of wornout gear. This suggests that the calculations of repayment schedules should be preceded by a thorough investigation of the nature and extent of capital sources in the village; to which can be added a conservative - a very conservative - calculation of the capital which the innovation might produce. Aid agencies can then decide in advance whether they will provide the massive subsidy or abandon the innovation.

An associated problem concerns the 'lumpiness' of capital. Peasant communities may possess considerable capital, but be unwilling, or unable because of the form in which capital is held, to invest in a new and therefore risky technology. A partial solution to this problem is to break the gear down into smaller parts. A boat, engine and nets may be required for effective fishing, but there is no reason why they should be owned as a unit.

However, while there are many specific ways in which a better understanding of local communities can improve fisheries planning, there remains an essential tension between the productive and the equity objectives. All things being equal, the introduction of new fishing methods which will give large catches of high value fish (if they won't, why bother?) must have radical effects on the distribution of wealth, income and power within the village. Innovations will make some owners richer, and, in displacing other fishing methods, make others poorer.

A possible way to ameliorate these consequences is not a closer integration of fisheries and social development planning, but a clear separation of the two. The equity implications of development are extremely important, but they should be dealt with by mechanisms designed for that purpose, including taxation or royalties. The most common method of trying to combine equity and productive objectives, the creation of co-operatives, has failed because the co-operatives have been forced to meet too many goals simultaneously. Fisheries co-operatives are expected not only to manage the craft, but also market the catch, provide repair facilities, run insurance schemes, alter the sexual division of labour and imbue the citizens with a co-operative spirit. It may be considered that introducing an expensive and very risky technology is a sufficient task for any institution: co-operatives, like planners, should restrict their aims rather than expand them.

REFERENCES

Alexander P, 1975a Do Fisheries Experts Aid Fisheries Development?, Maritime Studies and Management 3 pp5-11.

Alexander P, 1975b Innovation in a Cultural Vacuum, Human Organisation 34 pp333-344.

Alexander P, 1982 Sri Lankan Fishermen: Rural Capitalism and Peasant Society Canberra: ANU South Asian Series.

Bavinck M, 1984 Small Fry: The Economy of Petty Fishermen in Northern Sri Lanka. Amsterdam: Free University Press.

Bavinck M and van Dijk F M, 1978 The Transformation of a Fishing Community: The Case of Kadalur, Sri Lanka. Research Report, Amsterdam: Free University.

Director of Fisheries, 1955-77 Administration Reports. Colombo: Government Press.

Emmerson D, 1980 Rethinking Artisanal Fisheries Development: Western Concepts Asian Experiences. Washington: World Bank.

FAO, 1977 Assessment of Problems and Needs in Marine Small-Scale Fisheries, Sri Lanka. Colombo: FAO report.

Pietersz, U., 1978, "Development of Offshore and Deepsea Fisheries in Sri Lanka" Bulletin of Fisheries Research Station, No 28.

Stirrart R, 1974 Fish to Market: Traders in Rural Sri Lanka South Asia 7, 3:5-13.

Stirrart R, 1975 The Social Organization of Fishing in a Sinhalese Village Modern Ceylon Studies 6, 2:23-44.

Chapter Six

GIANT CLAMS IN THE PACIFIC - THE SOCIO-ECONOMIC POTENTIAL OF A DEVELOPING TECHNOLOGY FOR THEIR MARICULTURE

Clem Tisdell

It is now technically possible to farm giant clams (tridacnids). Methods for the breeding and rearing of giant clams under human management have been developed in the last decade and by the end of the next decade commercial farming in the Pacific is likely to be established even though there are still some socio-economic hurdles to be overcome. Further developments in the technology for raising giant clams can also be expected to improve the economics of clam cultivation.

These developments come at a time when tridacnid stocks are seriously depleted and a number of species have disappeared from their former range in the Indo-Pacific area. The IUCN has placed Tridacna gigas and Tridacna derasa, the two largest sized clams, on its endangered list (IUCN, 1983).

The possibility of farming giant clams is of particular interest because (except in the veliger stage), they are autotrophic due to their symbiosis with algae embedded in their mantle. This means that they do not require artificial feeding and in particular the import of food as, for example, prawn mariculture does (cf Uwate et al, 1984). The ocean grow-out phase appears technically simple and requires little capital investment beyond the purchase of juvenile clams and as far as is known clams of 'grow-out' size have few predators. Furthermore, clams are well adapted to the sunlit waters of coral reef areas low in nutrients. They are therefore of particular interest to atoll countries in the Pacific which have limited resources available to them for development but which often possess significant reef areas (Tisdell and Fairbairn, 1983; 1984). According to estimates made by Heslinga et al. (1984) edible meat production per hectare per year from clams almost equals that for mussels (which are heterotrophic and intensively managed) and far exceeds that for tilapia. In some of the Pacific islands, limited husbanding of clams by the indigenous population already takes place and this may provide useful skills for expanding the mariculture of clams.

THE STATUS OF GIANT CLAMS (TRIDACNIDS)

Giant clams (F Tridacnidae) are confined to Indo-Pacific waters of sufficient warmth for their survival but some species are restricted in range to waters in the vicinity of the Malaysian-Indonesian Archipelago through to Fiji in the west and bounded in the south by the tropical waters of Australia. The range of Hippopus hippopus, Tridacna gigas and Tridacna derasa as suggested by Rosewater (1965) are indicated in Figure 5. The range of Tridacna maxima and Tridacna squamosa is much greater. It includes most of the Indian Ocean above the Tropic of Capricorn and some portions below it (eg along the South African coast) and most of the West Pacific (see Rosewater, 1965, for details). However giant clams do not occur in the East Pacific nor in the Hawaiian Archipelago.

The largest sized clams are T gigas and T derasa. They reach a maximum shell length of approximately 100cm and 50cm respectively. Other species with likely maximum shell lengths include: T squamosa (40cm) Hippopus hippopus (40cm) and T maxima (30cm). T crocea, the burrowing clam, is much smaller.

Greatest recent interest has been expressed in the possiblity of cultivating T gigas and T derasa. Preference for T gigas is based upon the proposition that the biomass increase in these clams is greater than for other species during their initial growth years. Yet, there is a possibility that T derasa is hardier than T gigas. Nevertheless, the relatively small clam T crocea is reported to be commercially cultivated in Okinawa, Japan (pers. comm. Uday Raj, February, 1986).

Although Rosewater (1965) indicates that the range of Hippopus hippopus includes the Fiji Islands, there is no indication that it has extended to this area in historic times. Extensive surveys by the Fisheries Section, Department of Primary Industries, Fiji have failed to find any evidence of recent presence of Hippopus hippopus. Furthermore, T gigas seems to have disappeared from Fiji in

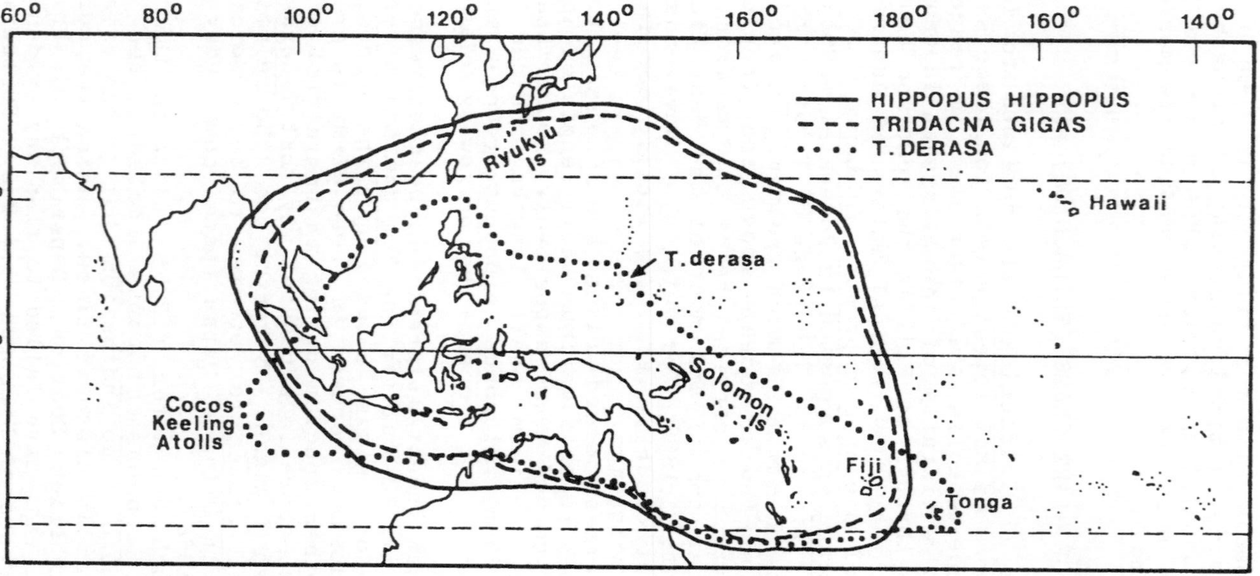

Figure 5 Generalised distribution of <u>Hippopus hippopus</u>, <u>Tridacna gigas</u> and <u>T. derasa</u> in historic times after Rosewater (1965) and Munro and Heslinga (1982).

recent times, possibly as a result of overharvesting. It has also disappeared in other parts of its range and has almost been eliminated in other places, eg the Philippines. Poaching by Taiwanese vessels especially in the Northwest Pacific seems to have played a significant part in this (Dawson, 1984). However, commercial sales and greater subsistence use may have contributed.

Australian waters now hold the largest stocks of giant clams in the world. Tridacnids are protected in Australian waters and effective action has been taken to curb Taiwanese poaching in the Australian fishing zone. Stocks, however, continue to be depleted elsewhere in the Pacific.

Domestic use of giant clams in the Pacific varies but in all cases the kidney is discarded before they are eaten. In some areas they are eaten raw. This seems to be especially common amongst Micronesians and Polynesians. In some cases they are also eaten dried e.g. in Ontong Java, or pickled in Tuba vinegar, e.g. in the Federated States of Micronesia. Many Melanesians, however, will only eat cooked clam whereas cooked clam is unacceptable to many Polynesians. In the Solomon Islands, the clam is cooked in coconut milk by the Melanesians and in some areas the seeds (fruit) of a particular mangrove may be added for extra flavour. In Serea, Fiji clams (vasua) are quite often smoked to help preserve them. The first cooking may be in water, recooking is in coconut milk, but in some parts of Fiji clams are eaten raw, in some instances, after being marinated in lemon or lime juice.

On a recent visit to the Solomon Islands and to Fiji (February, 1986), it was found that frozen clam adductor muscle is being exported by air to Australia. Much of this appears to be re-exported from Australia after being given health certification. While exports of mantle (meat) from Fiji was not significant, frozen meat was being sent by sea from the Solomon Islands to Australia. In Fiji the meat of the mantle is attractively packed by Feeders of Fiji in frozen form for sale in Fijian supermarkets. The export volumes from Fiji and the Solomon Islands however appear to be relatively small. Nevertheless, if farming should develop in either of these countries, local companies do exist which have experience in processing and marketing giant clams. It might be noted that clam meat is also intermittently on sale at municipal markets in Fiji, the Solomon Islands and other Pacific islands.

DEVELOPMENT OF THE TECHNOLOGY FOR GIANT CLAM CULTIVATION

Techniques for the controlled breeding and rearing of giant clams have been developed relatively recently and are still evolving. In 1972, LaBarbera of Duke University artificially spawned T maxima and T squamosa using stock collected in Fiji and reared the larvae through to the juvenile stage (LaBarbera, 1975). This was the first time that Tridacnidae had been successfully spawned and reared. Between 1973 and 1974 Jameson of the University of Guam successfully spawned and reared T crocea, T maxima and Hippopus hippopus and showed that giant clams may be stimulated to spawn by adding macerated gonads to the water (Jameson, 1976). The research was conducted at the University of Guam Marine Laboratory and in Palau at the Micronesian Mariculture Demonstration Center (MMDC). In 1978 and 1979 N Beckvar (1981) successfully spawned and reared T gigas and T derasa at MMDC, Palau, either relying on natural spawning or using macerated gonads and hydrogen peroxide as stimulants. The way for mass hatchery production of juveniles was opening up even though no reliable method for inducing spawning was yet available.

Between 1977 and 1981, experiments were also in progress at the University of Papua New Guinea on spawning induction of tridacnid clams and rearing of their larvae. In 1979, Gwyther and Munro (1981) found that freeze-dried gonad could be reliably used to induce spawning in T maxima. However, the problem with using gonads (macerated or freeze-dried) continue to be that it required the sacrifice of donors. In 1984-1985, Braley (1985) of the University of New South Wales showed that serotonin (a commercially available chemical product) can be used to induce spawning in giant clams. The chemical has been used successfully at the Orpheus Island Laboratory of James Cook University for this purpose.

Over a 4-year period commencing around 1980 and following Beckvar's successful breeding of T gigas and T derasa, the Micronesia Mariculture Demonstration Center developed techniques for the mass culture of giant clams (Heslinga et al, 1985). The method developed relies on the natural spawning of the clam broodstock and the rearing of clams at least to the juvenile stage of 10-20 mm shell size in raceways through which seawater is pumped at relatively low speed commencing 3-4 days after fertilisation. In the early stages the clam larvae obtain nutrients from the unfiltered plankton-rich lagoon water pumped into the raceway. No artificial feeding of clams is involved. While this method makes maximum use of local resources and involves relatively simple techniques, it has the disadvantage that the success rate in breeding and rearing juveniles to the macroscopic stage varies considerably.

In 1983, Dr J L Munro as Director, Resource Assessment and Management Program, International Centre for Living Aquatic Resources (ICLARM) put forward the description of a project entitled "The International Giant Clam Mariculture Project". Its aim is to be to promote and co-ordinate various international efforts in developing giant clam mariculture (Munro, 1985a) either formally or informally. In that respect, ICLARM has established links with James Cook University of North Queensland (JCUNQ) where Dr J Lucas and Dr Munro jointly co-ordinate a project of the Australian Centre for International Agriculture Research (ACIAR) investigating "The Culture of the Giant Clam (Tridacna Sp) for Food and Restocking of Tropical Reefs". Amongst other things, the ICLARM project envisages the establishment of a pilot hatchery, possibly in the Solomon Islands, to adapt techniques developed elsewhere to local conditions, materials and economic circumstances.

In June 1984, the Australian Centre for International Agricultural Research began funding the clam culture project (mentioned above) under the co-ordination of James Cook University (1985). Partners in the research are the Fisheries Division, Department of Primary Industry, Fiji, Silliman University, Philippines, the University of Papua New Guinea and the University of the Philippines. A basic aim of this project is to improve and develop techniques for the mass culture of giant clams, on an experimental basis. Work at the Orpheus Island marine research station of JCUNQ has concentrated on the adaptation to clam culture of intensive techniques similar to those used for the initial breeding of oyster spat. The methods involved are more reliable than those used at MMDC but require more skill and equipment and the use (at least, currently) of cultured algae rather than natural phytoplankton. Several other practical aspects of mariculture are also being studied. At the University of New Guinea and in the Philippines some research is aimed at improving the MMDC 'low-tech' approach to clam culture. In Fiji and in the Philippines effort is being put into the study of natural clam populations and the determination of their status. This ACIAR sponsored clam culture project was expected to terminate in June of 1987 and will have involved the expenditure of around $A0.9m. Its main economic benefits should be to improve techniques for giant clam mariculture and to spread knowledge about these methods.

ALTERNATIVE MEANS OF MANAGING THE SUPPLY OF CLAMS

The supply of giant clams may be maintained or increased by humans in many different ways. These include

(a) by controls on the harvesting of natural stocks
(b) reseeding of reefs or other habitats suitable to tridacnids
(c) ranching, and
(d) farming

Various controls may be placed on the taking of natural stock. McKoy (1980) at the time that he wrote was of the opinion that the most effective and economic means of maintaining supply of clams was to impose controls on the taking of natural stock rather than, say, farming clams. Little is known about optimal harvesting policies for giant clams in the wild e.g. the harvest levels corresponding to maximum sustainable yield. Should there be minimum size limits on clams taken from the wild? If so, how can these be enforced? Should various techniques such as scuba diving be banned? Hopefully some of the studies being undertaken as part of the ACIAR project will provide more information in this respect e.g. the Fiji module. In some areas, it is possible that villagers or traditional reef owners would vary their harvesting procedures if this would improve their sustainable yields and they had reliable knowledge of what is needed. For example, Robert Satu, a leader from a village on Malaita, Solomon Islands, informed me (February, 1986) that such control is feasible in his village at the village level.

Some limited attempts have been made in the Pacific to reseed reefs using juvenile clams from MMDC, Palau. While this is technically possible, if the juveniles are too small, the mortality rate is very high. Again even when reseeding is successful in re-establishing a clam population, its future will depend upon access to it for harvesting purposes. If there is common access or little concern with conserving the clam stock, a re-established population may be wiped out or exploited at a greater rate than optimal.

Ranching involves taking juveniles or other stock from the wild and growing it under managed conditions. This is a technical possibility for tridacnids. In Manus (MacLean, 1978) and in the Solomon Islands (as reported to me by villagers from Malaita and Savo Islands), villagers collect "medium-sized" clams and hold them in clam gardens until they are required. In this respect Johannes (1982: p.240) comments "In Manus giant clams are collected and held in walled enclosures on the reef until they are needed in rough weather when fishing is difficult. This practice may perhaps be said to constitute a limited form of conservation inasmuch as it increases available food near the village. But this practice cannot legitimately be referred to as aquaculture.... in the absence of any evidence that it actually promotes the growth of the clams". Johannes points out that the people of Andra Island, Manus Province believe that the growth rate of clams is somewhat reduced by this procedure. However, the procedure establishes a way of obtaining property rights to particular clams. This could result in clams being held longer before harvest than would be so if they could not be held in clam gardens. However, there is a general risk with ranching that if a product becomes very valuable, natural stocks will be collected at a faster rate than otherwise and animals left for breeding purposes seriously reduced in numbers.

Farming of animals is another possibility. Here we could distinguish between a closed system in which brood stock are domestically reared and an open system in which brood stock are taken from the wild. At present experimental clam hatcheries rely on brood stock taken from the wild. However, once the first batches of hatchery juveniles begin to mature these could be used as brood stock. In the long term, the breeding system can become a self-sustaining (closed) one and it should become possible to select superior stock for breeding purposes. While hatchery, nursery and grow-out farming could be combined in a contiguous area, at the present time it is envisaged that a combined hatchery and nursery at one location would provide juveniles for a number of different grow-out farms or grow-out points.

Although farming is a technical possibility, its potential depends upon economic and social factors. In the Pacific, particular attention needs to be paid to land (including reef rights) and sharing arrangements. Farming requires the establishment of property rights in the farmed animals and sharing arrangements that encourage the appropriate husbanding of them. Some attention will be given below to this as far as the Pacific is concerned.

BASIC ELEMENTS IN THE HATCHERY, NURSERY AND GROW-OUT PHASES OF CLAM MARICULTURE

The basic mariculture of clams as it has currently evolved requires several on-land tanks or raceways (containers) of approximately a metre or so in depth (exposed to sunlight) and a means of pumping seawater through them. Some means of filtering the water is also beneficial.

At least one tank is required to hold the broodstock. Heslinga et al, (1985) suggest that a batch of about 18 mature animals would be required for this approach involving natural spawning. If the intensive method of rearing larvae is used a smaller broodstock may suffice but an air-conditioned room and other equipment is needed to nurse the larvae through the first 7 days.

After 7 days (or earlier if Heslinga's approach is used), the larvae are transferred to a tank of seawater and held there for 60-90 days. At the end of this period, the juvenile clams are macroscopic (5-10 mm) and have settled on the floor of the vessel. They are scraped from the bottom and placed in Nestier shellfish trays containing basalt chips (or a similar substrate) to which the developing clams can attach and these in turn are placed in another tank containing seawater.

Subsequent operations involve reducing or rearranging densities of the juveniles as they grow. Also algae growth can be troublesome and a grazer needs to be added to the tank to keep fouling down. At MMDC, Trochus niloticus has been used for this purpose but other grazers may also be suitable. The culture of a suitable grazer could provide a small source of additional income.

After a post-fertilisation period of about 8-10

months, _T gigas_ juveniles appear to reach a shell length of around 3 cm. By the age of 2-2 years, _T gigas_ and _T derasa_ appear to reach a length of 10-15 cm. The preliminary finding of Heslinga _et al_ (1985:211) "suggest that unless some form of protection is provided, clams smaller than 100-150 mm may suffer unacceptably high losses from predators in nature". This implies that the nursery phase must last for 2-2.5 years and that reseeding of reefs with juveniles smaller that 10-15 cm in length is likely to be a waste of resources.

Although juvenile clams can be held in land-based tanks for the whole of the nursery stage of 2-2.5 years, this can take up considerable space and may be much more expensive than transferring juveniles at 8 months or so of age to an 'ocean nursery'. The ocean nursery involves placing juveniles in covered trays or protected containers on the ocean floor in a relatively shallow protected position e.g. just below low tide mark. However, alternative methods are still being investigated for the ocean nursery phase (Munro, 1985c).

Once juvenile clams reach 10-15 cm in length they can be placed out unprotected on the ocean floor to grow. They should be in a protected position (e.g. leeward side of an island) with clean water, for instance on a fringing reef. _T gigas_ and _T derasa_ should retain their position due to their weight but the impact of cyclones on their location is not known. If the juvenile clams are suitably spaced to begin with no further attention should be required prior to harvesting except to prevent them from being stolen. The harvested clams are likely to be valuable for their meat (adductor muscle and mantle) and for their shells.

UTILISATION AND VALUE OF CULTURED CLAMS

All portions of the clam except the liver can be utilised by humans. The adductor muscle, the mantle and shells are internationally traded. For example, the Solomon Islands exports small quantities of frozen muscle and mantle to Australia and Fiji exports frozen muscle to Australia. It is believed that some of this is re-exported after obtaining Australian health certification. Taiwan and Hong Kong are possible markets as well as Japan and the USA. The Philippines appear to be an important centre for the shell trade and clam shells are exported from here to many places (including to

Australia) to be sold in shell shops and souvenir shops. Most of the shell exported from the Philippines is obtained either within the country or imported from Indonesia. As natural stocks are dwindling in this area, the shell is likely to become scarcer, and while no exports of clam shell from Fiji appear to have taken place (or from other islands in the South Pacific) a potential seems to exist for export.

Estimates made by Munro (1985b) suggest that after five years' grow-out the value of a clam for its shell could almost be as great as for its meat. He estimates on the basis of Fiji data for adductor muscle and mantle that the meat would be valued at $5.99 and the shell (using Philippines data) would be valued at $5.06 making a total value of $11.05, in US dollars. This is most likely an overestimate of the value to the primary producer but if it was realised and given a mortality rate of about 10 per cent per year in stocks of clams grown-out, clam farming would appear to be potentially very profitable. Approximately 60 per cent of grown-out clams could be expected to survive five years and thus the average realisation per grown-out clam would be around 0.6 x $11 = $7.26. If a 10-15 cm juvenile costs $1 and if husbanding costs are virtually zero, the internal rate of return on the investment would be almost 40 per cent compounded. However, Munro's 'computer-trail' figures would greatly overestimate the current value obtained by primary suppliers of clams in Fiji. In the absence of shell sales and given current prices, $3.00 would be an optimistic allowance for the value of the clam in Fiji at the end of 5 years (that is, its meat value) (James Cook University, 1985; T Adams pers comm). Allowing for a 60 per cent mortality after 5 years, this would reduce the internal rate of return on a farming (hypothetical) outlay of $1 per juvenile clam to just over 11 per cent compounded. If the rate of interest was much in excess of 11 per cent, farming would then not be economic. However, meat prices could improve, a market might be found for Fijian shells and the cost of juvenile stock might be lowered.

It should be noted that production does not end with primary production if the clam products are destined for urban or international markets. For international markets, the clams have to be collected, prepared and packed. The muscle must be separated from the mantle, the kidney discarded. These products have to be frozen and packed for shipment, and stored under controlled cold-room conditions until shipment or sales. The exporter needs skills in arranging international exchange. The required infrastructure is present in Fiji and to some extent in the Solomon Islands since exports of frozen clam meat are taking place. In both cases a structure exists that could be expanded to cater for exports of maricultured clam meat.

SOCIO-ECONOMIC CONSIDERATIONS IN THE PACIFIC

The rate of expansion of clam mariculture in the South Pacific is likely to be constrained by several factors. The supply of juveniles from hatcheries can be expected to be a basic constraint. There is as yet no hatchery and nursery in the South Pacific for the supply of clams for commercial farming although experimental hatcheries exist. However, plans have been mooted for a pilot hatchery in the Solomon Islands. If a hatchery were to begin operation tomorrow about 7 to 7.5 years would be required before its progeny would contribute to clam supplies, assuming that the normal length of the grow-out phase is 5 years. Hence, it is likely to be around a decade before cultured clams can add appreciably to supplies.

Initially hatcheries in the South Pacific are likely to be under institutional or government control although in the longer term private hatcheries may be viable. If clam farming is to be established, it is important that growers be not misled about economic prospects and that juvenile clams released for farming have a high chance of survival. Possibly this is more likely to be achieved by government hatcheries and nurseries rather than private ones.

The success of farming depends upon property rights being established in grown-out clams. Many areas in the Pacific suitable for farming clams belong to traditional owners (cf Carrier, 1981). While the Crown may claim all the area below high tide mark, in practice governments in many Pacific countries cannot ignore the claims of traditional owners. The right of an outside person or company to use a marine area may depend upon consent from traditional owners (village groups, tribal groups, etc.) as well as the government. In most places, in the Solomon Islands and Fiji the consent of traditional owners would be required and in some cases ownership may be disputed. In Fiji, a check may be made with the Native Land and Fisheries Commission as to owners according to their records but in addition further local checks are advisable to determine whether village groups accept the Commission's allocation (pers comm Asesela Ravuvu).

It would be possible for a village group or co-operative to farm clams in its own right or to make arrangements with others to do this in a marine area belonging to the village. In the latter case the success of the venture is likely to depend on village involvement in it and the establishment of incentives to prevent others from raiding the stock or the villagers from taking it themselves. In places where marine areas have been alienated, the government may be able to give property rights to commercial growers as is for instance done for oyster farmers in Australia.

The integration of clam farming into traditional social and economic structures would probably tend to maximise employment of family groups especially women. In commercial large-scale cash enterprises in the Pacific, there appears to be a tendency for men to be employed in preference to women (Schoeffel, 1984:6).

There are many other issues that could be considered. For instance, in what ways can the technology for clam mariculture be made more appropriate to LDCs in the Pacific? Where should nurseries be located and how large should they be? Would large clam plantations be desirable? To what extent should villagers depend on clam cultivation as a cash crop? To what extent could clam cultivation be at the expense of other products taken from reef and shallow marine areas?

CONCLUSION

The basic technology for giant clam farming now exists. Advances are likely to be made in the next few years which will reduce the costs of seed clams and improve the economics of giant clam farming. A portion of the Indo-Pacific through from Malaysia to Fiji seems to be ecologically very suitable for tridacnid culture. This marine mariculture appears to have significant economic potential, the actual farming is low-tech and does not require imports and can be integrated into existing socio-economic structures and practices. It has the potential to make at least a small contribution to the output of LDCs in the region, provide increased cash incomes and some extra foreign exchange earnings. However, it will be at least a decade before we start to see these effects even though at least one large scale hatchery may be established soon.

REFERENCES

Beckvar N, 1981 Cultivation, spawning and growth of giant clams Tridacna gigas, T derasa and T squamosa in Palau, Caroline Islands, Aquaculture, 24 pp21-30.

Braley R D, 1985 Serotonin-induced spawning in giant clams (Bivalvia:Tridacnidae), Aquaculture, 47 pp321-35.

Carrier J G, 1981 Ownership of productive resources on Ponam Island, Manus Province, Journal de Societe des Oceanistes, 72 73 pp206-217.

Dawson R F, 1984 Can Australia expect a resurgence of Taiwanese clam boat activity? Australian Fisheries, February pp20-23.

Gwyther J and Munro J L, 1981 Spawning induction and rearing of larvae of tridacnid clams (Bivalvia:Tridacnidae), Aquaculture, 24 pp197-217.

Heslinga G A, Perron F E and Orak O, 1984 Mass culture of giant clams (F Tridacnidae) in Palau, Aquaculture, 39 pp197-215.

IUCN, 1983 The IUCN Invertebrate Red Data Book (Gland, Switzerland: International Union for the Conservation of Nature and Natural Resources).

James Cook University of North Queensland, 1985 The Culture of the Giant Clam (Tridacna Sp) For Food and Restocking of Tropical Reefs: Progress Report 2, Australian Centre for International Agricultural Research, Canberra.

Jameson J C, 1976 Early life history of giant clams Tridacna crocea (Lamarck), Tridacna maxima (Roding), and Hippopus hippopus (Linnaeus), Pacific Science, 30(3):219-233.

Johannes R E, 1982 Implications of traditional marine resource use for coastal fisheries developments in Papua New Guinea, pp 239-249. In: L Morauta, J Pernetta and W Heaney (eds), Traditional Conservation in Papua New Guinea: Implications for Today (Boroko, P N G: Institute of Applied Social and Economic Research).

LaBarbera M, 1975 Larval and post-larval development of the giant clams Tridacna maxima and Tridacna squamosa (Bivalvia: Tridacnidae, Malacologia, 15(1) pp69-79.

McKoy J L, 1980 Biology, Exploitation and Management of Giant Clams (Tridacnidae) in the Kingdom of Tonga, Fisheries Bulletin No. 1, (Nuku'alofa, Tonga: Fisheries Division, Ministry of Agriculture, Forestry and Fisheries).

MacLean J L, 1978 The clam gardens of Manus, Harvest, 4(3) pp160-163.

Munro J L, 1985a The International Giant Clam Mariculture Project, Annex N(A) In: James Cook University of North Queensland, op. cit. A revised version of ICLARM, mimeo, 1983.

Munro J L, 1985b Economics and social aspects of the development of mariculture systems for giant clams (Tridacnidae: Bivalvia) in the Australasian Region and the West Pacific, International Giant Clam Mariculture Project Discussion Paper No 2 (Townsville:ICLARM, South Pacific Office).

Munro J L, 1985c Ocean nurseries for giant clams : options and problems, International Giant Clam Mariculture Project Discussion Paper No 1 (Townsville:ICLARM, South Pacific Office).

Munro J L and Heslinga G A, 1982 Prospects for the commercial cultivation of giant clams (Bivalvia:Tridacnidae) presented at 35th Annual Meeting of the Gulf and Caribbean Fisheries Institute, Nassau.

Rosewater J, 1965 The Family Tridacnidae in Indo-Pacific. Indo-Pacific Mollusca, 1(6) pp347-394.

Schoeffel P, 1984 The Fisheries of the South Pacific: Strategies to Assist the Participation of Women in Fish Marketing, Small-scale Aquaculture and Fish Processing (Canberra:Australian Development Assistance Bureau).

Tisdell C A and Fairbairn I J, 1983 Development problems and planning in a resource-poor Pacific country: The case of Tuvalu, Public Administration and Development, 3 pp341-359.

Tisdell C A and Fairbairn I J, 1984 Subsistence economies and unsustainable development and trade: Some simple theory, Journal of Development Studies, 20 pp227-241.

Uwate K R, Kunatuba P, Raobati B and Tenakanai C, 1984 A Review of Aquaculture Activities in the Pacific Islands Region (Honolulu: Pacific Islands Development Program, East-West Center).

Chapter Seven

WOMEN IN FISHERIES. WHY WOMEN COUNT: PROSPECTS FOR SELF-RELIANT FISHERIES DEVELOPMENT IN THE SOUTH PACIFIC COMPARED TO THE INDIAN OCEAN

Caroline Ifeka

With the notable exception of Penelope Schoeffel's (1984) pioneering report on women in Pacific fisheries, and Leila Gulati's (1984) detailed studies of women in Kerala coastal fisheries, women's role in in-shore fisheries in the Indo-Pacific is relatively unresearched, though some work is now in progress. This essay draws on my field enquiries in Kiribati and southwest India down to 1985. These data show that Kiribati women make a crucial contribution to subsistence and commercial production in the atoll fishing economy.

In what follows the potential for self-reliant development in artisanal fisheries offered by Kiribati women's pivotal participation is emphasised by means of brief comparison to the Muslim-dominated atolls of the Maldives and to the religiously mixed (Hindu, Muslim and Christian) fishing communities of India's southwest coast. In both these latter regions, but for different reasons, women's role in the economic development of the fishery is limited. Indeed, in the southwest Indian case, women's declining contribution to artisanal fisheries is associated with deepening regional dependence on external capital, growing economic impoverishment, pollution of coastal waters, and marine resource depletion (Angle 1983). By way of contrast in Kiribati women's continuing involvement is a major reason why prospects are bright for self-reliant development through ecologically effective and economically parsimonious policies.

THE BASIS OF THE STUDY

Esther Boserup's (1970) classic study of African and South Asian women's role in economic development subsequently stimulated a feminist appraisal of androcentric rural development programmes (Dixon 1978; Nelson 1981; Rogers 1982; Jaquette 1984; Mukhopadhyay 1984). These studies have added considerably to our knowledge of the different ways in which, in various African and Indian rural communities, women as well as men contribute to the development process (Sharma 1980; Gulati 1984; Swantz 1985). Nowadays women's important role in food production, processing and post-harvest storage is incontrovertible.

The same cannot be said of women's economic contribution to artisanal fisheries (Thompson 1982). With certain exceptions (Firth 1943; Firth 1975; Gulati 1984(a), 1984(b); Schoeffel 1984) women's work in this field is muted, if not completely obscured (Johannes 1981; Alexander 1982), partly because the term 'artisanal fisheries' is used uncritically. In general the term is taken to mean labour-intensive, shallow-water capture fisheries (Lawson, 1980, 1985; Gopalkrishnan 1984).

My quarrel is not with the assumption that 'artisanal' indicates labour intensive small-scale production. Rather, it is with the cognate assumption that firstly only men fish, or that if perchance women do fish their catch makes an insignificant contribution to household consumption. Secondly, I question the notion that the work of catching fish encapsulates the entirety of labour involved in exploiting a fishery.

The artisanal fisheries considered here are exploited for a variety of purposes - subsistence, social and cash - by both men and women; these fisheries also entail a wide range of work in producing, managing and processing fish resources necessary to livelihood (cf., Wallman 1979). Subsistence production refers to the labour or time and energy expended in making a living; social production denotes the work of investing in social relationships; economic production indicates the labour entailed in making a living for cash (see Brookfield, 1972, 1984; Wallman 1979). Landed fish cannot be translated into subsistence, social and cash or commodity value without additional labour to process and distribute them (Firth 1975). Consequently, a fishery deemed to involve only the work of capture is incomplete, whether regarded from a subsistence or a cash-oriented perspective. Therefore, exploiting a fishery by labour-intensive techniques for subsistence and cash-oriented purposes requires consideration of the work of men and women in processing and distributing as well as catching the fish.

For present purposes then, a wider definition of artisanal fisheries will be adopted that accords with actual work practices in catching, processing and distributing fish in many inshore fisheries in the Indo-Pacific. In the fisheries surveyed productive labour involves fish capture, processing by means of gutting, salting and sun-air drying, and preparation for consumption by means of cooking, baking, or roasting and 'smoking'. Distributive labour, on the other hand, involves apportioning to others fresh or dried fish surplus to subsistence needs either in the social form of give-away offerings for which no return is expected, or of gifts for which a return is expected, or in the economic form of fish made ready for cash sale.

The foregoing conception of artisanal fisheries assumes that women as well as men may be involved in various tasks associated with catching, processing and distributing fish for subsistence, social and economic production.

This is the case in Kiribati, the South Pacific island state considered here. As in other atoll economies of the region (Brookfield 1979; Bayliss-Smith 1977, 1978; Schoefel 1984, 1985) Kiribati women's contribution to artisanal fisheries production and distribution is essential to subsistence. Women's continuing involvement in all areas of the subsistence economy, including fisheries, means that most households currently have the capacity to expand labour in one kind of production while maintaining inputs to other sectors. Largely through women's customary role in fishing with nets in reefs and lagoons, as well as in processing and in distributing fresh and dried fish, households are empowered to contribute to the following productive activities : to social production which strengthens the fabric of community life and thus reproduces the social means of existence, to subsistence production which satisfies the material means of existence, and to economic production which secures the cash with which to expand the market-oriented production. Women's contribution is thus a sine qua non of outer-island development in all sectors including artisanal fisheries production processing and marketing.

The potential importance of women's economic role in facilitating flexible development strategies in Kiribati is highlighted if we consider some figures. These indicate the small resource base of this island state, and hence the need for relatively labour intensive, low-cost forms of development, at least in the initial stages of capital formation. The figures point up the tiny volume of income relative to total capital inflows, generated by export-oriented activities. In 1985 Kiribati earned $7-9 million from sales of tuna and copra, and from tuna fishing licence fees (out of an estimated total capital inflow on foreign account in 1985 of over $26 million. (Fisk 1985 : 7; Government of Kiribati 1985 : 7-9, 17)). On account of Kiribati's narrow resource base, government policy is to promote self reliance on the outer islands. (Government of Kiribati n.d.: 69ff). In addition to strengthening subsistence capacity, it is hoped that outer-island households can expand their cash earning powers (at present limited largely to selling copra and fish as well as to receiving remittances) so as to generate savings for investment in small enterprises (Government of Kiribati : n.d. 71). These ventures should diversify outer-island economies and thus may help moderate the emigration of literate youth to peri-urban South Tarawa. Government believes that economic diversification will strengthen outer-island capacity to develop without excessive reliance on external aid: policies outlined in the national development plan (1983-86) are intended to promote self-sufficiency through economic diversification.

It is in the light of the foregoing considerations that the following account is offered of Kiribati women's work in the inshore fishing economy. These data will be contrasted with material pointing out women's increasingly restricted inputs to artisanal fisheries in the Maldives and south-west India. A concluding section evaluates prospects for self-reliant development in Kiribati, based on recognition of women's as well as men's contribution to artisanal fisheries.

OVERTURES TO CHANGE

In the pre-colonial period the people of Kiribati (known to Europeans as Gilbertese) subsisted on fish, coconuts and - the water lens permitting - giant taro (cyrtosperma known locally as babai) grown in flooded pits (Grimble 1952; Catalla 1957). Titles to coconut palm trees, babai pits, fish traps on the windward side of the reef, and to stretches of lagoon and reef foreshore were often inherited cognatically through either parent and their relatives, and distributed among sibling sets (Lundsgaarde 1974; Crocombe 1971; Geddes et al 1982). Cognatic or bilateral inheritance rights thus enabled most, if not all, people to exercise a significant stake in subsistence resources.

The subsistence economy continued largely unchanged in the colonial period. The main economic innovation concerned a terrestrial resource, the coconut palm. People sold to European or Chinese traders those nuts which were surplus to their immediate subsistence and social needs. In exchange for nuts, and later on, dried coconut meat (copra) Gilbertese obtained goods or cash which they then deployed in traditional gift exchange (bubuti) and in offerings during important rites of passage and local political ceremonies (Grimble, 1952, 1955). For the most part people were uninterested in systematically investing the cash obtained from the copra trade in improvements to coconut trees so as to increase yields. To the Gilbertese coconut trees were - and still are - a resource to be used primarily for subsistence and social purposes. (Fisk 1985; Government of Kiribati n.d.).

During the run-down to independence in 1979 the colonial government made a more concerted effort to diversify outer-island economies. In the area of artisanal fisheries this took the form of largely unsuccessful attempts to increase output by upgrading techniques for harvesting fish. The post-independence government has been more successful in promoting craft motorisation and gear upgrading. Recently fisheries officials have become interested in exploring appropriate technologies for fish drying; on this matter more will be said later.

Thus far technological change in artisanal fisheries is not very advanced in comparison, for example, to southwest India. In 1984 the Fisheries Division, South Tarawa, organised a survey of three outer atolls and found that between 5 and 7 per cent of fishing households surveyed owned motorised craft; the majority used traditional canoes and gill nets. Depending upon the density of fish stocks in the reef in particular, and people's degree of dependence on fishing for subsistence, a household landed on average between 44 and 85kg during the survey week (Marriott 1984: 6-12). With an outboard motor sufficiently powerful to allow ready access to grounds further off the reef, and with the use of larger nets rather than traditional hooks and lines, yields rose to 90-120 kg per week

(Mees n.d.:3-4(10). In the outer islands surveyed an average of 1.00 to 1.50 kg of fish was eaten per capita per day (Marriott 1984; 13) compared to 0.45kg, on South Tarawa (Mees 1984:19-20). These figures are supported by surveys of fishing households elsewhere in Kiribati (Mees n.d. 4; 1984:11). The major part of the fish protein consumed was derived from reef fish i.e. snappers, groupers, goat fish (Marriott 1984: 18). At least 46 per cent of cash income in surveyed households came from fishing and the sale of dried or fresh fish surplus to the household's immediate needs (Marriott 1984 : 12).

In the outer islands surveyed reported mean incomes in 1984 from fishing amounted to around A$25 a week per household (Marriott 1984 : 12-18). Some of this cash was used to buy a limited range of trade goods, but most households used cash obtained by selling copra and fish to pay school fees, island taxes, village committee levies and the like (Geddes et al.1982:68-89).

These data for 1984 may be compared usefully to income figures collected in the early 1970s in two relatively 'advanced' outer islands, Butaritari in the northern tip of Kiribati, and Abemama in the centre. At the time Butaritari households interviewed reported that in addition to money from remittances, copra, handicrafts and babai, mean household income from fishing amounted to A$0.03 to A$1.54 a week (Sewell 1983:165). Reported annual household incomes from all sources in Abemama ranged from A$84 to A$1218 a year (Watters and Banibati 1984:106-7); in Butaritari household incomes varied from between A$3.11 to A$125.2 a week (Sewell 1983: 167). These data indicate there are significant differences between households in the kind and quantity of labour available, which partly account for inequalities in income distribution.

Income inequality is even more marked in peri-urban South Tarawa. Here the economy is largely though not entirely monetised - many households still have access to craft and can secure fish protein from the reef and lagoon, thus reducing the amount of cash expended on food items - and cash incomes are more unevenly distributed than on the outer islands. Households interviewed in 1983-4 reported incomes from fishing that averaged out at A$20-30 weekly per household (Mees 1984:5-7), or A$1200 a year. In 1985 south Tarawa households could earn from A$500 to A$1800 a year from part time fishing[1]. At the top of the fishing income scale in South Tarawa in 1985 were less than a handful of households that owned four to five motorised craft each; these households fished full- time for commercial purposes, and their annual fishing incomes may gross A$25,000 - 50,000 a year[2].

Other estimated sources of annual (gross) incomes in 1985 range from: A$1600, seaweed farming in south Tarawa lagoon[3]; A$1200, employment as a clerk in a government office on South Tarawa; A$520, copra selling[4]; $104, small holder vegetable production on Butaritari[5]. Compared to these latter sources of income, fishing and seaweed farming are relatively rewarding.

The above figures represent earnings in the monetised sector of artisanal fisheries, and should be evaluated in the light of the cost of living in in the early 1980s in peri-urban South Tarawa[6]. On the outer islands people live in small communities where everyone is interlocked through a multiplicity of social ties, and many households produce fish first and foremost for subsistence. However, at the same time the volume of fish landed is also intended to allow for people's need to give away some fish to others. Through this strategy people hope to accumulate 'social capital' i.e. good will in the community, which they can draw on in the future when they need extra hands in cutting copra, or financial assitance in paying school fees. Finally, households will also try to catch a larger quantity of fish than that needed for subsistence alone, so as to allow for the need to produce fish to raise cash. The portion left over after subsistence and social needs are satisfied will be sold for cash either immediately, if fresh landed, or preserved and marketed during the rainy season when the supply of fish is less than demand.

It is in this context of a predominantly subsistence economy in the outer islands, where there is also some social and economic production of fish, that we must situate women's economic role in fisheries development.

TRADITIONAL TECHNOLOGY

Fishing

Islanders distinguish several marine zones. The people of Tamana, a reef island that lacks a lagoon and is located at the most southerly tip of Kiribati, think of the marine environment as being divided into five overlapping zones. On account of the gradual decay this century in reef tenure (i.e. titles inherited through either parent, which give the right to fish certain areas and to own the produce), today anyone can fish where they wish to so long as they belong to the approved social category. Today all families claim unlimited access, but looked at another way, from the viewpoint of individual members of the household, actual access is limited to persons belonging to specific sex and age groups. Each sex and age group is allocated a proper place or zone in which to fish from boats and with nets, to collect bivalves from the foreshore, to trap and dive for species of fin fish in different areas of the reef, and to collect crustacea and molluscs from coral rocks. In Tamana women appear to be excluded from fishing at the reef edge, though as described shortly women elsewhere do fish in this zone.

The following fishing zones are recognised by Tamana people:

(a) the beach zone: the sand is visible beneath the clear water. Anyone may fish here with hand nets and from outrigger canoes;
(b) the reef flats: anyone may fish these;
(c) the reef edge: this area comprises the grooves or holes in the reef edge between the flats and the narrow shelf in the reef slope. According to the tide young and old men fish here with gear;
(d) the 'verandah' or 'eye lid': the reef overhang where boys and young men fish with floats, lines, nets and spears;
(a) the deep ocean: only men fish beyond the reef line. The 'dark' or deep waters are sub-divided into several levels according to ever-increasing depth and people's eventual inability to reach the bottom with even the longest line. Here skipjack tuna, yellow fin tuna, striped tunny fish (bonito) and king fish may be caught (Lawrence 1983:98).

Elsewhere, for example the atolls of Butaritari and Abemama where lagoons are relatively large, women play a greater part in fishing deeper waters. In the 1950s Catalla (1957:124-5) observed women as well as men fishing with hooks and lines on very long poles at the reef edge for an especial species of fish called <u>te reitati (Cirrhitus)</u>. (Carcasson 1977). Furthermore, women often joined men at night on expeditions beyond the reef to catch flying fish. Women and men paddled canoes into the deep ocean on the windward side, where they caught flying fish in dip nets[7]. The value placed on women's contribution is acknowledged in the northern islands, for here a large portion of the catch is reserved customarily for preservation by sun-drying and salting (Catalla 1957:122).

The extent of women's contribution to subsistence fishing and household consumption is indicated in the following data:

(a) out of an estimated annual catch in South Tarawa in 1982 of 6,000 tonnes, women collected over 1,000 tonnes of shell fish (Marriott n.d.: 7);

(b) half of the estimated annual catch in South Tarawa in 1982 was landed in the lagoon. There women were observed to spend more hours per day than men with encircling nets and caught the smaller fishes. These are a significant though unreported proportion of the total lagoon catch (Marriott n.d.:7);

(c) fisheries division officers found that the greater portion of fishing protein consumed in the outer islands surveyed came from the reef. Observations indicate that a significant, though unenumerated, portion of reef fish are caught by women and children (Marriott n.d.:14-17; Schoeffel 1984:9-10)[8].

These findings highlight the importance of women's fishing contribution to household protein intake and nutritional well-being. Adequate supplies of fish protein on the outer islands help secure a reasonably nourished population. It appears, therefore, that the interdependent labour of women and men in the local fishing economy is the key to self-reliant development, as the work of both sexes contributes to household reproduction whilst also providing some spare capacity for extending subsistence into cash-oriented activities.

Fish processing, woman's especial provenance, is one such activity that non-government organisations in particular are exploring for its income-generating potential.

Fish Processing

With one or two reported exceptions (Watters and Banibati 1984:78-80), it is women's work to salt and sun-dry that portion of the household catch surplus to daily needs. Fish preservation is an important part of the household economy. Women's technology reduces waste - as when the catch is in excess of daily consumption - and thus promotes the conservation of precious lagoon and reef stocks. Women's work in curing fish enables the household to raise cash by selling dried fish to neighbours, and if sufficiently proximate, to markets in peri-urban South Tarawa. Preservation also caters for social production, as when women dry prized delicacies and then store them away for future distribution on ceremonial occasions such as marriage and festivals.

Among the several non-ice methods of fish preservation and handling currently in use in the outer islands and South Tarawa the following are representative of women's technical repertoire. These skills were either observed by the writer or reported to her by local women. Ifeka (1986); Catalla (1957:134) and Schoeffel (1984) provide supporting data.

'Dry' Salting

In large fish over 1kg (i.e. the tunas, bonito, and king fish) the head is cut off but not discarded, for it is considered a great delicacy. The fish is gutted, washed and split into two (i.e. butterfly filleted), incised for salting (one incision on the outer, one on the inner flesh), and then salted by rubbing in crystals.

Depending on the species of fish, and flesh texture desired subsequent to the drying process, the fresh landed weight of the fish will reduce between one and two-thirds. Thus, the relatively oily species as tuna and castor-oil fishes may reduce by up to two-thirds their fresh landed weight (which may well include the head, guts, etc); the bone fish (ikare) loses up to one half of fresh landed weight; the smaller reef and lagoon fish lose from a third to one half, (King pers. comm. 1985).

Later, the fish are exposed to the sun and air, and placed on bushes, pandanus logs or coconut tree branches where the circulation of air at the skin surface has the effect of providing heat by convection and removing water. Temperature, relative humidity and air velocity are important inputs in the drying process. When the fish is dried to low water content it is hard and dense, and depending upon the extent of moisture loss, may take from several minutes to several hours to reconstitute.

Reported shelf life without mould growth or maggot infestation due to fly contact during low moisture evaporation (most likely to occur on sunless days) can extend from a few months to two or three years.

'Wet' Salting

Fish may be preserved by curing in a very salty 'pickle' of extracted fluids. Or they can be soaked in prepared concentrated salt solution poured into a wooden barrel, or other suitable container, and kept there for several weeks.

'Smoking' Techniques

These methods require the use of heat, at least in the initial stages, and subsequent exposure to the sun to achieve further moisture loss. 'Traditional' methods are essentially a variant of food preparation by baking fish wrapped in leaves on hot stones, but with the addition of sun-air drying to further reduce moisture and so extend shelf life. As explained below 'modern' techniques involve the addition of heat and smoke that circulate around both sides of the free-standing filleted fish.

A hemispherical hole is lined with flat stones on which coconut husks are placed and lighted. When the stones are well heated, a basket of fresh coconut leaves containing the fish to be cooked is placed on the stones in the hole. The whole is covered with babai leaves, then with an old mat, and finally with earth. When the odour indicates the fish is cooked as required, the basket is removed - generally after several hours - and the fish dried in the sun. A variant of this baking method produces a Butaritari delicacy, the aua 'smoked' fish. (Ifeka 1986.

A small fish, the aua (sprat) has a flesh somewhat similar in texture and oiliness to the much larger skipjack tuna. Butaritari women catch the fish (aua) by using coconut leaves woven to form a net matting. On bringing the catch from the lagoon, leaves are placed around about 20 of these little fish. Then they are put in a coconut string net and tied together inside a pandanus leaf. About five bundles, containing about 100 fish in all, are placed on top of a low-flame, smouldering fire with their heads down and tails up. (See Figure 6). A pandanus mat is placed on top, and the whole left until morning.

Figure 6 Traditional method of 'smoking'; Butaritari Island

The fish are subsequently dried in the sun for 3-5 days until very hard, when they can last for a year or more.

WOMEN'S TRADITIONAL TECHNOLOGY ASSESSED BY COMPARISON TO THE MALDIVES

The foregoing are some of the traditional (i.e. customary, pre-European) processing techniques still in use among women on the outer islands and South Tarawa. These methods are used by female members of the household in subsistence production to increase food security and nutritional well-being. Indigenous preservation techniques also enable household members to participate in social production or gift-giving between families that contribute to community cohesion.

At the same time non-ice methods of fish preservation described above were selected as examples of techniques which might be extended by judicious fusing with western fish processing technology. In this way Kiribati women's traditional technical skills could become part of a new 'blended' fish processing technology. Recent trials initiated by local non-government bodies indicate that this technique could produce modest increases in yields sufficient to satisfy inter-island and even limited external demand.

However, this foundation for upgrading yields by 'marrying' women's indigenous fish processing techniques with western technology does not always exist. In the Indian ocean atolls of the Maldives there is at present no significant women's contribution to artisanal fisheries upon which subsistence-supported development could be based, and yet the marine environment of the Maldives is most favourable and does not of itself indicate a very restricted economic role for women.

A detailed survey in the early 1900s by the scientist Agassiz (1903:1-xxxv) of Maldivian atoll geology showed that the 'fragmented landscape' (Maloney 1980 : 178) of this island state contains far more luxuriant coral branching than observed in the atolls of the South Pacific. This finding implies that at the time there were more abundant (and easily accessible) lagoon and reef fisheries in the Maldives. Beyond the reefs, too, Agassiz sighted extensive shoals of sea bream, bonito, the albacores and, in the principal passes to the lagoons, his team observed many shoals of flying fish, masses of micro-algae, various gasteropods, bivalves, large blue shrimps and floating fish larvae. Many fish species would have been then, as is the case today, common to the southerly latitudes of the Indo-Pacific oceans (Randall 1955 :x-ix).

In the remote past the rigours of atoll existence in the Maldives may have facilitated a mutual interdependence between the sexes comparable to that still extant in Kiribati. In the early twelfth century the Dhivehi-speaking peoples of the Maldives were converted to Sunni Islam. Information about peoples elsewhere, for instance hunter-gatherers and swidden cultivators, who produce their own means of material and social existence by very labour-intensive means (Lee and deVore 1969; Collier and Rosaldo 1981) suggests strongly that although the precise impact of Islam on the sex division of labour would have depended in part on then-prevailing conditions in the Maldives, conversion to the conservative doctrines of Sunni Islam probably altered quite radically the sex division of labour on the northern and southern atolls.

In the early seventeenth century the French explorer, Pyrard, observed that women assisted men only in weeding and harvesting millet and tubers, while in inshore fisheries they were restricted to smoking the dark-fleshed bonito into the product known for centuries as 'Maldives Fish' (Pyrard 1984: 2(2): 117-8; Maloney 1980 : 279). The women of a household de-gut and fillet the bonito according to custom in a hot dank shed in the back yard. Owing to shortage of salt the most common method of curing used in the past and nowadays is wet-salting; the fillets are boiled in salt water, smoked for two days or more over a fire made with wood collected by the women, dried for two or three weeks until the desired loss of moisture is attained, and then stored in a cool place prior to shipment.

Since 1977 demand for 'Maldives Fish' from the major buyer, Sri Lanka, has declined sharply, though dry-salted tuna produced by men only and exported to the Middle East is increasing in volume and value (Infofish 1983; IFAO 1988; Far Eastern Economic Year Book 1985). However, economic changes associated with the modernisation of craft and fish processing facilities have further limited Dhivehi women's inputs to preparing fish for household consumption and social exchange. Compared to Kiribati women's extensive activities in artisanal fisheries Dhivehi women make a small contribution indeed to subsistence and economic production.

Whereas in the Maldives at present there is no significant women's contribution on which to build appropriate i.e. 'blended' fish processing technology, in Kiribati the interdependence of the sexes in artisanal fisheries means a platform exists for small-scale, self-reliant development through the implementation of 'blended' techniques that are economically sensitive to ecological and social conditions (cf., Clarke 1985).

'BLENDED' TECHNOLOGY

Since the early 1980s, various groups in Kiribati have experimented with appropriate techniques of smoking and drying fish. Their stated intention is to increase the volume of fish cured weekly and so to improve productivity, that is, output per woman hour. They hope also to produce a cured product that conforms more closely to western quality standards and is therefore potentially marketable outside Kiribati (Ifeka 1986; see also Government of Kiribati n.d. 69-71, 98).

Smoking

New methods of smoking fish (i.e. blue mullet, aua, and milk fish, awatai) in either a 44-gallon tin drum (Figure 7) or in an especially constructed smoke house made of coral bricks and imported cement entail some modifications to traditional methods.

Figure 7. Smoke house, South Tarawa

Innovations include the following:

(a) the fish are placed in a 'man-made' container or smoke house;

(b) the fish are separated from direct contact with the fire by being suspended high above low, smouldering embers;

(c) the fire and heat are kept at a stable temperature for several days so the fish are thoroughly dried and imbued with a 'smokey' flavour and characteristic darkish colour.

Certain technical problems will have to be resolved before these 'blended' techniques can be used more widely. First, the cement fire box cracks in the heat and so interrupts the smoking process.

Second, to ensure a perfectly smoked product, it is necessary to maintain constant heat and air convection against the flesh of the suspended fish; so far this has not been achieved (Ifeka 1986; c.f. Borgstrom 1965; FAO 1981).

Solar Drying

In 1984-85 a non-government organisation installed some trial driers on one of the outer islands. Apparently these have been successful in the sense that dried fish production for sale in South Tarawa has been maintained now for over a year. The driers are made of a wooden or coral brick frame (Figure 8).

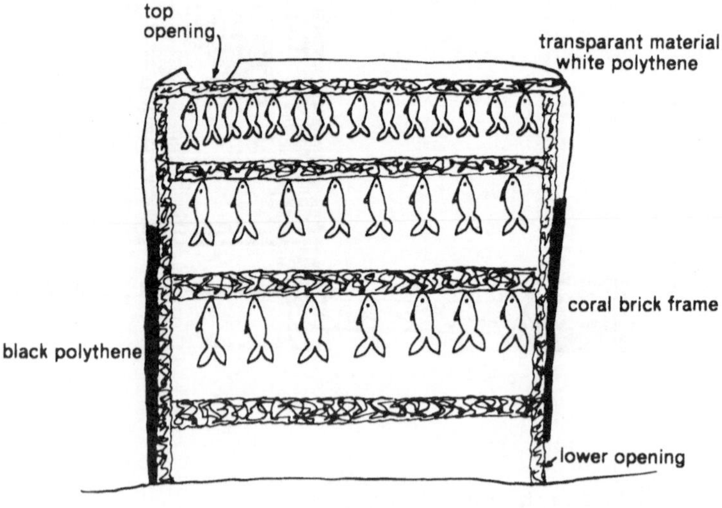

Figure 8. Design for small-scale brick-frame solar drier

Peter King, formerly of Butaritari Island, has commented on solar driers in general. He writes that the frame:

> is enclosed on its upper surface by a transparent material which permits solar radiation to enter. The lower surface is a dark coloured material which absorbs the solar radiation and is heated by it. The heated dark material is in contact with the lower layers of air within

the drier, so they absorb heat from it and rise to the top of the drier....to be replaced by higher levels of cooler air which are in turn heated, and so on. So far the air is simply circulating within a closed system which will eventually achieve equilibrium and prevent further drying of the fish. So the drier must have at least two openings: one at the top for moisture laden warm air to leave the drier, and one at the bottom to allow cooler air to enter, thus creating a draught through the drier. The drying is caused by the air flowing over the fish and absorbing moisture from it; the heat is primarily a means of creating the air-flow. (King, pers.comm. 17.7.86).

Trial driers on the outer island in question have a holding capacity of approximately 40kg. About 86 goat fish may be dried at any one time on three racks (Ifeka 1986).

Other types of low-cost solar driers used elsewhere in the Third World include the polythene sheeting tent. This could cure 3kg of fresh fish per m^2/day (ICLARM, 1981). These, however, share some of the technical disadvantages of the solar drier built with a wooden or coral brick frame and covered with black plastic sheeting (See Figure 9)

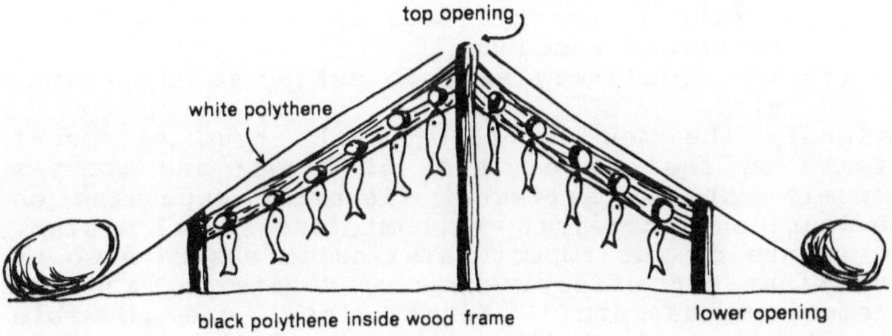

Figure 9 Design for small-scale polythene tent solar drier

Technical problems include:

(a) the plastic sheeting is liable to become brittle and tear;

(b) the inside temperature drops when the sheeting tears, so the fish retain moisture;

(c) in changeable weather and with 100 per cent undamaged tent, the internal temperature can be difficult to maintain at some degrees higher than the outside temperature so that the air flow is maintained and drying continued;

(d) in the wet season inside temperatures are relatively low and air flow is slower. If the insect screening over the openings gets torn and flies enter, the internal temperture is insufficiently high to kill them. A mechanical fan could keep flies off the fish to prevent infestation, and also increase air flow to maintain the drying process.

(e) it is unclear that drying in solar driers will eliminate the risk of flies attacking fish unless it is also heavily salted. Of course most people prefer to eat less rather than massively salted fish.

Some people in Kiribati believe that the proposed new technology will be advantageous to women processors because in their view solar driers:

(a) save women's labour time;

(b) avoid fly infestation by direct contact;

(c) facilitate faster drying;

(d) enable use of less salt so the product suits modern palates;

(e) entail no energy costs as they use a 'free' renewable resource;

(f) are relatively easy to set up in the community.

Obviously the new technology will have different effects on the sex division of labour and women's economic role in artisanal fisheries depending on the local environmental, economic and social system. The nature of the impact entailed is shaped also by the extent and effectiveness of monitoring and management mechanisms. Nevertheless, one possible scenario is indicated in accounts of recent events among fishing castes living along India's Malabar and Konkan coasts; here largely unsupervised technological change undermined women's traditional economic autonomy and deprived many of a productive role whilst giving some women new (dependent) roles as day labourers in prawn-peeling sheds.

TECHNOLOGICAL CHANGE ASSESSED BY COMPARISON TO SOUTHWEST INDIA

Whether they belong to the better-off and credit worthy net and boat sub-caste or the poorer boat-less, hook and line fishing sub-caste, Muslim 'Mopplah' (i.e. Mappila) women de-gut, de-head and preserve fish landed by their menfolk by means of dry and wet salting techniques. (Mathur 1977:293). Craft motorisation schemes directed towards Mopplah men have benefitted some of the boat Mopplahs who, equipped with outboard motors, are able to reach newly discovered prawn grounds in deeper waters offshore.

Women of the poorer, fish and line communities have been incorporated as processing outworkers into the new, technologically advanced and capital intensive inshore fishing economy. In return for minimal pay women shell and winnow prawns for merchants of the boat-owning sub-caste. Working for cash for outside men in their own homes poor Mopplah women have lost the capacity to produce dried fish for social production. They are unable nowadays to shape household decision-making vis-a-vis the distribution of surplus fish. As in the Maldives, Mopplah women's work in this area is increasingly devoid of influence-conferring powers.

In fishing communities along the Konkan coast, in Goan territory, the situation for women is likewise sombre (Ifeka 1985; Ifeka and Chiragakis 1985). Traditionally Hindu women of the fishing sub-castes played a part in artisanal fisheries; once their work included net making, sail repairs, fish salting and drying, and of course marketing. (Muslim women, though, had and have a very circumscribed economic role, living as they do in virtual seclusion in households whose menfolk are arch-conservative practitioners of Sunni Islam.) Today, though, increasing control by outside capitalist interests over inshore fishing, processing, and marketing has reduced most Hindu women to small-time sellers of fish at wayside markets, in other people's houses, and to fish headloading for a few paise (c.f. Braganca Pereira 1940; Soeiro e Brito 1966).

Women of Christian fishing castes still glean the foreshores and tidal flats of Goa for crustacea, molluscs and small fishes trapped in tidal pools. However in Quilon district, Kerala, the 'factorisation' of prawn processing and winnowing in conjunction with the development of fish processing 'outwork' has had the effect of removing fish processing from women in Christian households into centrally controlled workplaces (Gulati 1984a,b). Although fishing is still carried out by the menfolk, ostensibly on a household basis, craft with outboard motors or small trawlers bought on credit are often effectively owned by financiers, banks, and local merchants rather than by the household head. The household's loss of control over production, processing and distribution in inshore fisheries reduces the fishing community, women and men alike, to extreme dependence. New kinds of livelihood for some are emerging, but, in this writer's opinion, many people's ability to feed themselves and thus to promote self-sufficient development in the community is now severely impaired[9].

CONCLUSION

The foregoing suggests that unsupervised introduction of western technology can take work away from women (and men). It can also weaken household capacity for subsistence-supported self-sufficient development, and on the other hand stimulate rapid economic differentiation.

And yet in Kiribati the pivotal role of women in all aspects of artisanal fisheries, excepting deep sea fishing, provides a sound platform for self- sufficient development. In fact, given supportive policies, development outcomes in Kiribati may be more beneficial for women and society as a whole than in the Indian ocean cases considered above.

Today Kiribati is poised at the cross-roads of the development process. In their desire to strike a balance between on the one hand, production for profit and on the other, social value by means of planning strategies that build on traditional conservationist prescriptions adaptive to the fragile atoll ecosystem, Kiribati women and men will be deciding whether they opt for increasingly dependent or for progressively self-reliant development. As the Kiribati government has noted 'The final outcome must be one which takes into account the sensitivity of the people ... It will have to be a Kiribati solution' (Government of Kiribati n.d.:62).

ACKNOWLEDGEMENTS

Field research in Goa in 1983 was funded by the Gulbenkian Foundation and a Faculties (ANU) research grant. Data were collected in Kiribati during a three-week visit in late 1985, sponsored by the Australian Development Assistance Bureau. I am grateful to Fred Fisk for detailed comments on an earlier draft, and to various people in south Tarawa, Abemama and Butaritari for their truly generous assistance. I owe an especial debt to Peter King for very informative comments on an earlier draft, and to Mary Day and Winnie Powell for friendship in the field. None of these people is of course responsible for any errors. Thanks also to Val Lyons who transformed my inadequate sketches into publishable format, and to Sue Nolan for speedy typing.

FOOTNOTES

1 Part-time fishing household income: estimate based on Mees (n.d.:10). In 1984 on Tamana an average fishing household operating part-time for commercial purposes landed 30kg per trip x 4 times a week = 120kg per week. People 'ate' an average of 1.7kg per head per day in surveyed households; this figure may or may not include fish given away and dried, and so may overestimate the quantity consumed. At current prices this catch, less amount deducted for daily portion 'eaten', generated an annual fishing income of A$1400 per annum.

2 Full-time fishing household income: estimate based on figures provided by Mees (1984:5-7, n.d.:7), and Marriott (1984). The volume of fish landed is multiplied by current (1985) prices of fish to arrive at estimated gross income. Current prices of fish to the consumer in south Tarawa in 1985 were 50c per lb on average, and in outer islands 37c. Prices vary according to species of fish.
To determine gross income deduct a variable proportion to allow for fish retained for household use, and not exchanged for cash. A full-time fishing household with five motorised craft will net c.1 metric tonne of fish per trip. Two trips per week = 1,000 mt per annum. At 50c per lb - A$50,000 per annum (gross) (Mees, pers. comm., 1985). NB. There were no more than three such large-scale operators on South Tarawa in 1985.

3 Seaweed farmers' income: estimate assumes farmer plants 30 plants per line weighing 20gm; farmer manages 30 lines. Within 10 weeks the 30 lines, if planted simultaneously, are harvested. Assume 5 plantings of 30 lines a year. Farmer will gross c.A$1600 per annum (Why pers. comm., 1985).

4 Copra producer's income: conservative estimate based on current low copra prices.
3-4 nuts = c.1 lb of copra.
1 bag (rice/flour) of c.350 nuts = 100 lb copra.
At 10c per lb (i.e. 26c per kg) 1 bag of nuts = A$10.
Assume modest size plantation, low proportion bearing good sized nuts on account of prevailing drought (in 1985): A$520 (gross) per annum.

5 Vegetable grower's income: Income arrived at by assuming, as was the case in 1985, that the grower will sell to buying agent vegetables at 20c per lb. If the grower maintains production at 510 lbs per annum he will gross an annual income of A$104. (King, pers. comm. 1985).

6 Retail commodity prices late 1985, South Tarawa. These are government regulated.

flour	32c per lb.
rice (calrose)	34c per lb.
kerosene	35c per litre.
salt	25c per lb.
sugar	35c per lb.

Fresh fish prices, late 1985, south Tarawa.

skipjack tuna	A$1.10 per kg.
violet squirrel	A$1.21 per kg.
spangled emperor	A$1.08 per kg.
bonefish	A$1.04 per kg.

7 As Schoeffel notes, it is less that women are not allowed to fish from outrigger canoes or motorised craft, and more that they are not encouraged to do so, and therefore often lack the knowledge that most men have of the art of fishing from canoes (1984:9-10). Nevertheless a Butaritari woman told me in 1985 that some especially adventurous women do join the men on nightly fishing trips, and if necessary they can sail canoes themselves.

8 Bayliss-Smith reports that in Batiki, Fiji, in the 1970s 'women's fishing methods are usually the more productive' yielding 0.5kg per hour or an annual female catch of 6 metric tonnes per annum. This represents 37 per cent of the islanders' protein intake (Bayliss-Smith, 1978:116). Women spent 5.3 hours per week in subsistence fishing; men 3.8 hours a week (Bayliss-Smith, ibid). See also Bayliss-Smith, 1980.

9 In the early to mid 1970s Kerala fisherfolk consumed on average a mere 15kg of fish per capita per annum (Gulati, 1984(a):5). Compare this figure to an estimated annual per capita fish consumption in Kiribati of between 157.50kg to 525kg. (See Mees 1984:20).

REFERENCES

Angle P S, 1983 Goa: An Economic Review (Bombay:Goa Hindu Association Kala Vibhag)

Agassiz A, 1903 The Coral Reefs of the Maldives, vs 1 and 2 (Cambridge: Harvard)

Alexander P, 1982 Sri Lankan Fishermen (Canberra: ANU Monographs on S Asia No.7)

Bayliss-Smith T P, and Feachem R M, 1977 Subsistence and Survival (London: Cambridge University Press)

Bayliss-Smith T P, 1978 'Batiki in the 1970s: satellite of Suva', in R.D. Bedford et al (eds), The Small Islands and the Reefs (Paris: UNESCO), 67-128

Bayliss-Smith T P, 1980 The Price of Protein : Marine Fisheries in Pacific Subsistence (Unpub. paper Cambridge)

Borgstrom G (ed), 1965 Fish as Food, V.3, Pt 1 (New York: Academic Press)

Borgstrom G (ed), 1965 Fish as Food, V.4, Pt 2 (New York: Academic Press)

Boserup E, 1970 Women's Role in Economic Development (New York: St Martins)

Braganca Pereira, 1940 A Ethnografia da India Portugesa V.2 (Panjim:Bastora)

Brookfield H C, 1972 'Intensification and disintensification in Pacific agriculture : a theoretical approach', Pacific Viewpoint, 13(1), 30-48

Brookfield H C, 1983 'Intensification revisited', Pacific Viewpoint, 25(1), 15-44

Brookfield M, 1979 'Resource use, economy and society: island at the cross-roads', in H C Brookfield et al (ed), Lakeba: Environmental Change, Population Dynamics and Resource Use, 127-99

Carcasson R H, 1977 A Field Guide to the Coral Reef Fishes of the Indian and West Pacific Oceans (London : Collins)

Catalla R L A, 1957 'Report on the Gilbert Islands: some aspects of human ecology'. Atoll Research Bulletin No 59, 1-187

Clarke W C, 1985 'The fabric of the world farm: in I. Farrington (ed), Prehistoric Intensive Agriculture in the Tropics (Oxford : British Archaeological Reports No 232, 865-81)

Collier J and Rosaldo M, 1981 Politics and Gender in Simple Societies. IN Ortner S and Whitehead H (eds) Sexual Meanings pp 275-330 (Cambridge: Cambridge University Press)

Crocombe R (ed), 1971 Land Tenure in the Pacific (Melbourne OUP)

Dixon R, 1978 Rural Women At Work : Strategies for Development in South Asia (Baltimore : Johns Hopkins University Press)

Dixon R, 1980 Assessing the Impact of Development Projects on Women (Washington : Office of Women in Development)

FAO, 1981 The Prevention of Losses in Cured Fish, FAO Fisheries Technical Paper No. 219 FIIU/T219 (Rome : FAO)

Far Eastern Economic Review, 1985 'Fishing', FEER Yearbook, 42-3

Far Eastern Economic Review, 1985 'Maldives', FEER Yearbook, 198-202

Firth R, 1943 Housekeeping Among Malay Peasants (London : LSE)

Firth R, 1975 Malay Fishermen : Their Peasant Economy (New York : Norton)

Fisk E K, 1985 The Economic Independence of Kiribati (Canberra : Australian Development Assistance Bureau)

Geddes W H, 1983 Tabiteuea North (Canberra : Australian National University, Development Studies Centre)

Gopalkrishnan C (ed), 1984 The Emerging Marine Economy of the Pacific (Boston : Butterworth)

Government of Kiribati, n.d, National Development Plan 1983-86 (South Tarawa)

Government of Kiribati, 1985 Statistics Bulletin for the Kiribati Aid Donors Meeting, May (Tarawa : Ministry of Finance)

Grimble A, 1952 A Pattern of Islands (London : John Murray)

Grimble A, 1955 Return To The Islands (London : John Murray)

Gulati L, 1984(a) Fisherwomen on the Kerala Coast (Geneva : ILO)

Gulati L, 1984(b) Profiles in Female Poverty (Delhi : Hindustan Publishing Corporation)

Hill P, 1970 Studies in Rural Capitalism in West Africa (Cambridge : Cambridge University Press)

ICLARM, 1981 Alternative Energy Sources in Fisheries and Aquaculture, Vol. 4(2) (Metro Manila, Philippines)

Ifeka C, 1983 Field Notebooks Nos. 1-2

Ifeka C, 1985 Hierarchal Women : Towards Rethinking Woman's Role in Development in India (forthcoming)

Ifeka C, 1986 Report on Women and Fish Processing in the South Pacific with special reference to Kiribati and Tuvalu. Australian Development Assistance Bureau, Canberra.

Ifeka C, and Chiragakis L, 1985 Christian and Hindu Households in a Changing World : the case of Goa, southwest India. (Unpublished paper)

IFAD 1985 Report of the Project Identification Mission to the Republic of Maldives Oct. 1985 (Asia Division)

INFOfish, 1983 Improving product quality in the Maldives', INFOfish, 2, 16-17

Jaquette J, 1984 Women and Modernisation Theory. World Politics 34(2) pp267-64

Johannes R E, 1981 Words of the Lagoon (Berkeley : University of California Press)

Koch G, 1965 Materielle Kultur der Gilbert-Inseln (Berlin : Museum Fur Volkerkunde)

Lawrence R, 1983 Tamana (Canberra : Australian National University, Development Studies Centre)

Lawson R, 1980 'Development and growth constraints in the artisanal fisheries sector in island states', In: R Shand (ed) Island States of the Pacific and Indian Oceans (Canberra : ANU), 41-60

Lawson R, 1985 Economics of Fisheries Development (London : Printer)

Lee R and I deVore (eds) 1968 Man the Hunter (Chicago : Aldine Publications) and I.deVore (eds)

Lundsgaarde H P (ed), 1974 Land Tenure in Oceania (Honolulu : University Press of Hawaii)

MacLean R F, 1980 'The land-sea interface of small tropical islands : morphodynamics and man', In: H C Brookfield (ed) Population-Environment Relations in Tropical Islands: the Case of Eastern Fiji (Paris : UNESCO), 125-30

Maloney C, 1980 People of the Maldive Islands (Bombay : Orient Longman)

Marriott S, n.d., The South Tarawa Artisanal Fishery (Tarawa : Fisheries Division)

Marriott S, 1984 Rural Fisheries in Kiribati, (Tarawa : Fisheries Division)

Mathur P R, 1971 The Mappila Fisherfolk of Kerala (Trivandrum : Historical Society)

Mees C C, n.d., The Fisheries of Tamana and Aror (Tarawa : Fisheries Division

Mees C C, 1984 A Fisheries Related Market Study of South Tarawa (Tarawa : Fisheries Division)

Mies M, 1982 The Lace Workers of Narsapur (London : Zed Press)

Mukhopadhyay M, 1984 Silver Shackles (Oxford : OXFAM)

Nelson N, 1981 African Women in the Development Process (London : Cass)

Pyrard F, 1964 The Voyage of Francois Pyrard of Laval to the East Indies, the Maldives, the Moluccas and Brazil V.2, Translated and edited by A Gray and H C P Bell (New York : Burt Franklin)

Randall J E, 1955 'Fishes of the Gilbert Islands', Atoll Research Bulletin No. 47, 1-242

Rogers B, 1980 The Domestication of Women (London : Tavistock Publications)

Schoeffel P, 1984 The Fisheries of the South Pacific : Strategies to Assist the Participation of Women in Fish Marketing, Small-Scale Aquaculture and Fish Processing, Regional Summary, Kiribati (Canberra : Australian Development Assistance Bureau

Schoeffel P, 1985 Women in the Fisheries of the South Pacific. In H Hughes (ed) Women in Development in the South Pacific, pp156-175 (Canberra : Development Studies Centre)

Sewell B, 1983 Butaritari (Canberra : Australian National University)

Shand R T (ed), 1980 The Island Stages of the Pacific and Indian Oceans ; Anatomy of Development (Canberra : Australian National University)

Sharma U, 1980 Women, Work, and Property in North-West India (London: Tavistock Publications)

Soeiro e Brito R, 1966 Goa e as Pracas da Norte (Lisbon : Junta de Investigagcoes du Ultramar)

Swantz M, 1985 Women in Development : A Creative Role Denied? (London : Hurst)

Thompson P, 1985 Women in Fishing : The Roots of Power Between the Sexes. Comparative Study of Society and History 27(1) pp3-32

Watters R and Banibati K, 1984 Abemama (Canberra : Australian National University)

Wallman S (ed), 1979 Social Anthropology of Work (London Academic Press)

Chapter Eight

OCEAN MINERALS - PROSPECTS FOR PACIFIC ISLAND NATIONS

Cruz A Matos and Jioji Kotobalavu

The land masses of CCOP/SOPAC member countries fall into two broad geological categories: islands on volcanic arcs; and seamounts or atolls. Volcanic arc islands have, as a rule, greater land mass and more diverse geology and hence are more likely to have a greater potential for non-renewable natural resources than seamounts or atolls whose superficial basic fabric is often just coralline sand and carbonate rock. Nevertheless, with a few notable exceptions, the small insular countries of the South Pacific have only limited land-based resources. Thus, for many of these states, their long term economic prospects are seen as linked to the potential bounty of the surrounding seas which, due to the advent of extending maritime zones, outstrip the land area in some countries by a ratio of more than 7000:1. Whether such hopes are in fact justified or will prove illusory depends very much on what marine resources, living and non-living, lie off shore. Given the importance attached to the economic potential of their offshore areas, it is vital to the Pacific island countries that they base their development on a realistic appreciation of what the sea has to offer.

Lack of knowledge about the region's oceanic environment is perhaps one of the most salient features of current South Pacific development planning. In contrast with the land areas, very little is presently known about the geology of the South Pacific seabed. There is tantalising but fragmentary evidence to suggest commercial resources may exist in the area - such as of hydrocarbons, seamount mineral encrustations, beds of manganese nodules, finds of detrital minerals and the like. Nevertheless, the present geological picture is seriously deficient in many areas. Since the location of just one modestly-sized, commercially exploitable mineral deposit would have a profound impact on any of the smaller island states in the South Pacific and because a major discovery could affect the entire region, there is a clear need to complete the picture as expeditiously as possible. Mineral discoveries leading to an economic transformation would be gratefully received by all states, but few if any expect such success to come overnight.

The need to better understand the offshore areas of the South Pacific may be economically crucial for some of the island states and desirable for all but this is not the only reason for supporting marine research at this stage. Whatever benefits the new Law of the Sea Treaty may confer on coastal states, it also imposes responsibilities. These responsibilities require considerable knowledge of the offshore areas to permit domestic legislation to be drafted, patrol and surveillance regimes to be established, and fundamental baseline data to be developed for the enforcement of quality control regulations.

These and related needs, however, create a demand for advanced technical information which few if any of the South Pacific countries could satisfy individually. It is for this reason that most of the region's countries have joined together in CCOP/SOPAC to address collectively the problems of offshore research into their non-living marine resources and the problems associated with the development of these resources. The united effort helps to promote not only greater self-reliance by the island states of the South Pacific but it also contributes to more effective research.

CCOP/SOPAC - an acronym standing for "Committee for Co-ordination of Joint Prospecting for Mineral Resources in South Pacific Offshore Areas" - was founded in 1972 under the auspices of the United Nations Economic and Social Commission for Asia and the Pacific (ESCAP). The membership is composed of governments mainly from the South Pacific region and at the present time consists of Cook Islands, New Zealand, Western Samoa, Tonga, Tuvalu, Fiji, Kiribati, Vanuatu, Solomon Islands, Papua New Guinea and Guam from the North Pacific. Since its inception the Committee has acted as the regional mechanism for co-ordination and stimulation of marine research in the region. With encouragement from ESCAP and financial support from the United Nations Development Programme (UNDP) and interested donor countries, CCOP/SOPAC carries out scientific research, marine mineral surveys, baseline coastal studies, workshops and seminars, and in co-operation with others - specifically the University of the South Pacific, Victoria University of Wellington, the United States Geological Survey, New Zealand Geological Survey, and Australian National Mapping Agency - conducts training activities at the technician level to upgrade marine expertise available in support of the national programmes. Many member countries in the beginning had no geological expertise whatsoever, a situation now changing as national geological graduates emerge, in many cases selected from outstanding students of the CCOP/SOPAC training sessions.

The Committee meets annually to conduct its business and to establish or review its work programme. The work programme consists of national projects for each member state depending upon that state's own requirements and priorities, and regional projects which overlap member states or are desirable goals for part or all of the region. Currently, there are 101 national projects and 36 regional projects in various stages of activity.

The annual meeting is also attended upon invitation by representatives and observers from supporting countries such as Australia, China, France, Germany, Japan, Norway, USSR, UK and USA. These representatives and observers provide advice and guidance to the Committee on the technical aspects of its activities.

The activities of the Committees set out in the Work Programme are carried out by the Technical Secretariat housed at Mineral Resources Department in Suva, Fiji. Initially, the UNDP provided a marine geologist the first of whom commenced duties in 1973. In 1979, major funding was provided by UNDP to enable a much enlarged programme of operation over a three year period. A further three-year funding period was granted in 1982 and later extended to the end of 1986. CCOP/SOPAC in 1984 became a legal regional governmental body by enactment of a Memorandum of Understanding signed by all members.

Beginning in late 1978, a 65 foot steel schooner 'Machias' out of Honolulu, was chartered to assist the work programme for 6 months a year until 1981. This vessel regularly logged 25,000 miles per charter working through the CCOP/SOPAC area to take single channel seismic profiles, magnetics, echo soundings, bottom samples of sediments and manganese nodules, and precious coral dredgings. For many areas, this was the first research vessel to obtain such data.

Using the data from 'Machias' and other available information, a database was built-up and specialist consultants contracted to study and report on resource aspects of highest interest, such as the deep sedimentary basins in the central intra-arc areas of Vanuatu and Solomon Islands, on precious coral prospects of the region, and on manganese nodule enrichments and metalliferous sediments. Other work was also being carried out on projects such as detrital gold prospects in the Solomon Islands, bauxite in Rennell Island, clay minerals in Vanuatu; sand and gravel deposits in Tonga, and many more.

Meantime, research vessels from institutions and organisations of many countries had been periodically visiting the area to extend knowledge of their own particular interests in geo-science. Often, the Southwest Pacific countries in whose waters they worked were not even aware of these operations, and did not derive any direct benefits from their presence or their findings. This became a more serious matter in the early 1970s when, following the discovery of genuine oil seeps in Tonga in 1968, several major oil explorations were made to determine if a potential existed for economic deposits of oil. None of the SOPAC countries was prepared with legislation pertaining to oil exploration or development, and much of the data from the efforts of the early 1970s were lost to some of the governments of the time because they did not realise their value, and were not aware that they could be obtained from the explorers legally, and usually easily, under the proper conditions.

CCOP/SOPAC provides a means of exchanging experiences, obtaining expert advice and assistance in matters relating to exploration and development, and is a forum for discussing and determining the respective obligations and requirements of both governments and industry in relation to mineral and hydrocarbon exploration. Legislation is now in place in almost all CCOP/SOPAC member countries in this regard. The few that have not yet enacted legislation, are close to doing so.

In 1981 Australia, New Zealand and the United States offered a multi-million dollar programme to assist the CCOP/SOPAC countries in assessing their marine resources which became known as the "Tripartite" Programme. Working from CCOP/SOPAC's base of knowledge and advice from scientists interested in the region, investigations of potential resource areas were quickly formulated in two main fields: petroleum, and deep-sea mineralization. The United States Geological Survey with their seismic research vessel 'SP Lee' and their immense technical and professional manpower resources were given the task of conducting the petroleum part of the programme with the assistance of Australia and New Zealand, under the general co-ordination of CCOP/SOPAC. The Hawaii Institute of Geophysics, University of Hawaii conducted the deep-sea projects using the HIG vessel 'Kana Keoki', also with assistance of the other Tripartite partners and co-ordination by CCOP/SOPAC.

The final results of the Tripartite I cruises are just becoming available, first as reports to CCOP/SOPAC, then as publications in the Earth Science Series of the Circum-Pacific Council for Energy and Mineral Resources. The petroleum-related manuscripts alone total seventy-four papers in three volumes, truly a monumental work.

In the meantime Tripartite II, a continuation of the Tripartite I programme, began in 1984. Again, the 'SP Lee' came to the South Pacific, this time for an operation of 100 days' duration covering areas of Tonga, Fiji, Vanuatu, Solomon Islands and Papua New Guinea. The studies carried on from the 1982 work, but also included additional coverage in basins not studied previously, and provided data in new areas of possible resource potential. The data from the Tripartite II programme are still being studied.

The minerals project under Tripartite II did not begin until late 1985, this time using Hawaii Institute of Geophysics' new vessel 'Moana Wave'. Due to funding and scheduling restrictions, this project was completed over several periods of ship-time during 1986. The first leg of the work was accomplished in the Solomon Sea at the triple junction of the Woodlark spreading centre and the Solomon Arc, and in Manus Basin, Bismarck Sea, another young spreading area.

Other major programmes have been developed with Japan. One of these was concluded in 1985 and involved two periods of shiptime of 30 days each with the Japanese vessel R/V "Natsushima". The first period studies tectonics and resources in the Solomon Sea including the New Britain Trench, the Trobriand Trough, and their collision zone in the western Solomon Sea area, and on the Trobriand Platform, an area where petroleum exploration leases were recently put up for bid by the Papua New Guinea government. The results of this study will be published in a special issue of Geo-Marine Letters. The second study area was in the northern Lau Basin and north Tonga Arc. The results of the second cruise will be published in a bulletin of CCOP/-SOPAC.

Another programme with Japan commenced in late 1985. This programme will study the manganese resource potential in the extended economic zones and adjacent waters of Cook Islands, Kiribati and Tuvalu. The Metal Mining Agency of Japan's Research vessel 'Hakurei Maru No. 2' is scheduled to operate systematically through selected areas in these waters for 50 days per year for 5 years.

As noted above, considerable interest in the geology and resources of the Southwest Pacific has been generated during the past several years, much of it due to the concerted efforts of the small nations of the region banded together in CCOP/SOPAC, where they speak as one voice. The CCOP/SOPAC region still remains a frontier where data in many areas are very sparse. Considering the size of the region, more than 5 times greater than the Mediterranean Sea, not counting international waters between member countries, much more effort must be spent before its resources are known with confidence, but after fourteen years of CCOP/SOPAC, a brief synthesis of activities in the resource fields of interest, and some of the knowledge gained to date can be provided.

MANGANESE NODULES

Despite several survey cruises undertaken in the South Pacific in respect of manganese nodules, the available data are still sparse and inadequate. About 300 analysed sample points exist, or less than one for each degree square of ocean floor. That is equivalent to one sample from an area the size of the State of Tasmania. For ore-grade nodules the combined metal content (Cu+Ni+Co) should be greater than 2.4 per cent. Nodules from northern parts of the Southwest Pacific exceed this value. The maximum grade found to date in the SOPAC region is 3.55% in the East Central Pacific Basin. The maximum concentration of nodules in many places in the SOPAC region exceeds the established minimum economic level of 10 kilograms per square meter. The maximum concentration found to date in the Southwest Pacific is 62 kilograms per square meter in the South

Penhryn Basin, but abundances appear to be variable through the region.

A synthesis of all available Southwest Pacific nodule data by the CCOP/SOPAC Technical Secretariat in 1982/83 indicated that best locations for economic grade and concentration appear to be in the areas of the East Central Pacific Basin north and east of the Phoenix Islands of Kiribati, and in the eastern North Penrhyn Basin of Kiribati and the Cook Islands. Considerable areas of deep water lie within the Exclusive Economic Zones of Kiribati, Cook Islands and Tuvalu that have potential for economic deposits under the jurisdiction of the adjacent state and not under the UN International Seabed Authority.

The CCOP/SOPAC compilation has heavily influenced the manganese nodule work being done under the current Tripartite programme of cruises which is searching for nodules in some of the areas identified as being of interest. It has also been instrumental in bringing a Japanese Government manganese nodule exploration programme into the region over the next five years. In addition, based on the CCOP/SOPAC work, a proposal has been made by a consortium of United Kingdom research groups to bring a British vessel into the Kiribati region for detailed manganese nodule studies in 1987 or 1988. By 1990 enough data on manganese nodules within the area should be available for a major appraisal of future mining possibilities to be undertaken.

COBALT-ENRICHED CRUSTS

The existence of manganese crusts containing a high percentage of cobalt (up to 2.6% or more) on seamounts at water depths of less than 2000 metres has only recently been recognised as being potentially economically attractive. A compilation of all available data has been done in the SOPAC to look for good potential. Cruises have been scheduled under the Tripartite programme for 1985 and 1986 to investigate the waters of Kiribati, Tuvalu and the northern Cook Islands for cobalt-crust bearing seamounts, and a West German group is investigating the cobalt potential of crusts in the Line Islands in eastern Kiribati.

Without substantially more work however, the full evaluation of the cobalt-rich crust potential of the region will probably not come before the end of the present decade.

Although the economics of mining manganese nodules and cobalt-rich crusts do not appear favourable at the present time, this will probably change before the end of the present century. Investigation of these minerals is therefore part of the long-term objectives of CCOP/SOPAC.

METALLIFEROUS SEDIMENT AND SULPHIDE DEPOSITS

Considerable attention to exploration for metalliferous sulphide deposits is now being given to back-arc basins behind volcanic arcs, where new crust is being injected as at mid-ocean ridges. Hydrothermal deposits including sulphides such as are known to occur at some mid-ocean rift systems, are being found in these back-arc basin settings.

Until the CCOP/SOPAC Technical Secretariat synthesised all available chemical data on sediments in the Southwest Pacific in 1981 very little was known about metalliferous sediments within the region. This compilation demonstrated two settings in which the deposits occur: back-arc basins (as mentioned above), and in the volcanic arcs themselves. The former setting is considered to have the potential for higher grade deposits.

This work, coupled with a near simultaneous joint New Zealand/UK cruise in the Tonga region which discovered hydrothermal manganese deposits and provided indications of metal sulphide occurrences, led a West German group to explore the Lau Basin within the Tongan EEZ in which metal sulphides were discovered early in 1985. A further West German cruise is scheduled and there are also plans for a British research vessel to explore the area. In addition, cruises have been scheduled under the Tripartite II programme, the target areas being the waters of Tonga, Fiji, Papua New Guinea and the Solomon Islands. All of these cruises are following up the indications in the 1981 CCOP/SOPAC synthesis.

At the present time, such deposits are a scientific curiosity rather than an economic resource, but it is becoming more and more apparent that they are much more widespread than previously considered, and like many other ore bodies, could become a resource when better understood. The potential for their occurrence in other areas of the Southwest Pacific is demonstrably good.

DETRITAL MINERALS

Normally, an extensive hinterland is required for placer mineral occurrence, so many of the small islands of the South Pacific would not be expected to have offshore placers because of insufficient land areas. Furthermore, coral reef development dissipates wave energy needed to concentrate placer minerals, thus further reducing the likelihood of their occurring extensively off the smaller islands. Even so, investigations of beach sands and shallow offshore areas have been made by CCOP/SOPAC for placer gold and magnetite sand in the Solomon Islands, Vanuatu and Fiji. The samples collected give indications that economic deposits may exist. At present, work is being done to establish the quantity and grade over wider areas than those sampled up to now.

Gold has been sought in offshore sediments transported from the Gold Ridge area of Guadalcanal, Solomon Islands, but results so far are disappointing. In Vanuatu, iron-rich beach sands occur in the vicinity of Port Patterson, containing up to about 15% iron. Values up to 14% have been found in sediments off shore. In Fiji, magnetite bearing sands occur off shore and on beaches near Sigatoka and Ba. Reserves of 1.8 million tons of magnetite minerals have been established for the deposit near Sigatoka. Small placer deposits have been found near a number of other islands. In Papua New Guinea, work by the Geological Survey there has found significant deposits of titanium-bearing magnetite in the beach sands in southeast Papua. Alluvial chromite has been located in bays on the Morabe coast south of Lae. So far, four and one half million tons of chromite have been reported.

The CCOP/SOPAC Technical Secretariat is currently analysing geochemical data for 17 elements on over 600 offshore sediment samples collected throughout the region, for indications of mineralization. An early result of this work is the finding of titanium enrichments off Western Samoa.

PHOSPHATES AND PHOSPHORITE DEPOSITS

Phosphorite deposits, of potential use as fertilisers, occur in a number of island groups within the CCOP/SOPAC region, and in major abundance on the Chatham Rise off New Zealand. Many small onshore deposits were exploited in the early part of this century. A number of CCOP/SOPAC cruises have included phosphorite exploration as part of their work, and the analysis of geochemical data mentioned above, is looking at phosphorus as one of the elements of interest. The main situation in which phosphates might occur in the CCOP/SOPAC area is on oceanic islands and on seamounts, or in the lagoons of atolls which were above sea level prior to the last sea level rise. The large commercial deposits of Nauru, Ocean and Christmas Islands are well known, and nearing exhaustion. Drilling in coral atoll lagoons has been done for a number of islands by exploration companies. In French Polynesia a large reserve was found in Matahiva lagoon which now awaits an improvement in prices to make it economic. A new phosphorite discovery is being tested in the Chesterfield Group west of New Caledonia. Although these deposits are not in territories of CCOP/SOPAC member countries, they lend encouragement to the search within that region. The CCOP/SOPAC Technical Secretariat has programmed lagoon drilling in promising areas of the Cook Islands, Tonga and Tuvalu in the near future.

CORALLIUM AND BLACK CORAL

Although not properly a subject of marine geology, corals do offer a source of income which reaches into the village level, especially where there are artisans and craftsmen who can work in the medium of coral carvings. It is also a resource which can be sought by marine geologists in the course of other work, and harvested with minimal equipment by the local people. Thus CCOP/SOPAC has been active in the search for corallium, and more recently, for black coral.

Corallium, or precious coral, including pink, red and gold members has been found in the CCOP/SOPAC region, but although the colours are excellent, their size is too small to be commercially important. The indications are that precious corals of commercial value may exist in the western areas of the Southwest Pacific, such as in the Solomon Islands and possibly Papua New Guinea, but so far no important beds have been located. They occur in deep water at about 100-300m or deeper.

Black corals, on the other hand, are common in many areas and occur within 50m of the sea surface. Small black coral industries have sprung up in Tonga, Fiji and Solomon Islands which provide incomes from carvings sold to tourists, although some raw coral has been exported for carving elsewhere.

SAND AND GRAVEL

On some islands, development needs for aggregate exceed the supply of easily obtainable material. On one island in Tonga sand has been mined both legally and illegally from beaches which have taken many years to be formed and a recreational and tourist asset has been lost. In other areas, planned development such as runway extensions for airports, port expansion, and hotels and tourist facilities require new aggregate sources to be found for the developments to proceed. Projects to locate offshore deposits have been successful in most areas, but the costs of extraction and transportation will no doubt be greater than merely removing sand from the beaches, a financial problem with which some island governments with tight budgets may have to find ways to cope.

HYDROCARBONS

It was formerly thought that volcanic arcs had no petroleum potential because they were mainly composed of volcanic rocks. Those ideas changed with discovery of oil seeps in Tonga, and the potential for petroleum resources is now of high interest to the CCOP/SOPAC member states. It is accepted among them that the potential in seamount and atoll provinces such as Western Samoa, Kiribati, Tuvalu, and Cook Islands is not significant.

Since oil seeps were found in 1968, exploration by industry has been intermittent and mainly confined to a few areas where definitive targets were found early, mostly in Papua New Guinea, Fiji and Tonga. A number of test holes were drilled on shore in Tonga and Papua New Guinea and some off shore. Since the Tripartite programme began in 1982 there has been a quantum leap in available high quality data, including many thousands of kilometres of new multi-channel seismic reflection data. Many smaller sedimentary basins have been found but remain unexplored. Much work remains to be done and we are looking forward to and hoping for an as yet undefined Tripartite III programme. Major oil companies have followed the recent programmes closely and have expressed strong interest in the results. The petroleum exploration programme in each member country is at a different stage of development, but there appears to be greater potential throughout the arc areas than had been considered even a short time ago. There are problems which we hope will be addressed in greater detail, such as lack of strong indications of source rock. However the few studies carried out have been on the land areas whereas there is reason to believe that the marine basins have had somewhat different histories and direct extrapolation of land studies into the offshore basins may not be reliable. Another problem is the depth of water covering these basins. Much of their area is in water from 1000 to 2000m depth but it is only a matter of time before the technology for drilling and completion has advanced into these depths.

This outline has given an overview of the various research activities that CCOP/SOPAC has undertaken to assist the island countries in the South Pacific in identifying the hydrocarbon and other mineral potential of their ocean floor. Obviously, more research is needed for a more precise appraisal and assessment of the economic viability of the undersea mineral potential of these countries.

This is why the CCOP/SOPAC Technical Secretariat warmly appreciates the generous support that is being provided by Australia, New Zealand, the United Nations, the United States, France and others to enable these research activities to be undertaken.

The UN Law of the Sea Convention, by extending the maritime and resource jurisdiction of coastal states over their adjacent seas, has given the small island countries in the South Pacific new opportunities to develop a viable economic future for the exploitation of their marine resources. It has been our task at the CCOP/SOPAC Technical Secretariat to provide support and assistance to these countries, not only in the identification and assessment of the economic viability of the mineral and hydrocarbon potential of their seabed but also in helping them to acquire and develop the capability to be self-reliant in marine mineral resource exploration and exploitation.

Chapter Nine

OCEAN ENERGY DEVELOPMENTS: PROSPECTS FOR PACIFIC ISLAND NATIONS

M Ellis

Until colonised by Europeans, Pacific islanders lived in a technologically simple stone age culture. Their requirements for energy and materials were slight. The only substantial energy sources were their own muscle power for fishing, gardening, etc., and wood and coconut shell and husk for cooking. On the "high" volcanic islands a limited amount of evening lighting was obtained from torches of resinous material such as candlenuts. On coral atolls sources of light were even more limited.

Colonial administration had profound effects on some aspects of island life but, for many decades, little on energy use. Only in recent decades, and particularly since the Second World War has the use of kerosene and other petroleum fuels become significant. Steadily declining petroleum prices through the 1950s and '60s encouraged the adoption of kerosene and white spirit lanterns as the standard light sources, followed by the rapid growth of electricity consumption, almost entirely from diesel generators. The use of LPG as a cooking fuel also put in an appearance at this time.

That the price declined in the face of rapidly increasing consumption was largely the result of the opening up of the vast and low cost resources of the Middle East. By 1970 the price of oil was so low that almost every other energy source was uneconomic by comparison. However, consumption was catching up with production capacity. A gradual price rise turned into a giant leap under the psychological impact of the Arab-Israeli war of 1973. The world's perception of the importance of energy supplies was revolutionised.

Energy conservation, and the development of alternative sources of energy suddenly became fashionable. The new attitudes were powerfully reinforced by the second price leap following the Iranian revolution. As this is written, the collapse of the OPEC cartel has allowed prices to drop to some $US16 per barrel. In "real terms", ie after allowing for inflation, this is their lowest level since 1973. There is a serious danger that attitudes will revert to their pre-1973 condition in which the maintenance of adequate energy supplies was regarded as someone else's concern. Once again only the companies immediately involved will concern themselves, and then only with sources suited to immediate exploitation.

If this is permitted to occur, the scene will be set for the last 15 years to be repeated, starting in the late 1990s. It is important that this does not occur: that attempts to improve the energy efficiency of industrial process, of transport and travel, and of building functions are maintained, that attempts to facilitate the development of non-petroleum, and especially non-depleting energy sources, are maintained.

The world's greatest potential source of non-depletable energy is the radiation from the sun. Most of that sunshine falls on the oceans. This vast energy flux, plus a few lesser energy sources, produces a wide variety of energetic phenomena. In theory at least, each of these could be harnessed as a source of energy useful to man.

At present none of them is being exploited except in either very small-scale specialist applications or experimental installations.

The energy being dissipated in the ocean greatly exceeds that required for human use. The figures in Table 1, taken from Constans (1979) give estimates of the dissipation rates "commonly found in the literature".

Table 1 Marine power dissipation rates

	MW x 106
Thermal Gradients	40,000.0
Salinity Gradients	1,400.0
Bioconversion	10.0
Currents	5.0
Tides	3.0
Waves	2.5
Offshore winds	20.0

However, like many "well known facts", these should be treated with care. Other texts give distinctly different estimates. In relating these to human consumption rates account needs to be taken of the environmental effects of large scale exploitation, as well as practical limits on the efficiency. In comparison with the total world electricity generating capacity, which would now be of the order of 2 x 106 MV, it is clear that the smaller sources could make only a modest contribution. The largest is much more than sufficient to supply all the world's needs.

This energy is, however, generally not available in the places where energy is most needed. It is most available where there is the most ocean. Consequently, it is particularly available in the Pacific.

OCEAN THERMAL DIFFERENCES

Solar radiation raises the temperature of surface waters between 23 and 26°C in favoured areas. Water chilled in the Antarctic between 4 and 5°C underlies this at depths of 600 to 1,200m. The temperature difference between these bodies of water is capable of driving a suitably designed heat engine to generate electricity. Such an "ocean thermal energy conversion (OTEC)" system uses the surface water as a heat source, and the cold deep water as a heat absorber. The temperature difference is only some 18 to 22°C. Consequently the theoretical limit on the system's efficiency is only 7 per cent. Practical systems will only achieve between 2 and 3 per cent. By comparison conventional nuclear or coal stations use a temperature difference of 400 to 500°C to obtain efficiencies of 30 to 35 per cent. The "fuel" is free, but this low efficiency is still important because it means that very large volumes of warm and cold water must be circulated through the system, relative to its useful output. The warm water is readily available, but the cold water must be piped, and pumped, up a vertical pipe some 1,000m or so long.

The cost of this essential component effectively precludes the economic development of small-scale OTECs. Other components, especially mooring, also show strong economies of scale. Most designs to date have been based on a unit size of around 100MW. This is too large to be employed in the national grids of any of the Pacific island countries. The only prospect for utilising such a plant would seem to be in conjunction with a very large-scale mining and processing development.

Smaller plants could be feasible if other factors are favourable. One important element is the length of the underwater transmission link. Some Pacific island countries have deep water much closer to shore than do the larger land masses. Temperature differences are also favourable in the Western Pacific. Indeed the only substantial region of the world with a year round average temperature difference in excess of 24°C runs in a broad band roughly from Guam to Tuvalu. All the member countries of the South Pacific Forum lie in waters with at least a 22°C temperature difference (Ocean Data Systems, 1978).

As Foster pointed out as early as 1972, ocean thermal energy is "The Most Abundant Natural Resource of the South Pacific", and he could have left out the word "South".

Nauru has tried the OTEC concept. The steepness of the offshore slope is such that the plants can be built on shore. This avoids the otherwise difficult and expensive underwater transmission link.

A pilot plant was built in 1981. This had a gross output of 100kW, and a net output of 15kW which was supplied into the country's public supply. (Mitsui et al, 1983). The plant was closed at the completion of testing.

Major problems remain to be solved before OTEC systems become commercially available. One of the most intractable is marine fouling of the heat transfer surfaces. Corrosion also severely constrains the use of low cost materials. Most proposed designs have been based on conventional steam turbine technology. Some innovative alternative ideas have been suggested which might overcome some of these problems. However, they have yet to be developed into detailed design studies.

There are those whose technological optimism is unbounded. Clay (1981) has even gone so far as to be concerned about the leasing of sites and the need for instituting criminal penalties for poaching. Such concerns are remote from the situation at present.

Tropical surface waters have very low nutrient levels. The deep cold water, by contrast, is nutrient-rich. Some enthusiasts have suggested that a valuable by-product of an OTEC scheme would be to produce an artificial upwelling of this deep water, greatly enhancing the biological productivity of the surrounding area. Brodie (1982), following an analysis of deep water off the coast of Viti Levu, has even gone so far as to warn of the possibility of undesirable algal blooms and eutrophication. These effects are not likely. The cold deep water would be only warmed by 2 or 3°C by an OTEC. It would be likely to be released at a depth of 100m or more to reduce pumping penalties. Even if it were released at only say 30m, its greater density would cause it to rapidly sink too deep to substantially affect biological activity. Indeed it is essential to the success of an OTEC as an energy producer that this cold water does not reach the surface, since it would then be drawn into the intake in place of warm water, sabotaging the plant's ability to function.

WAVES

In spite of the comparatively modest total amount of energy dissipated world wide by waves, this energy source has important advantages. In deep water the energy in a wave can travel long distances with little energy dissipation. In effect waves act as natural energy collection and delivery systems, collecting energy over a large expanse of ocean and delivering it to the surrounding shores. This reduces the energy transmission problem which is inherent in most ocean based energy development. Waves are a more steady and predictable source than the winds from which they draw their energy. Nevertheless the variations are still very substantial.

Wave energy is concentrated at the sea surface. Consequently a wave energy collection device needs to be of substantial extent in only one dimension. The potential of wave energy has excited the imagination of investors for more than two centuries. Constans (1979) records that hundreds of patents have been issued and comments that 70 to 90 per cent of efforts are made on the machine while only 10 to 30 per cent are spent on the energetic characteristics of sea waves. Consequently, far too many proposals are put forward without proper consideration of the system's basic element, the sea.

The Pacific is particularly badly off in this respect. Virtually no serious data relevant to energy production from waves have ever been collected. A number of proposals have been put forward to install various types of plant. However, these have usually been based on no more than a visual site inspection, often of only a single day at any given location. Estimates of any system's performance, when based on such inadequate information, must be regarded as highly suspect.

The great bulk of the development work put into wave power devices has gone into systems intended to be moored some distance off shore. This seems to reflect mainly the North Atlantic situation where tidal ranges are typically three or four metres, so that most types of fixed installations are not workable, and coastlines which are either closely developed or reserved in various ways. Several systems have been studied in detail. Easily the most elegant would be the Salter Duck. This has a cam-shaped float which nods in the waves like ducks on a breezy lake. Attractive results from early work stimulated enthusiasm for the concepts. One author was moved to title his book "Energy from the Waves; the First Ever Book on a Revolution in Technology" (Ross 1979). In this he claimed that wave power development was "as important as the discovery of steam power"!

A review of these systems by the Energy Technology Support Unit at Harwell, England, in 1979 (Dawson, 1979) indicated "that wave produced electricity is likely to be expensive compared with either nuclear or fossil fuels unless some major breakthrough in the engineering can be achieved". The British Government subsequently drastically reduced its funding for wave power development.

These massive and sophisticated offshore structures would be severely out of proportion to the technical capabilities of Pacific island countries. Economies of scale effects also indicate that installations of well over 100MW would be needed.

Most Pacific islands have low tidal ranges and, due to their small size, large ratios of coastline to land area and population. Hence onshore systems are much more interesting than for the North Atlantic. Two distinctly different systems have been proposed.

What is effectively a low head hydro scheme can be built by providing a sloping ramp which waves run up and spill over. In a "Mauritius" type arrangement the ramp would be built along the edge of a coral reef. The raised waters of the lagoon behind this would provide some useful short-term storage. Several islands have been examined with a view to installing such systems. Three sites on the south coast (the "Coral Coast") of Viti Levu, Fiji, have a total potential estimated at 50 to 75MW. Similarly a survey of the south Upolu, Western Samoa, identified three suitable sites (Crown Agents, 1980). The requirements for prospective sites are listed by that consultant:

1. An unbroken reef of at least 1KM
2. Acceptable levels of wave activity
3. Wide lagoon, at least 100m, with a quickly rising coast
4. No low-lying roads, villages or other structures.

Sites satisfying these requirements could probably be found around nearly all the larger islands. Such a development is probably precluded on atolls by the flooding that would result from raising the lagoon level by some three metres.

Some ancillary benefits from a "Mauritius" development could be increased recreational and tourist value from the deeper lagoon, which would facilitate activities not attractive in shallow water. Biological activity in the lagoon could also be stimulated (USP 1980).

A fundamental problem with the "Mauritius" scheme is the low head, only some three metres, from which electricity can be generated. Turbines operating at such a head are very large and slow-moving in relation to their energy output. The high costs of such machinery make even conventional hydro schemes unattractive at such a low head. A wave power plant would also have the problem of marine fouling to contend with, and the need for what is effectively a dam far longer than would be considered tolerable for a hydro station. Overall it is clear that such a scheme would produce power only at a high cost.

A variation on this idea which attempts to overcome some of these problems is the Tapered Channel. This uses a funnel-shaped channel to concentrate the wave's energy. By this means a considerably greater head can be developed. Unfortunately this improvement is somewhat offset by an increase in the length of wall required. Natural formations, such as tapered gaps in a raised coral reef, could occasionally be used to advantage to reduce costs. A pilot plant of this type is reported to be under construction in Norway (Rodke, 1984).

A quite different scheme is also being developed in Norway. This is the Multiresonant Oscillating Water Column (MOWC). A water piston in a vertical column pumps air back and forth through a symmetrical turbine. The bottom of the column is connected below sea level to a rectangular "harbour" facing the incoming waves. The water column and the harbour are tuned to somewhat different frequencies so that the system resonates over a range of wave frequencies. This considerably increases the system's energy output. The MOWC is designed to be installed on a steep coast such as a cliff face. It could be adapted to the edge of a raised coral reef provided deep water is available alongside the reef. Energy costs for a design developed by Kvaorner Brug A/S of Norway have been estimated at 6-7 US cents per kWh. This assumes installation in a situation with a very good wave regime. A prototype is being constructed and tested in Norway, with completion due late 1985. This is designed to produce 500kW maximum output.

A Wave Energy Utilization Mission visited several Pacific island countries in late 1984. The mission concluded that there was considerable potential for wave power in all the countries. Technically the best site found was the south coast of Savaii, Western Samoa. Eastern Tongatapu, Tonga, also has a suitable coastal configuration and wave availability.

A possibility raised by this mission was the harnessing of the spectacular blow holes which occur in Southern Tongatapu and Savaii. These are, in effect, natural oscillating water columns. They require only the fitting of a suitable turbine and generator to the vent, plus some relatively minor works to seal leaks and improve the effectiveness of water and air flows, to produce significant amounts of energy. The cost effectiveness of this could be quite attractive. However, the blow holes have substantial cultural and tourism values. The effects of development on these values would need to be fully incorporated into any assessment of the desirability of such a scheme.

TIDES

The standard model of tidal behaviour is of two bulges on opposite sides of the earth, each of which circle the globe once per lunar day. This model explains the usual tidal period of 12.5 hours, but otherwise has little connection with actual tidal behaviour. The continents so obstruct the circum-global movement that the tides are forced into circulatory patterns within each ocean. Relatively high tides occur where these patterns intersect major coastlines, while near-zero tides occur at the nodes of the pattern. A mean tidal range in excess of 1.5 metres is rare for a mid-ocean situation.

Much larger tides occur at the margins of bodies of water which have a natural period close to 12.5 hours. Exceptionally high tides also occur in the upper reaches of suitably oriented funnel-shaped inlets. Tides up to nine metres occur in particularly suited locations. The latter situation is analogous to the tapered channel wave power system, except that its characteristic period is 12.5 hours instead of some 10 to 12 seconds.

The theoretically available energy from a given sized tidal embayment is proportional to the square of the tidal range. In practice the effect of range is even greater than this since around one metre of head is unavoidably lost: the water leaving the turbines must be left with sufficient kinetic energy to move it away from the turbine. In addition, the range of water levels in the controlled pool must be less than the natural range if generation is to be spread over a long enough period each day to be useful.

Consequently the amount of energy, which could practically be generated from a tidal range of 1.5, or even 2.5 metres, is negligible.

CURRENTS

The ocean's currents transport enormous quantities of water at rather low velocities, and usually far from land. The kinetic energy of this moving water is a substantial, but very dilute energy resource. In some locations these currents run up against continental shore lines. This confinement causes the currents to run at a somewhat greater pace. Even so the energy density is very low. As a result devices to extract this energy would need to be very large in relation to their energy output. One inventor's design requires huge turbines rotating at just one revolution per minute. Inevitably, materials inputs will be very high in comparison to energy produced.

A further difficulty is that of long distance underwater transmission. At present this restricts the possibilities for obtaining energy from ocean currents to a small number of close-to-shore situations. In principle the energy could be used to synthesize a chemical fuel such as hydrogen or ammonia. However, the engineering and cost penalties associated with siting a major chemical plant in mid-ocean have deterred serious consideration of this.

A further limitation is the possible environmental effects of substantial development. Ocean currents play an important role in determining the world's climates. Any significant modification of a current's flow, velocity or direction could have highly-undesirable consequences.

No Pacific island countries are favoured with concentrated ocean currents close to shore. Hence the potential of this resource from their points of view is essentially zero.

OFFSHORE WINDS

Winds on shore frequently suffer from wind-shading, at least for winds from some directions. All winds are less near the surface than at higher levels due to friction. Both these factors are much less severe well off shore than on land, due to the ocean's large-scale smoothness. Even quite small differences in wind velocities are important, since the energy available from a given size of wind machine depends on the cube of the wind speed. Offshore siting also has the advantage that competition for land space is avoided.

To date these advantages have not proved sufficiently convincing for any significant offshore wind power plants to have been built, even near major cities where land space is at a premium. The difficulties of marine corrosion, the high cost of either a floating base or a sub-sea tower base, and the greatly increased cost of maintenance are serious economic penalties. The difficulties of power transmission to shore make it impractical to site a generator far enough off shore to get full benefit from increased winds, while even close to shore, underwater transmission is a substantial cost item.

All these difficulties apply with accentuated force in the Pacific islands. The benefit of increased wind speed is virtually non-existent on the low atolls, while the high volcanic islands can in some cases offer inland ridge-top sites with concentrated wind flows.

Tropical temperatures further accelerate marine corrosion rates, while cyclones, and the waves they can generate, are a further and expensive design problem. The small size of most island electrical systems make the integration of highly variable wind power difficult unless the amount is small relative to their small system. Offshore wind power generation is not a small scale technology.

Offshore winds can be, and are being used in another, and more successful way. This is to provide motive power for shipping. This is a technology with a long history. It is salutary to remember that sails lost out to steam power for the bulk of the business long before the days of cheap oil. Furthermore, modern diesel engines and especially the big slow-speed diesels, are a vast improvement on the coal-fired steam systems which saw off the clipper ships. There is no point in trying to just re-introduce the sail technology of the late 19th century. A successful wind-powered shipping technology of the late 20th century requires both major technical and materials improvements, and careful selection of vessel sizes and duties.

Materials improvements are available in high strength air-proof and rot-proof synthetic materials for sails, synthetic ropes, and corrosion resistant metal alloys. Technical improvements have also occurred, notably in the sealed, sea-water-proof electric motor. Sails can now be furled, unfurled or reset at the push of a button, or command of a computer, instead of a rush of manpower.

At present sails show little economy of scale. This may be only because of the undeveloped state of modern large-scale sail technology. However, in the meantime the most appropriate application for sails is to relatively small vessels, such as fishing boats and those transporting between small communities. These are classes of boats of particularly high importance to Pacific islanders.

Technologies other than sails have been tried. In the first rush of enthusiasm for alternatives to oil after 1973, a Japanese group tried using aeroplane wing style aerofoils. These rapidly proved a hopeless failure. The efficiency of a well set sail is much higher than this group had appreciated. The marginal gain in efficiency with a rigid aerofoil was nowhere near to justifying its clumsiness, and inability to adapt its size and shape to varying wind conditions.

A deck-mounted wind turbine driving a conventional propeller seems to have more to offer. It can be independent of wind direction; a ship equipped in this way can "sail" at full speed directly into a strong headwind. Its lift-to-drag ratio is higher than for sails, so that more power can be obtained from crosswinds for a given list. Turbines show economies of scale, so this may be the way to go for large vessels.

SALINITY GRADIENTS

The difference in salt concentration between fresh and sea water represents a major potential source of energy. The source of this is the difference in osmotic pressure between the two. Desalination plants consume large amounts of energy in working against this pressure difference. An "osmotic power station" would generate power by reversing the process. The pressure difference is remarkably large, about 25 atmospheres. The energy released at the mouth of every major river is equivalent to a waterfall some 240 metres high. Even greater pressures are available between fresh or sea water and concentrated salt solutions such as in the Dead Sea, or produced artificially with rock salt. The processes for which substantial research has been carried out all require vast areas of special membranes. Due to the high cost of these, current estimates of the cost of developing salinity energy run at around ten times the cost of alternatives. Even this may not be the full story. The estimates do not appear to be fully developed. Ancillary equipment and civil engineering costs could send them even higher.

Non-membrane systems have been suggested, e.g. by Wick et al (1981), but have not progressed past that stage.

Even apart from its unsatisfactory technical and economic state, salinity energy is of little interest to Pacific island countries. The atoll countries have insufficient fresh water, while the large islands have undeveloped hydro potential which is more appropriate than salinity.

There are a few islands in an intermediate situation. For example Christmas Island (in Kiribati) could conceivably combine salinity power generation with salt production.

BIOMASS

The only significant form of undeveloped zoological biomass in the ocean is the sub-Antarctic krill. Arguments continue about the scale and best use of this resource. However, it would be a clear waste to use it for energy.

Interest in botanical sources centres on kelp. It has a very high growth rate and regenerates naturally after harvesting. Trials off California have been moderately successful with the kelp being used to feed an anaerobic digestor, producing methane. The Pacific islands have many sites where kelp could potentially be grown, such as submerged reef areas and lagoons. Unfortunately kelp's rapid growth depends on a good supply of nutrient-rich water. Tropical Pacific water is extremely low in nutrients. Indeed the resulting sparsity of biological activity underlies the famous clarity of this water.

This limitation could be overcome by either pumping up nutrient-rich deep water, or by supplying artificial fertilisers. Both would be costly. For most countries land grown biomass makes more sense. However, for the atoll countries, with high population densities per unit of dry land, and little soil, but vast areas of ocean, it is a possibility worth keeping in mind.

SOLAR PONDS

Solar ponds utilise a strong salinity gradient to suppress convective mixing of a body of water heated by the sun. This enables highly saline water to reach temperatures of 80 to 90°C. Heat loss at the water surface is reduced by an overlying layer of cool fresh or low salinity water. Solar ponds are not usually regarded as an ocean technology. However, the lagoons of many Pacific islands would readily lend themselves to adaptation to solar ponds. A substantial supply of salt would be needed to set up and maintain the required highly saline bottom layer. However, many lagoons are a suitable depth and sea water could be used as the low salinity insulating layer. The cleanliness of the air on small islands and the clarity of the sea water, would greatly reduce one of the problems with land based ponds: heat absorbing dirt, leaves, etc. accumulating in the surface layers.

Nevertheless, substantial cost problems remain, e.g. experimental plants can use titanium heat exchanges to handle hot concentrated saline solutions, but this is unlikely to be viable for a production plant.

NON-RENEWABLE ENERGY FORMS

Deuterium

Potentially the largest energy resource in the oceans is its deuterium content. Extracting deuterium is an energy-intensive large-scale industry. The scientific feasibility of fusion power has seemed to be on the verge of being proven for some 20 years, still without a clear success. Even apart from this problem, the hypothetical fusion power station designs that have been produced indicate that individual fusion machines will be very large indeed, 10,000MW or more. Only the world's largest countries could utilise such a station. They are certainly not for Pacific islands.

Uranium, Thorium

Sea water contains enough uranium and thorium to keep a substantial world nuclear programme running for centuries. The resource is very dilute. Processes to concentrate the fissile material have been studied but not brought to full-scale operation. Pacific islands are unlikely sites for extraction plants, and totally inappropriate locations for nuclear power stations.

Coal

Coal is mined, notably in Britain, by tunnelling out under the sea. Coal has not, to this author's knowledge, been discovered on any Pacific island, although its occurrence must be quite likely in Papua New Guinea (PNG). Undersea coal mining is, at this stage, a remote prospect in the Pacific.

Oil and Gas

Offshore areas have become major sources of oil and natural gas supplies in several areas of the world. In the Pacific a major gas and condensate field has been discovered off Papua New Guinea (PNG). More fields are quite likely on and near this semicontinental land mass. The other Pacific countries have a much more limited potential. However, any substantial volume of sedimentary rock has some possibilities, a substantial such mass occurs under and around Tongatapu, Tonga. Some drilling has been undertaken there, but so far with no hydrocarbon discovery.

IMPLEMENTING NEW ENERGY TECHNOLOGY IN THE PACIFIC

Since 1982, the South Pacific Bureau for Economic Cooperation (SPEC) has been implementing a programme to install a variety of prototype and other new and renewable energy technologies in South Pacific countries. These technologies have all been onshore; however, the experience of this programme has relevance to the implementation of any of the ocean technologies described above.

One of the most notable features of this programme has been the great length of time required to get a project from identification to commissioning. Not all the delays occur in the South Pacific. The programme is funded by the European Economic Community under the Lome Convention. Very severe delays have been incurred in getting proposals approved, and tenders called, by the vast and cumbersome EEC bureaucracy. Further delays, plus considerable increases in cost, have resulted from the EEC's requirement that all equipment and services be purchased from EEC sources. Nevertheless serious holdups have occurred in the recipient countries.

The programme has had a chequered history, with projects being abandoned, usually at a very early stage. Others have been radically revised, transferred to different sites, changed in scale and scope, etc.

Some lessons from this experience are:-

(a) The importance of high quality comprehensive initial investigations. This could have avoided instances of proposals which proved unable to be supported by the available resource, or poorly matched to the energy demand proposed to be supplied.

(b) Avoidance of optimism in initial cost estimation. When funding is arranged on the basis of estimated cost, and the estimate proves seriously low, or to have not been fully comprehensive, the programme is thrown away. In the present case an increase in the total funds available is not possible. This is not an unusual situation. Consequently a cost over-run in one project forces a cut-back or abandonment of that, or another project within the programme.

(c) Completeness of the scheme. It is of no use to simply have a piece of equipment manufactured and delivered to a site. It will be left to rust away. The scheme must be worked through and delivered as a complete package. If it requires wood as a fuel, then the package must include fuel gathering and processing equipment. The operators and other personnel involved in running the plant must be given appropriate training. A common fault is to assume that the recipient organisation has an adequate budget for the purchase of auxilliary or replacement items. A gasifier generation project can fail because no money is available to replace a tyre on the tractor. Another is to assume that persons with adequate expertise will be hired. If a good manager or mechanic leaves, there will not necessarily be anyone to take their place.

(d) The project must be integrated into its technical, social and institutional environment. For example equipment made from high strength alloy steel will be seriously damaged if repaired by an inexperienced welder whose previous work has been all with mild steel.

(e) The organisation taking responsibility for operating the project must have adequate technical and managerial resources. Many projects in our programme have failed to make progress because of an inadequate capability at the site to make basic preparations. In such situations it is essential that supply of equipment is deferred. It is useless to assume that imminent arrival will act as an imperative. It is more usual for the equipment to be left in "temporary" storage.

(f) The agency funding the project must have an adequate technical and managerial competence. Even the best of initial plans will not produce projects which can be successfully implemented without significant changes when working with new technologies. The agency funding the project must be able to process, and make technically competent assessments of, requests for project changes, including budgeting and funding changes.

CONCLUSION

The oceans of the world, and the Pacific in particular, are a vast reservoir of potential energy. There is no presently available low cost and simple means of exploiting this potential in substantial quantity. Numerous contending technologies may some day change this situation. With the exception of wind powered shipping, this does not seem likely to occur for at least another decade. Implementation of an ocean technology will be faced by the same difficulties as have been met in new land based technologies, plus others specific to the hostile marine environment. Success will be dependent on learning from prior experience.

REFERENCES

Batt A N, 1981 Preliminary Assessment of Seawave Energy Potential and Development Prospects for Tongatapu Island, Kingdom of Tonga. Crown Agents, London.

Brodie J E, 1982 Analysis of deep Ocean Thermal Energy Conversion Site, Coral Coast, Viti Levu, Fiji. INR, USP, Suva.

Clay G S, 1981 Ocean Leasing for Hawaii. Honolulu: Department of Planning and Economic Development, Honolulu.

Constans J, 1979 Marine Sources of Energy. Pergamon, New York.

Dawson J K, 1979 Wave Energy. HMSO, London.

Foster P, 1972 The Most Abundant Natural Resource of the South Pacific. Search. 3(10).

Mitsui T, Ito F, Sega Y and Nakamoto Y, 1983 Outline of the 100kW OTEC Pilot Plant in the Republic of Nauru. IEEE Transactions on Power Apparatus and Systems, PAS-102(9).

Ocean Data Systems Inc. Large-Scale Distribution of OTEC Thermal Resource, 500-m and 1000-m Charts. In: Wick G L and Schmitt W R, 1981 Harvesting Ocean Energy. UNESCO Press, Vendome.

Rodke B M 1984 Wave Energy Utilization Mission, 5-12 November, 1984. (Unpublished).

Ross D, 1979 Energy From The Waves : The First Ever Book on a Revolution in Technology. Pergamon, New York.

USP Satellite Network Seminar on Wave Power in the South Pacific, 1980 University of the South Pacific, Suva, Fiji.

Wick G L and Schmitt W R, 1981 Harvesting Ocean Energy. UNESCO Press, Vendome.

Chapter Ten

CHANGES IN PORT AND SHIPPING TECHNOLOGY IN THE PACIFIC AND THEIR SOCIAL IMPACT

A D Couper

This paper outlines some of the employment and social impact aspects of the new port and shipping technology being adopted in the Pacific islands, primarily as a result of external pressures. It refers also to the problem of outer island economic developments and social relationships in a new marine technological era.

For many of the Pacific islands sea transport and cargo handling costs are vital factors in determining standards of living. They represent deductions from the sale of primary products and additions to the cost of consumer goods. The quality and frequency of shipping services are, in turn, important for social reasons, and they influence the range of commodities which can be produced in the islands for sale at urban or overseas markets.

The problems of attaining reduced freight rates and more frequent services for remote islands which have limited resources and low cargo generation capabilities, have remained unresolved over many years. Only subsidised or poor quality, infrequent, and precarious shipping have allowed some outer island communities to survive in the commercial economy. The tendency now is for island governments, faced with so many other problems, to try to avoid subsidising transport, but also for outer island people to be less tolerant of high levels of freight rates and poor infrequent services. This makes the search for and choice of more economic and technically efficient forms of cargo handling, shipping and patterns of trade very pressing.

The situation regarding choice of technology has radically altered in the last few years. Emphasis worldwide is on integrated sea and land systems. General cargo carriage is by container vessel, RoRo and LASH, while in the bulk trades mechanical loading terminals and new types of self-unloading ships are more prevalent.

The main ports in the Pacific have had to conform to containerised requirements in their links with overseas shipping, and inter-island shipping is beginning also to be drawn in this direction.

IMPACT OF PORT TECHNOLOGICAL CHANGE

Containerisation has already had an enormous impact on the quantity and quality of port employment throughout the world. In the UK, for example, port labour was reduced from 40,000 to 13,500 in fourteen years, and in Australia from 17,688 to 7,944 between 1970 and 1982.[1]

In the Pacific islands only Guam has full container facilities with a gantry crane for ship-shore operations. Within the next ten years this is likely to be provided in Noumea, Papeete, Pago Pago and possibly Suva, where at all places containers are at present handled by ship's gear. Neither has the movement of full containers proceeded beyond the confines of the main island ports to any great extent, the practice is for containers to be unpacked and packed by port workers within these ports.

Despite the partial container systems the new technology has already transformed work at Pacific island ports. During the immediate pre-container period break bulk cargo handling was highly labour intensive. The work was hard and arduous and paid by tonnage. In Suva there was a ten-hour working day plus required overtime. Workers were drawn from the poorer sectors of the urban area on a casual basis. Many of them had their origins in Kadavu and were picked for physical prowess and relationships with each other and with the local trade union organiser, also from Kadavu. At peak periods supplementary casual labour was recruited daily from the Rewa delta villages. Port work had low status at that time and there were long periods of unemployment. On night shifts unofficial rest periods, and consumption of alcohol, were common and accidents frequent. For the loading of bagged sugar it was the practice for ships to call at Suva and pick up labour. The workers lived on deck and loaded the ship at the western and northern sugar ports. Wet, insanitary and unhealthy conditions prevailed.

The port workers at Suva emerged from this industrial environment as a cohesive group with a strong identity, a suspicion of employers, and a proprietary interest in port work. Under these circumstances it was obvious that new technology would not be readily accepted unless there were clear benefits in it for port workers. The conditions greatly improved in the early 1970s after a period of strikes, negotiations and enquiries. These culminated in the end of casual employment, the registration of dock workers, a guaranteed 40-hour week, a 7-hour working day, and increased wage rates. Such conditions of employment spurred the speed of introduction of labour saving technology by the port employers, but they were also to prove difficult when the port had to induce workers to leave the industry. Only by quite generous severance payments was this possible during the introduction of containerisation. Table 1 shows the reductions in the labour force which were achieved.

Table 2 Decline in Port Labour at Suva

Year	Registered Workers
1971	600
1977	338
1980	307
1984	192
1985	178

Source: Port Authority of Fiji.

Workers who decided to accept voluntary redundancy payments and leave the industry have, from all accounts, remained in Suva. Some joined the body of casual labourers who periodically work the small inter-island vessels, others have entered the ranks of the unemployed who hang around the port area. At Lautoka the bulk sugar conveyor has replaced much of the labour formerly required, although for general cargo and, especially during the planting season for discharging fertilisers, Fijians from designated villages are periodically recruited.

The Papua New Guinea ports have shown similar trends in mechanisation and unitisation. Currently, there are about 1400 registered and 100 casuals working in PNG ports. Elsewhere in the Pacific, port worker numbers are much reduced. In Honiara 160 men are registered and employed by the port authority, but in Noumea most workers are still recruited in the villages on a casual basis.

IMPACT OF CHANGES IN SHIPPING

The choice of technology for improvements in island shipping is also being influenced by events outside the island economies. Over recent years there has been more externalising of marine technology. There have been drastic reductions in village boat building and in the repairing and crewing of boats as part of integrated village activities. This decline has been due to the adoption of new designs, construction materials, motorisation, and more rigorous regulations.

Recently there has also been a deterioration in the sail and motorised wooden cutter sector owned and operated by small-scale entrepreneurs at the port towns. These vessels for long provided services around villages even in quite remote areas. Cutters were generally badly maintained and as they aged they became more precarious. They were overloaded with passengers at peak periods, and often they were manned by untrained and overworked crews. Many cutter services have disappeared due to bankruptcies, foundering of vessels at sea, grounding on reefs, and stricter marine regulations.

On the more profitable inter-insular liner routes, larger, steel-hulled, coastal-type vessels were owned and operated by merchant companies. They likewise have become fewer in number due to ageing, stricter surveys and the withdrawal of the companies from shipping. There have also, in any event, been difficulties in replacing this class of vessel, due to its reduced availability on the second-hand markets in Europe and Australia as a result of the technological changes now well established in these areas.

Most of the older types of 10 to 100 GRT vessels which operated in the Pacific islands carried crews of 7 to 18. Accommodation was poor and the crew manhandled cargo over long hours during unloading and loading around island ports and anchorages. Employment was often on a casual basis, although crews tended to be drawn from specific islands. Government owned vessels and the bigger merchant company ships had better conditions, articles of agreement, and some systems of planned maintenance.

There is still a considerable range of craft, in a variety of physical conditions, in the Pacific; but the ships acquired most recently are technologically very different from the past. They have included modern RoRo ferries, such as the 677 GRT

'Princess Ashika' purchased by a Fiji firm from Japan.

These new types of vessel are becoming relatively plentiful on the second-hand market and are often available at low interest rates and long term repayments. But by island standards their capital costs are high and the operational and maintenance requirements complicated. They can carry 300 to 400 passengers and up to 50 or so vehicles. They have bridge-controlled twin engines, are easily manoeuvred in confined spaces, and have bow and stern ramps for lying at simple T-jetties. Containers can be packed at, or transhipped from, island main ports on trucks or chassis to be driven on board. Passengers may carry larger quantities of goods than can be taken by air, and fares are half the price of air tickets. For the islands there are opportunities in these new vessels to receive freezer cargoes by truck and to market fish, fresh produce and livestock. The benefits of such vessels are immediately apparent.

On the negative side of this technological transfer are the high capital, maintenance, and fuel costs. This makes it less worth while for the ships to call at remoter coastal villages and islands for small quantities of cargo. The modus operandi is short stays at jetties where large quantities of cargo and passengers have concentrated. Maintenance has to be regularly carried out on these ships, and it is likely that repairs, maintenance costs and spares will exceed the capital costs of the vessel by three to four times within its life. There have to be higher levels of seamanship, and navigational and engineering professionalism, and particularly close attention paid to stability, the integrity of the watertight bow ramp, and the securing of road vehicles on board. Island commercial ships have not been noted for these measures, or for planned maintenance, in the past.

The social traditions of island shipping can also present problems for new vessels. Socialising on the ship and waiting for passengers at villages are part of more complex relationships between island shipping and island communities (Couper A D, 1973). An example of both the social function of the ship, and the pressures on the captain to maintain good relations with the local community by holding the vessel, was witnessed during a voyage on 7th December, 1985 when eight firemen on behalf of 'Green Watch' at Suva Fire Station were presenting sports gear to a village in Kadavu. They received the traditional mats, pigs and other items in return, together with a small feast. The occasion was of some significance for the village, but the vessel was delayed.

Newer ships with higher capital and depreciation payments have to maintain schedules and they need more highly trained crews. The human factor has also to be improved for meeting the requirements of Conventions on safety, dangerous and hazardous cargoes, load line, collision, tonnage, and standards of training, certification and watchkeeping (STCW) which apply to the larger class of ship.

The profile of the Pacific seaman is thus becoming very different from that of the past - when physical stamina was a basic requirement of the sailor, and rudimentary navigation using a magnetic compass and visual observation of reefs and coastal landforms, was all that was required of the captain. Now, new types of vessels, and a uniform Pacific Maritime Standards Code, with formal certification for various grades, demand different types of seafarers.

CONCLUSIONS

The changes coming about in Pacific island main ports are similar to those that have taken place in all of the developed country ports under the impact of new technology. There have been reductions in the numbers employed, and increased requirements for higher levels of skills. The hard physical labour has been taken out of port work, there is more security for the worker and more job status. But the majority of main ports are still overmanned and only the retention of cargo handling from and to containers in the port maintains some jobs.

The reduction in employment at ports has affected families in the urban areas, and to some extent the nearby villages. It may be argued that the improved turnaround of ships, and the somewhat less significant improvements in the speed of goods flowing through the ports, will have stimulated exports and cheapened imports, and thereby benefited the community as a whole and created work opportunities beyond the port. This has yet to be proven.

Conversely, it may be argued that the new mechanical appliances and their spares requirements have added to balance of payment deficits, that unemployment has resulted in port communities, and the employment creating multiplier effects of new technology have been transferred abroad to the centres of equipment and container manufacturing.

It must be concluded, however, that in a competitive situation port unemployment would have ensued if no technological changes had taken place in some Pacific ports, and this would have had more serious wider impacts on the community.

The question which remains is how far to press ahead with further technological advances in the island ports. It is possible to have an almost fully automated port with computer controlled systems, and this is the way many of the most advanced ports of the world are heading. On the other hand, a highly automated terminal in Rotterdam has made the decision not to introduce even more technology but, in the interests of job satisfaction and employment, to allow some tasks and decision-making to be carried out under human control, even if they could be more efficiently performed by automated systems. It is important that Pacific ports also decide on an appropriate point beyond which they are not pushed by technology.

In relation to island shipping, it is difficult to predict whether the new types of vessels can survive physically and economically in the island marine environments. Two aspects are certain. First, survival and viability depend on improved qualities of seamanship and navigation, and on changed attitudes to ship maintenance and operation. Second, the needs of the poorer, remoter outer islands cannot be met by these vessels. In this latter respect simpler tug-and-barge systems, self-sustained powered barges, or new designs of sailing vessels are all being considered as options. But it is also necessary to acknowledge certain facts of geography and admit that for many such places only subsidised transport or goverment vessels are the alternatives to high freight rates and infrequent services.

The only underutilised resources in the outer islands are the fisheries and the human resource potential available as seamen. Seafarers are already drawn from the outer islands of Lau in Fiji for local ships, and for crews and officers on regional shipping. Seafarers from the eastern islands of Vanuatu man local Vanuatuan, New Caledonian and French owned shipping, and Kiribati has been supplying about 1000 seafarers to West German shipping companies.

Pacific islanders from these and other outer

islands have proved to be intelligent, strong and fearless seamen. With proper training courses to international standards the islands can not only provide crews for the operation of local vessels, but can offer competition to the seafarer-exporting countries of the Philippines, South Korea, Hong Kong and increasingly the PRC. This market is large, the Philippines provides about 70,000, and South Korea 30,000, seamen for foreign flag ships.

An example of the possible levels of seafaring remittances to island economies may be appreciated from the agreements between the German companies and the Kiribati Overseas Seamen's Union, which is affiliated to ITF. In 1984 Kiribati seamen received 88 per cent of the level of wages of a West German seaman, in 1986 the level was ninety per cent and for 1987 the agreement is for 93 per cent.

The increased employment of outer islanders as seafarers is not without social problems for villages. Men return to their home islands with much wider horizons and experience than exists in the family circle of wives and children. But cash remittances generate demand for imported consumer goods and travel in island communities, and as commercial shipping to the islands responds to effective demand for imports this income may provide the basis for more adequate shipping, with concomitant transport opportunities for marketing dried and frozen fish and other island exports.

It seems that part of the key to both the guarantees of adequate shipping to the smaller islands, and the survival of outer island communities, lies in the further development of the natural marine and human resources which exist in the Pacific. Part of the key to this, in turn, lies in the provision and appropriateness of maritime training for fishermen and merchant seamen.

REFERENCES

Couper A D, 1973 Islanders at Sea in Brookfield, H.C. (ed) Pacific in Transition, Edward Arnold pp229-247

Couper A D, 1986 New Cargo Handling Techniques: Implications for Employment and Skills in the World Port Industry, ILO, Geneva

Chapter Eleven

TRADE AND SHIPPING NEEDS FOR ISLAND ECONOMIES

Paul McDonnell

There are considerable similarities between the islands of the South Pacific and those of other areas, notably the Caribbean, and some lessons can be drawn from these other areas in considering the particular problems faced by South Pacific islands in identifying and meeting their shipping needs.

It is also particularly important at the outset to appreciate the differences in situation and circumstances of larger island countries, which, generally, have more or less self-sustaining economies and resources that can be developed in a modern economic context, and the smaller islands that have no realistic hopes for future self-sufficiency, and which have, generally, distorted internal economies. In the Pacific the former, consisting of Papua New Guinea, Solomon Islands and Fiji, have economies so different in size, type and scale from the rest of the South Pacific islands that it is very difficult to compare them in any meaningful way, and especially to address their shipping problems from a common point of view.

Shipping certainly has a profound effect on the economies of the larger island countries, just as it does on the smaller ones, the difference is that in the smaller islands shipping has a more fundamental impact and is much more significant for day-to-day life. In the larger economies to a considerable extent the effect of shipping is more diffused and indirect. The large economies have an internal dynamism of their own of which shipping services are but one component whilst in the smaller island countries the economy, such as it is, is excessively dependent on a number of individual factors, of which a significant one is shipping. Between the two extremes lie a few countries that have the potential to develop a workable and active economic structure but which, for various reasons, not the least being lack of manpower, political will and cultural constraints, have yet to reach their apparent potential. In this group we might include Vanuatu, Western Samoa and Tonga. The effect of shipping on their economies, while not as profound as it can be on that of the smallest group of islands, is nevertheless very significant and has perhaps a more direct bearing on the everyday operation of those countries' economies. For two countries (Western Samoa, Tonga) it is particularly significant with regard to the development of exports, and the role these two countries have played in the Pacific Forum Line is indicative of the central importance this sector has in their own view of economic development.

A fourth group, essentially outside the ambit of this paper, are the non-independent territories. These have economies that are considerably distorted by military requirements and generally do not fit the South Pacific pattern, except inasmuch as places like French Polynesia, Guam or American Samoa are overwhelming examples of the general South Pacific pattern of imports dominating shipping services. These countries export very little and because of the high standard of living they enjoy, sustained by the military expenditure of the metropolitan power, maintain very high levels of imports. This is an extreme example of what is a common case in the region.

BACKGROUND

It is important to relate South Pacific trade and consequently shipping services, to their place in the world scene. Trade with South Pacific islands represents a very small fraction of world trade, probably about 0.5 per cent. Of this amount, by far the greatest proportion is generated by five regional countries (Papua New Guinea, New Caledonia, Fiji, Nauru and Solomon Islands) which together account for approximately 98 per cent of total regional exports. Thus the remaining percentage exported by the other regional countries is insignificant. About 75 per cent of the region's export consists of bulk products, particularly phosphate, copper, nickel, and timber which, of course, accounts for the predominance of the countries mentioned previously. Three countries alone (Papua New Guinea 53 per cent, Fiji 27 per cent and the Solomon Islands 13 per cent) accounted for 93 per cent of the total regional agricultural exports and increases over the last five years have principally been due to increased exports of timber from Papua New Guinea and sugar from Fiji. Agricultural exports from the remainder of the South Pacific region have remained largely static. Thus the preponderance of a few large South Pacific island countries is emphasised even more when the export figures are considered, and it is clearly very difficult to draw a parallel between the situation of Papua New Guinea and the impact shipping has on its economy and the situation of a small island country like Tonga or Cook Islands.

THE SIGNIFICANCE OF IMPORTS

If the non-independent territories are left aside, which, because of the the reasons explained above, have a very distorting effect on the regional pattern, it can be seen that dry general cargo imports into the region, at approximately three million tonnes per annum, exceed the general cargo exports in the ratio of approximately 6:1 (if sugar, molasses, lumber and mineral exports are excluded). Thus it is clear that in most trades it is the level of imports that largely determines the nature of the region's liner service and not the level of exports. This is the most significant single factor in evaluating regional shipping services. Once again it is clear from the charts that the major countries predominate to an overwhelming extent in the level of imports. However, the relative level of imports into any single island country, particularly the middle-sized and smaller islands, has a significant local effect. It is this level of imports that basically determines the type of shipping service available, and the key to maintaining an appropriate level of imports, to justify what is perceived as an adequate shipping service, is the maintenance of a sufficiently high level of spending power in the community to sustain the appropriate level of imports.

Petroleum product imports are significant and once again illustrate the differences between the larger developed economies and the smaller. There is some difference here if one considers the per head consumption of the non-independent but economically advanced territories, for example, Hawaii or French Polynesia consumption, and by analogy, development, and the smaller independent territories of the South Pacific.

Total imports into the smaller island countries are truly insignificant (at a level of approximately 180,000 tonnes per year in total if the four main consumers are excluded) and, because of the effect of a static or even declining income level in real terms, have not shown any tendency to rise. Generally speaking the larger and more developed countries have the best potential for economic development and consequently a rate of real growth sufficient to sustain an increase in imports at least proportional to population growth. The smaller islands, however, have limited economic prospects and their future performance is likely to be modest, with a consequent effect on the demand for imports and thus shipping services.

THE SIGNIFICANCE OF EXPORTS

The South Pacific is a marginal area in world trade terms. Exports, dominated by a few major producers of bulk commodities, are generally shipped in specially designed ships that have little impact on import trades. For the other smaller island countries that have comparatively insignificant exports, mainly agriculturally based, the key to maintaining satisfactory levels of shipping services depends on maintaining or increasing the level of imports. Paradoxically these small island countries are also dependent on the same shipping services to maintain the level of exports they are able to sustain at present, although this is small in real terms and proportionately not significant when compared to imports. The objective must be for these countries to attempt to maintain direct services at a level which permits their small, although economically vital, quantities of exports to be shipped out. The key then to sustaining adequate shipping levels for the needs of island economies rests on three points. These are, respectively, the need to maintain direct shipping links to the major sources of imports and destinations of exports, the need to sustain adequate spending power within the economy to sustain a level of imports that justifies adequate services and, finally, a need to increase exports where possible to improve the viability of existing and possible future services.

If we agree that the provision of general cargo shipping capacity is primarily determined by the volume of imports, and I suggest we must, the source of those imports is an important factor in ensuring continued maintenance of adequate shipping services. Since 1970 the importance of Australia has declined, together with that of the European Community, while Southeast Asia and Japan, and New Zealand have all enjoyed significant increases as sources of regional imports. Tonnage flows to and from the major island countries, regardless of source or destination, are probably sufficient to maintain adequate shipping services in the future. The concern of the medium and smaller island countries however, is to ensure that they do not suffer from inadequate services, which means, essentially, making the provision of those services sufficiently commercially attractive to operators to continue providing them. The very smallest countries, however, may not even be able to do this and it is probably unrealistic to expect countries such as Cook Islands, Niue, Kiribati and Tuvalu to be able to sustain commercially viable services at an adequate level particularly if they were to rely on exports to do this. Thus they will probably need some sort of subsidy to provide services that at once maintain a sufficient flow of imports and provide an outlet for exports which, although small, have a significant social and economic effect within those countries themselves.

THE IMPACT OF TECHNOLOGY

As we have indicated above, the South Pacific has a negligible impact on world trade, but the converse is not necessarily true, with the impact of modern world-wide technical development in shipping. We have already identified the difference in circumstances between the larger island states and the smaller, and the impact of the technological revolution in shipping, which is particularly directed at cargo handling methods and by that we mean containerisation, is also likely to be profoundly felt in this region. The larger island states with significant exports have a greater justification for developing the necessary port infrastructure to handle containers than the smaller islands. However, this is not completely the case, as a great proportion of the exports of the larger states consists of bulk items, which require specialist ships and often specialist loading methods. In the Solomons and Papua New Guinea for example, logs are often taken straight off the beach rather than being shipped through any developed port, and the cantilevers in

Nauru are an obvious example of new technology as far as cargo handling is concerned that does not have any relevance to containerisation. Nevertheless, since imports generally sustain shipping services in the South Pacific and, increasingly, containerisation is the mode by which most consumer products, and increasingly other general cargo, is handled, it is inevitable that containerisation will increase in the region.

The handling of containers is well entrenched in the major ports in the region. The question is how far down the chain of cargo movement will it penetrate? Almost every country in the region has a port capable of handling containers, the only exceptions being Alofi in Niue and Avarua in Rarotonga. This is one of the reasons the service to those two islands from New Zealand bears the highest subsidy of any South Pacific shipping operation per ton of cargo. There is, despite this, still a large amount of breakbulk cargo handling in other ports in the region. For example, the Pacific Forum Line trunk service, which is completely containerised, leaves cargo in Suva for transhipment by breakbulk to Tuvalu and Kiribati. This clearly adds greatly to transhipment costs and this is inevitably passed on to the consumer. There is therefore a strong imperative to increase the penetration of containerisation in an effort to reduce overall costs. If one end of the service, namely, the metropolitan source of imports is dependent on containerised operation to maintain a tolerable level of handling costs, it is necessary that the recipient state also be able to handle containers to constrain costs as well. The fact that breakbulk charges might be very low in the recipient state because of labour efficiency and low costs will have a negligible impact on the overall cost equation involved in providing the service. Importing states, and by that we mean all South Pacific island states, will be forced to accept containerisation because of external reasons and they will also have to accept the cost of establishing the appropriate level of infrastructure.

This is the least of the problem for the major states, which have the resources and access to funding to provide an appropriate level of infrastructure, for example, container handling facilities, berths, etc., and which will get a greater utilisation from these facilities, because of a much higher level of both imports and exports, than will the smaller states, which have few exports and a proportionately lower level of imports. There facilities would be used only infrequently and would show a negligible return for the capital costs required to establish them. Despite this, the only alternative to providing the necessary infrastructure is for smaller island states to accept less efficient and much more expensive breakbulk operations with an increased risk of losing their direct connections to the metropolitan rim countries as their shipping operations become incompatible with what is acceptable in those countries.

CONCLUSION

It is clear that the shipping needs of the island states' economies vary considerably depending on the islands themselves. There is not one set of problems that is common across the region nor is there a conclusion that will satisfy the shipping requirements of all the islands. There are, however, common problems that exist, particularly between groups of similar islands. A productive approach might be to divide the South Pacific islands into categories. In some cases shipping services are a developmental tool in increasing economic development where the potential exists for this, in others they should be seen more as a social service that sustains an existing distinct socio-economic group.

New technologies are having an impact in the region and this is providing difficulties for some of the countries. Since most services are provided by organisations that lie essentially outside the region, the South Pacific is, and is likely to remain, a service taker for its shipping requirements. The impact of containerisation has already had a significant effect, particularly in the major ports of the larger and more developed states, but it will eventually be felt right down the chain of cargo movement to the smallest ports in the smallest states in the region. This will require an inevitable amount of infrastructural development and some countries will need to adopt a least cost approach to this if they wish to remain part of the regional shipping network. As the economies of the island countries vary so do their shipping needs, and the solutions will be found only by examining the individual circumstances of each island state.

Chapter Twelve

AID FOR MARITIME DEVELOPMENTS IN THE PACIFIC

N T Riley

The region of the South Pacific was formerly administered as colonies and protectorates. The various colonial or protectorate administrations offered the necessary shipping, infrastructure and training to provide for the day to day transport and communication needs of the region. However, with the formation of the various independent nations in this area the responsibility for the maintenance of these services has become those of the countries concerned.

The equipment existing usually originated with the administering country, it was based on the technology appropriate to the metropolitan country and was re-designed to suit the expatriates in the colonial administration.

Much of the equipment provided by the external administrations was ultimately handed over to the local governments to maintain existing services and infrastructures. However, the necessary back-up for repair and maintenance no longer existed and the comparatively high level of maintenance required to keep this equipment operating has increased the burden of administration and expense of the various nations concerned.

In most instances the equipment was designed and in operation before the oil crisis of the early seventies and the cost of fuel for operation was not then a primary consideration. Since the region has no current oil-producing capacity the cost of importing fuel oil is a significant factor in the viability of the various national economies.

During the period of his consultancy to the Australian Development Assistance Bureau the author has been involved in a number of areas related to the provision of aid to the region. These include:-

(a) The survey and reporting on the status of existing craft and equipment;
(b) Assessment of the requirements of new craft and equipment;
(c) Procurement of new craft and equipment;
(d) Overseeing repairs on vessels owned by individual governments: and
(e) Advice on the planned maintenance of vessels owned by individual governments.

IDENTIFICATION OF PROBLEM AREAS RELATED TO THE MARITIME SCENE

As a result of his visits to the various regions of the Pacific the author has been able to identify a number of fairly general problem areas in relation to existing equipment and also problems associated with donor-furnished equipment.

Existing Equipment

It has already been mentioned that many of the existing vessels in the area date back to the days of earlier administrations and are now reaching what would be generally considered the end of their economic lives. In some cases it could be said that the economic life had been well exceeded. However, the necessity to keep a particular vessel or piece of equipment in operation, because of the lack of the ability to provide a replacement, forces this situation to exist.

The main problems observed in vessels taken over from previous administrations are:-

Deterioration of Structure

The majority of vessels operating on inter-island voyages are of either steel or timber construction. The tropical environment, which is both warm and humid, is not conducive to low cost maintenance on either of these materials.

In the case of steel, exposed areas are prone to mechanical damage, and unless the paint coatings on damaged areas are properly repaired immediately after damage then the steel will start to rust.

In internal spaces sweating of the steel structure will occur, particularly in damp areas and in spaces which are poorly ventilated. These conditions support corrosion and unless treated properly the corrosion will eventually cause holes in important parts of the structure, such as the shell plating, decks and tank tops.

In the environment already described timber hulls will suffer from dry rot if not properly ventilated. Unless properly and frequently slipped and antifouled the underwater hull will be attacked by toredo worm and other marine organisms.

Electrolytic action, which can be caused by the operation of defective electrical systems or the use of dissimilar metals will accelerate the deterioration of both steel and timber structures. In the case of steel, pitting of the affected surface will occur, while in a timber structure fastenings will be eaten away and the timber in the way of these fastenings will exhibit a form of rot.

Unserviceability of electrical and mechanical equipment

The most common factor observed which contributed to the loss of operational availability of vessels and their infrastructure was the unserviceability of electrical and mechanical equipment. As with the structural problems mentioned above the warm humid atmosphere contributes to corrosion of mechanical equipment. Unless positive steps are taken, this atmosphere will quickly render electrical equipment unserviceable.

However, two other factors were observed to contribute to loss of operational availability. These were the lack of adequate spare parts backing, and the casual attitude of operating personnel to the demands of continuing and regular maintenance of the hull, machinery and equipment.

The first of these can be attributed to either the lack of planning for an adequate spares inventory and re-ordering or the difficulty of timely procurement of spares due to the equipment going out of production.

The second factor is basically a matter of training and education of the personnel concerned and of their supervisors.

Donor-Furnished Equipment

In a number of cases of vessels and equipment provided under aid projects, the author observed that these particular vessels and equipment had been designed and constructed to suit the requirements and regulations of the donor country rather than the recipient country. This was evident in a number of ways, e.g.:

(a) the arrangements and accommodation were unsuitable for the climatic conditions of the region;
(b) the equipment supplied was more sophisticated than was necessary; and
(c) difficulty was experienced in obtaining spares in the area of operation.

Recurrent Costs

In the cases of both inherited vessels and equipment, and donor-supplied vessels and equipment there still remains the need for recipient countries to find the recurring costs of operation and maintenance.

One of these costs which merits close scrutiny is the cost of fuel. In general, the vessels and equipment inherited from earlier administrations were designed and in operation before the oil crisis of the early seventies, and energy conservation was not then an important design consideration. Since the region produces no oil of its own, the need to conserve fuel usage is important to the economy of the region.

In addition to fuel costs the recurring costs of maintenance of vessels and equipment are significant. Much could be done to reduce the cost of maintenance if routine repairs and maintenance were carried out on a regular and continuing basis, rather than when breakdowns occur.

SOME PROPOSED SOLUTIONS TO CURRENT PROBLEMS

From the observations already made it is believed that positive action can be taken to provide more effective vessels and equipment for the region and to reduce operating costs.

In the case of new projects it is believed that these objectives should be addressed at the inception of each project.

Suitability of Vessels and Equipment

As mentioned previously, it has been observed in some instances that new vessels delivered to the nations of the Pacific have reflected the standards of the donor countries rather than the requirements of the recipient countries. Therefore at the design stage the requirements for acceptable habitability, for both passengers and crew, should be given the strong consideration that is required.

Thorough attention should be given to the detail design of equipment and structure to minimise built-in maintenance problems. Some examples of these are:-

(a) structural details should be designed to provide easy access for effective painting in the building stage and maintenance after delivery;

(b) the arrangement of all equipment should be such as to provide easy access for maintenance and repair;

(c) items of electrical equipment should be protected against water impingement; and

(d) adequate ventilation should be provided to all spaces below decks and in the case of ventilation to machinery spaces a complete change of air every minute should be the minimum acceptable rate. In closed-in accommodation spaces a minimum of a complete change of air every two minutes should be taken as an acceptable rate.

Machinery and equipment should be chosen on the basis of its suitability for the purpose intended, rather than economic expediency. Further, all items of equipment should be suitable for operation in a salt-laden tropical environment and should be as simple as operational requirements will allow.

As most craft operating in the region will, in all probability, carry passengers whether they have been designed for this operation or not, consideration should be given in the design stage for such a situation.

The author has observed that in cargo vessels deck passengers are carried on the cargo hatch and are protected from the elements by a canvas tent. Such an arrangement is acceptable in the case where the vessel concerned is travelling from one port to another and the hatch is not subject to inundation. However, when a number of ports are serviced, then the passengers have to be moved to permit working of the cargo gear and the hold. In this situation provision should be made to carry the deck passengers in spaces away from the areas where cargo is to be worked.

Observations indicate that hydraulically-driven equipment is more reliable than electrically-driven

Observations indicate that hydraulically-driven equipment is more reliable than electrically-driven equipment. Also the expertise available to repair electrical equipment is not as prevalent as mechanical expertise. Finally hydraulic circuits, once set up, are reasonably trouble-free in comparison to electrical circuits and concomitant equipment. Therefore, hydraulic systems are preferable to electrical systems.

In all but the larger vessels operating in the region, the normal form of propulsion is by means of an automotive diesel driving a conventional propeller through a reverse reduction gearbox. While such an installation may be justifiable on a first-cost basis, other considerations should be addressed. In particular, maintenance requirements and fuel economy should be checked against the more expensive dedicated marine diesel engine. Almost invariably the dedicated marine diesel engine will prove to be the most attractive unit for use in the region.

It is a common occurrence for vessels of the region to operate in remote localities, where even basic maintenance facilities are non-existent. It is therefore mandatory that all essential services be provided with at least one back-up system. For this reason alone, twin screw propulsion should be a feature of any vessel operating in the region.

Fuel Economy

Lagoon Craft

During visits to the Pacific region the author has observed that high speed petrol engines, both inboard and outboard, are used for rapid transit. These types of engines are not fuel-efficient and the comparatively high speeds at which these craft travel only exacerbate the problem of inefficient use of fuel.

It is considered that action should be taken to introduce a scheme to change over to diesel propulsion and to accept lower speeds.

Inter-Island Vessels

Fuel economy can be achieved in two ways on diesel-driven inter-island vessels.

The first way is to travel at the slowest speed acceptable. The second way is to install dedicated marine machinery which has a lower fuel consumption than a commensurate automotive-type diesel.

Steam Propulsion

In areas which have extensive timber resources a strong case exists for using steam-powered vessels on relatively short runs.

While it is advocated that timber be used as the fuel source, it is not proposed that valuable forests be decimated for this purpose. Rather, it is suggested that the offcuts from the associated timber mills could be used, and where copra production is significant the old coconut trees and waste products from the coconuts themselves could provide a ready source of boiler fuel.

The advantages of steam propulsion should not be overlooked. If reasonable water depths occur in the area of operation being considered then a combination of low shaft R.P.M., obtainable from a simple steam engine, together with a large propeller diameter will provide a reasonably high propulsive coefficient.

Further, the limits and fits encountered in steam machinery of the type being considered are not as delicate as those encountered in diesel machinery. This results in the maintenance requirements being significantly lower than for a diesel installation of comparable size.

Besides reducing the maintenance load, the use of timber-fuelled steam machinery would not pose any drain on foreign currency. For countries having sufficient waste timber resources the internal cost of fuel for this mode of propulsion would be minimised.

Wind

Another source of low cost power is that provided by wind. There exists a body of enthusiasts who are keen to see the re-introduction of sail power.

The author believes there is a strong case for the use of sail power in certain areas of the South Pacific, particularly those areas which lie in the trade-wind belt.

However, sail power is not considered to be the panacea for all the propulsion ills of the region. Rather, it is a viable alternative in cases where favourable and consistent winds can be anticipated. Also sail power is an attractive form of propulsion assistance to an internal combustion system.

It is understood that some projects have been initiated which use high-technology type sails and materials. Whether such an approach is appropriate is open to discussion, mainly because of the need to provide a reasonable degree of maintenance, and the need to have a ready source of man-made fibres to replace and repair damaged sails and associated rigging. (See Dick, this volume)

Maintenance

It is axiomatic that all structural, mechanical and electrical equipment requires regular and effective maintenance. As previously mentioned, regular and timely maintenance is not a strong point of the region.

The solution to this problem should be addressed in three areas:

(a) adequate training and education of operating personnel;
(b) adequate spares backing; and
(c) operational profiles of vessels and equipment to be arranged to provide for reasonable out-of-service time for repairs and maintenance.

CONCLUSION

Due to the environment and remoteness of some of the areas concerned, there are a number of unique problems associated with the provision of effective maritime aid to the Pacific region.

The factors considered to be most important in overcoming these problems are:

(a) the use of materials and associated coatings to minimise corrosion;
(b) the use of simple, robust and easily-maintained machinery and equipment;
(c) the effective implementation of timely and adequate repair and maintenance procedures; and
(d) the provision of purpose-designed vessels and equipment to suit the needs of the region, rather than items reflecting the needs and practices of the donor countries.

ACKNOWLEDGEMENTS

The author gratefully acknowledges the opportunity given to him by the Australian Development Assistance Bureau to participate in this workshop. Any views expressed are those of the author and do not necessarily represent those of the Australian Development Assistance Bureau.

Chapter Thirteen

ALTERNATIVE TECHNOLOGY - SMALL COMMERCIAL SAILING VESSELS. A LOST CAUSE?

H W Dick

The arguments for sail power can be divided into the romantic, the technical and the economic/commercial. Among western researchers and advisers the romantic is probably a more compelling motivation than would be comfortable to recognise. A good deal of time and money has nevertheless been spent upon research into more efficient sail technologies and their adaptation to ships built in both modern and traditional ways. The conference on Sail and Motor Propulsion held in Manila in November 1985 was, like its predecessor, dominated by papers on technical themes. Ultimately, however, even the most technically oriented recognise that sail technologies must be commercially viable if they are to be any more useful than wings for flying pigs. An efficient technology is a necessary but not sufficient condition for commercial viability.

More than a decade after the first OPEC oil price rise, one is impressed by the amount of technical research that has been carried out and the evidence of the commercial viability of various prototypes. The fact remains, however, that the rate of adoption of sail technologies, whether of sophisticated computer-controlled auxiliary sails for modern bulk carriers or of 'appropriate' sail technology for less developed countries, has been agonisingly slow. Moreover, Indonesia - a country which ten years ago was the last stronghold of the commercial sailing vessel - has against all expectations witnessed a very rapid motorisation of the prahu fleet.

The first part of this paper puts forward a simple taxonomy of the possibilities involved in (a) adoption of sail technology, and (b) motorisation, as a basis for considering whether these two processes are in fact symmetrical. The second part considers why motorisation in Indonesia has run counter to what would have been expected by advocates of sail technology. The third part considers why sail-assisted power has made so little progress elsewhere despite the evidence of technical and commercial viability.

A TAXONOMY

The adoption of sail power logically encompasses three situations:

(a) motor vessel to (pure) sailing vessel;
(b) motor vessel to sailing vessel with auxiliary motor;
(c) motor vessel to motor vessel with auxiliary sail.

The first two of these situations need not be seriously considered. Reliance solely upon sail power no longer seems to be regarded as a viable commercial option. A sailing vessel with an auxiliary motor seems to forgo the advantages of both sailing and motor vessel (Dick, 1978:37-8). Given the capital cost involved in installing an engine in the first place, there seems to be little advantage in installing an engine so small that it cannot propel a vessel for substantial periods in the face of light or adverse winds, thereby permitting much greater flexibility of operation and reliability of schedule.

In terms of the third situation of motor vessel with auxiliary sails (i.e. wind-assisted propulsion), King (1985) argues that the best possibility is to be found 'at the top end of a vessel's speed range'. This does not, however, preclude fuel savings at lower speeds through improved stability or use of sail propulsion alone under favourable conditions. As King points out, the extent to which wind power can be relied upon must depend upon the parameters of acceptable performance. A small inter-island trading vessel is likely to have more flexibility in this regard than a large modern bulk carrier for which the profit margin on a charter depends critically on elapsed voyage time.

In the case of countries like Indonesia where pure commercial sailing vessels can still be found, the same three situations can be identified in reverse in the context of motorisation:

(a) sailing vessel to (pure) motor vessel;
(b) sailing vessel to motor vessel with auxiliary sail;

(c) sailing vessel to sailing vessel with auxiliary motor.

In Indonesia it was never clear which of these two latter options was intended. In practice, however, motorisation has resulted in most cases in situation (a). Although, as pointed out by Hughes (1984:40), so-called 'auxiliary sailing prahu' (prahu layar motor) still display the traditional stern quarter rudders and foremast, these features are intended primarily to enable such vessels to qualify for the manning and seaworthiness concessions applicable to prahus and are little more than decoration. The vessels perform poorly under sail alone and sail seems to be rarely used at sea even for auxiliary propulsion. It seems to make little difference whether the vessel has been retrofitted or newly built.

Motorisation in Indonesia therefore seems to have followed a course quite contrary to the modest achievements of re-introducing sail propulsion in the West or in other Third World countries. If the arguments of the proponents of sail technology are correct, one would expect sail-assisted motor vessels to be a preferred alternative to either a pure motor vessel or a pure sailing vessel. Yet sail-assisted power is still the 'missing link' in this evolution. It may therefore be worth while to consider whether this lack of interest in sail-assisted propulsion is explained by factors specific to Indonesia or whether it is part of a more general phenomenon.

MOTORISATION: THE INDONESIAN CASE

As late as the mid-1970s sail shipping retained an important share of inter-island shipping, with perhaps as many as 10,000 sailing vessels of more than $10m^3$ (i.e. excluding fishing vessels) (Dick, 1975a: 70). Although motorisation had been government policy as long ago as the 1930s, the results had been disappointing. Auxiliary sailing vessels (prahu layar motor) were confined to a few headwind trades in which pure sailing vessels were not viable. A few experimental auxiliary prahus built in the early 1970s had achieved only indifferent results in traditional sail trades. As late as 1975 it was therefore reasonable to be pessimistic as to the prospectus for motorisation, the more so in the light of the higher international fuel prices which had flowed from the formation of the OPEC cartel

(Dick, 1975b:94-103).

Yet in retrospect the mid-1970s were a turning point. In 1976, as part of the pork-barrelling before the following year's general election, the President had introduced a Presidential Assistance Scheme (Bantuan Presiden: BANPRES) to provide 100 engines on generous credit terms. The intention was that as each loan was paid off the funds would be reinvested in another round of motorisation. In these terms the programme was only modestly successful, but by the end of 1981 no less than 1130 engines had been sold for installation, of which 133 were under the BANPRES programme, 107 under prahu owner co-operative schemes (KOPELRA) and the balance of 890 (almost 80 per cent) under private arrangements (Hughes, 1984:37). Most of these engines were installed in the larger prahu pinisi. By the early 1980s these two-masted sailing vessels had all but disappeared and motorisation was rapidly spreading to the smaller single-masted prahu types.

The reasons why motorisation took off so rapidly in the late 1970s are not easy to identify. Chronologically the BANPRES program stands as a turning point, yet the number of engines installed under this programme was small compared with the number of prahu pinisi alone, the loss rate was high, and the repayment record was poor. Hughes (1984:35) suggests that BANPRES provided the 'impetus' for motorisation to become self-sustaining, but this merely begs the question. The mixed success of the BANPRES programme hardly constituted an unarguable demonstration effect. Another possibility, canvassed by Brookfield (1985), is that sailing vessels found themselves caught in a cost-price squeeze, notably by rising fuel costs and rising fixed costs. This does not, however, fit the Indonesian case. Until the 1980s domestic diesel fuel prices were insulated from soaring international prices (Dick, 1980b); by the time diesel prices were adjusted to reflect international parity, motorisation had proceeded so far as to be irreversible. Rising fixed costs are a red herring because the competitive strength of prahu shipping lay precisely in maintaining a flexible cost structure through such devices as payment in net revenue shares and use of crew labour for stevedoring (Dick, 1975b). Except for the subsidy offered under the very limited BANPRES programme, it is likely that until the end of the decade the relative profitability of sail and motor prahus did not alter significantly from that identified by Dick (1975b).

A more plausible explanation is one to which Hughes (1984:64, 66) refers in passing, namely the increase in the maximum permitted size of an auxiliary prahu (prahu layar motor). Under the old colonial regulations a sailing prahu had been restricted to 500m^3 while a p.l.m. had been restricted to only 100m^3, anything larger being classified as a motor vessel. The intent of these regulations had been to encourage motorisation without subsidising any effective competition for modern and mainly Dutch (i.e. KPM) owned inter-island shipping. Although consistent with the typical size of sailing prahus in the 1930s, this 100m^3 limit was nevertheless too low for the greater earning potential to recover the additional investment outlay (Dick, 1975b:98). In 1976 the government recognised that the 100m^3 limit was unrealistic and abolished the size distinction between prahu and p.l.m., while setting for the latter a maximum of 120 horsepower (Hughes, 1984:87). This change brought the capacity limit for p.l.m. into line with that applying to small wooden- or steel-hulled motor vessels (equivalent to the Fijian 'cutters') under the lokal (i.e. 'local') category, which was dominated by Chinese business interests. It was widely believed in the inter-island shipping industry, as reported by Hughes (1984), that most of the private capital invested in motorisation after 1976 was in fact Chinese capital more or less thinly disguised. While this is difficult to prove, it is obvious that the change in regulations created a strong incentive for businessmen to switch from lokal vessels to p.l.m. and gain the benefit of concessional manning and safety requirements without any penalty in vessel size. Moreover, while prahu owners and managers had previously been very successful in keeping Chinese capital out of the industry (Dick, 1975), the change in regulations created a common interest: traditional owners needed additional capital for motorisation whereas Chinese traders, seeking cheap freight rates, needed acceptable frontmen to act as nominal owners of their new p.l.m. If this analysis is correct, the very rapid motorisation of prahu shipping in Indonesia has been caused by nothing more remarkable than a change of regulations, thereby in effect releasing long pent-up forces. The outcome has not, however, been a fair test of the economics of sail versus sail-assisted or motor power because the concessions to p.l.m. are highly distorting. In view of the heavy loss rate of p.l.m. (Hughes, 1984: 984), they are also impossible to justify in any responsible way.

SAIL POWER: WHATEVER HAPPENED TO THE SECOND COMING?

The inconsistency between the alleged technical and economic efficiency of sail-assisted propulsion and the lack of commercial interest can logically be attributed to three possibilities. Firstly, it is possible that the technical calculations are wrong. The few prototypes, whether small or large vessels, nevertheless seem to have demonstrated superior performance over both traditional sailing vessels and conventional motor vessels.

Secondly, it is possible that the economic/ commercial calculations are wrong or incomplete. This possibility can be explored from two standpoints, that of cost structure and that of mode of operation. With regard to cost structure, King (1985) argued that analyses of commercial viability have often been simplistic:

> In the early nineteenth century some ship owners were reluctant to use power driven vessels, arguing that the wind is free, why pay for fuel. This attitude was as short-sighted as that adopted by those who would argue the reverse case (i.e. reversion to sail) today.

'What is the most appropriate form of propulsion?', he suggests, is therefore a more sensible question than 'how can fuel costs be reduced?'. in fact even this reformulation is too narrow. As McAlister (1985) points out with regard to fishing vessels, fuel costs can be reduced in a variety of ways: installing more energy-efficient engines, reducing horsepower or operating speeds and harnessing alternative sources of energy all relate directly to propulsion, but improvements in hull design (and maintenance) and modified methods of fishing can also save on fuel outlays. Ultimately, one must seek the most cost-efficient vessel in terms of total cost.

As McAlister implies, however, the most cost efficient vessel cannot be assessed without regard to the mode of operation. While motor vessels are by nature flexible in routing, being able to sail in a direct line wherever there is sufficient draught, sailing vessels are more restricted and, as in the last days of sail in the Indonesian Archipelago, tend to be squeezed into niches, such as the timber trade on routes where the prevailing winds are favourable (Dick, 1975a). The sail-assisted vessel cannot necessarily occupy the same niche because its higher capital and operating costs absorb much of the competitive advantage of pure sail power. Sail-assisted propulsion can return cost savings only on legs where wind conditions are favourable, and would perhaps justify the additional investment only if there was some likelihood of regular employment on such trades (e.g. the trans-Pacific trade). Similar considerations apply to inter-island trades, bearing in mind the complications raised in archipelagos like Indonesia or various Pacific islands groups by the monsoons. Estimates of profitability under ideal conditions may therefore give a misleading impression of a vessel's earning potential over an extended period.

The third and most likely possibility is that technological feasibility and conventional accounting calculations of profit and loss are not in the end decisive. It tends to be forgotten that a ship is not only a physical object for carrying goods and passengers and earning revenue but also part of a cultural matrix. Anthropologists have long recognised that in 'traditional' societies, sailing vessels (e.g. prahus) have an important role in the ceremony of life. Construction is by techniques handed down by word of mouth and sanctioned by ritual, manning is heavily influenced by kinship and communal ties, and sailing and navigation are part of folklore. In Indonesia, the impact of motorisation has been to remove the prahu from its traditional cultural matrix. Owners are increasingly urban Chinese rather than indigenous village patrons. Whereas traditionally the crew shared in the risks and the profit of the voyage, increasingly they have taken on the status of mere wage employees. The proportion of earnings taken by the owner has increased, while patron-client ties have weakened (Hughes, 1984: 244-5). With a more intensive schedule of operation, vessels now seldom return to their home village; communal ties are thereby broken and crews have become heterogeneous in origin (Hughes, 1984). The higher level of qualifications required and the addition of engine-room personnel have also changed relations between the crew themselves. Although new skills have been designed to operate engines, in respect of construction, sailing and navigation, there has been a sudden 'deskilling' which has made most of the old technology of folklore redundant.

These cultural processes are not reversible. The new p.l.m. are part of a more amorphous capitalist economy and society. That does not mean, however, that the cultural or social context can now be ignored, in Indonesia or anywhere else.

In the decision whether or not to adopt sail-assisted technology, the shipowner is obviously the critical decision-maker. It tends to be assumed by the advocates of appropriate technology that if an innovation can be shown to yield a higher rate of return, then market forces will automatically generate a demand. As with the old adage of the better mousetrap, customers are expected to beat a path to the door of the Appropriate Technology Institute. Yet the 'mousetrap' adage is so much quoted by marketing experts because it is wrong. In practice, having a good product is only the first stage in the marketing process. Anthropologists recognise the same thing when they refer to 'opportunity and response'. It is not difficult to understand why shipowners have been wary of committing their capital to sail-assisted technology. In many countries the technology is still untried. Shipowners, like many other 'rational' entrepreneurs, often have less faith in their own calculations of profit and loss than in what the herd is doing. If no one is adopting a new technology but foreign experts are promoting it enthusiastically, then there must be something wrong with it. The shipowner is all the more likely to be wary if the initial capital cost is higher for a sail-assisted vessel and the second hand value is likely to be lower.

Shipowners will be influenced by the attitude of shippers. Because sail-assisted technology would usually have no significant impact upon the quality of service, the attraction for shippers is likely to depend upon whether it leads to a reduction in freight rates. In minor feeder services served by only one or two shipowners, as is typical of the Pacific islands, the shipowner is not under competitive pressure to pass on any cost savings. If he did so, the return on investment would, of course, be correspondingly reduced. It is therefore hardly surprising if the shipowner perseveres with familiar motor vessels and continues to pass on to shippers his cost increases. This situation would be likely to alter only if the threat of new entry became more pressing and forced the shipowner to become more cost-conscious.

Although master and crew do not necessarily have any direct say in the investment decision, their attitude towards sail-assisted technology may well be an important influence. One of the things that has facilitated the introduction of engines and outboard motors in even the most remote corners of the Third World is that they both involve less work (until they break down!) than traditional oars and sails. Moreover, they are modern. Crews are unlikely to want to accept sail-assisted technology unless their earnings increase or they can exercise skills of which they are proud. The impact upon earnings will obviously depend upon the form of remuneration: crews are likely to be more enthusiastic in cases where they are shareholders in the vessel or earn a share of the profits. The pride in sailing skills will depend in the first instance upon whether the skills are in fact possessed. In Indonesia, a country where sailing skills are still widespread, motorisation has nevertheless resulted in crews making little use of the residual sailing capability still required of their vessels if they are to qualify as p.l.m. In countries where those skills do not exist, decisions would need to be made as to whether existing crew numbers would be re-trained or new members added. If existing crew members are to be re-trained, which members should be chosen and how should their responsibilities, status and remuneration be adjusted? If new members are added to the crew, how would shipboard society adapt?

Finally, the attitudes of government officials must also be taken into account. While foreign experts may have their romantic bias towards sail-assisted technology, officials often hold very strong prejudices the other way. There is a strong suspicion that the enthusiastic promoters of 'appropriate technology' are trying to palm off something that is second-best and extract some acknowledgement of inferiority. In Indonesia, determination to eliminate an embarrassing sign of backwardness has undoubtedly provided much of the official impetus for motorisation (Dick, 1975 a,b). At the same time, the Indonesian Government has supported the development of modern commercial sailing vessels through the innovative Indosail Project (Suleman, 1985). This is an all too rare case of appropriate technology research being carried out in the Third World. Thus, it cannot be presumed that governments would either support or oppose the introduction of sail-assisted technology. If such a project is to be successful, however, as in Fiji, the government clearly needs to be persuaded and involved.

CONCLUSION

The lack of progress made with sail technology under the favourable economic conditions of the past decade suggests that the experts have either got their calculations wrong or left something out. This paper suggests that there has been a preoccupation with the 'hard-headed' or 'rational' aspects of technology and conventional accounting profit and too little attention to the problems of innovation. Reintroduction of sail or sail-assisted technology has encountered all the problems of resistance to technological change which are as familiar in the West as in the Third World.

Due to the non-economic obstacles to the acceptance of sail-assisted technology, it may well be that the better commercial prospects lie not in the Third World but with sophisticated and cost-conscious shipowners in the West. The commercial benefits of computer-controlled, sail-assisted propulsion have now been demonstrated for large bulk carriers in the trans-Pacific trade. Whether interest will survive the recent collapse of oil prices and the bankruptcy of the Japanese shipowner who had taken the initiative remains to be seen.

REFERENCES

Brookfield, H C, 1985 Problems in inter-island transport, Regional Conference on Sail-Motor Propulsion, Manila.

Dick, H W, 1975a,b Prahu shipping in eastern Indonesia' (Parts I & II), Bulletin of Indonesian Economic Studies, XI(2&3), 69-107, 81-103.

Dick, H W, 1978 Inter-island and feeder transport services for developing island countries, United Nations (TD/B/AC.24/2).

Dick, H W, 1980a The oil price subsidy, deforestation and equity, Bulletin of Indonesian Economic Studies, XVI(3), 32-60.

Dick, H W, 1980b, The rise and fall of economic dualism: the Indonesian inter-island shipping industry, In: R G Garnaut and P T McCawley (eds), Indonesia: Development, Growth and Poverty (C of Pacific Studies, Research School of ANU).

Hamada, N, 1985 The technological development of modern sail-assisted ships, Regional Conference on Sail-Motor Propulsion, Manila.

Hughes, D, 1984 Indonesian cargo shipping vessels and the problems of technological choice for sea transport in a developing country, PhD thesis (Cardiff: UWIST).

King, J, 1985 Ship management and wind assistance, Regional Conference on Sail-Motor Propulsion, Manila.
McAlister, R G, 1985 Application of sail in fisheries development, Regional Conference on Sail-Motor Propulsion, Manila.
Suleman, W and Schenzie, P, 1985 The Indonesia-German Indosail Project, Regional Conference on Sail-Motor Propulsion, Manila.

Chapter Fourteen

IMPROVED EDUCATION AND TRAINING FOR NEW MARINE TECHNOLOGY AND SOCIAL CHANGE IN THE PACIFIC ISLAND NATIONS - A PRELIMINARY APPRAISAL OF THE TASK

D M Waters

During its first five years of operation, the Australian Maritime College (AMC) has concentrated on the establishment of programmes for sea-going and shore-based occupations in shipping, fishing, off-shore industries and ports. The College has not as yet contributed significantly to Australia's over-seas maritime aid projects.

The Secretary-General of the International Maritime Organisation (IMO) suggested that arrangements might be made under the auspices of IMO for the AMC to provide assistance to maritime colleges in the developing countries of Southeast Asia and the Southwest Pacific. Following this, discussions were held with officials of the Australian Development Assistance Bureau (ADAB), the Department of Education and the International Development Programme of Australian Universities and Colleges. These discussions covered possibilities for assisting students through sponsorship by ADAB, by international agencies and by other Governments. Also discussed was AMC's involvement in off-shore projects funded by World Bank, Asian Development Bank, and other agencies. AMC is anxious to ensure that it helps meet Australia's obligations to the developing countries. However, when one attempts to establish what is already being done, it seems there is a case for more co-ordination of effort before yet another 'expert' contribution is added to what appears to be a somewhat unco-ordinated field of endeavour. Certainly there is a need for caution when setting up training schemes that involve the certificate of competency requirements for personnel in the shipping and fishing industries. The history of marine education and training is markedly different in many of the traditional maritime countries. The resulting diversity of programmes and philosophies has been inherited by the various developing countries, without consideration of relevance to local conditions.

This paper highlights some of the issues that have to be taken account of in considering training schemes in the Pacific region. Central to the issue is the relationship between maritime education and the certificates of competence. This, and the historical reasons for different national approaches, are addressed in the following section.

DIFFERING NATIONAL PROVISIONS FOR MARITIME EDUCATION AND CERTIFICATES OF COMPETENCE

It is axiomatic that vocational education and training programmes must seek to inculcate an appreciation of the job to be performed. For the shipping and fishing industries, an important objective of the marine training programme must be coverage of the certificate of competence requirements. However, it is most important to appreciate that coverage of the certificate of competence requirements does not equate with a full training programme for the job at sea.

Certificates of competence or marine licences to serve in responsible positions on merchant ships and fishing vessels are generally administered by the Marine Authority of a country. These authorities are primarily concerned with safety at sea and, in recent years, with protection of the marine environment. They are not concerned with the commercial viability of maritime industries. A government's interests in the latter are generally administered by Shipping Policy or Trade Departments.

Since the knowledge requirements of certificates of competence are by nature narrow, one of the first considerations in planning a training programme for a developing country is: how comprehensive should it be? Should it be confined to preparation for the certificate of competence examinations, supplemented by some short courses, and with the assumption that most of the necessary training for the job is acquired through experience at sea, or should it be a more flexible programme of formal education, including 'hands-on' training with up-to-date equipment?

In addressing these issues it is important to appreciate that there is a fundamental difference between the alternatives. On the one hand, the syllabus requirements specified by the regulatory authority - result in a highly standardised programme with the emphasis on 'coaching' to pass the statutory examination questions. On the other hand the education-based programmes are flexible by nature enabling coverage of various requirements and changes of emphasis - but with the boundary condition that the course work must satisfy the general requirements or standard of the registration or regulatory authority. If the choice is a comprehensive programme of education and training, a secondary consideration might be whether it should take account of the fact that port, marine and survey authorities generally recruit maritime personnel for shore-based positions without requiring further formal training or qualifications. Should the curriculum, therefore, take account of the fact that many of the trainees will eventually fill senior technical positions ashore?

The reality of the matter is that such training as is currently provided in developing countries is likely to be based not so much on these objective considerations and local needs as on the system existing in the country providing the expert advice and assistance. For example, a maritime expert from the UK would probably advocate an 'examination-oriented' system, with separate preparatory courses for each grade of certificate of competence. If the expert was trained in the USA or in some of the European maritime nations, the system would more likely be 'education-oriented', with the formal training towards the front-end of the trainee's career. An appreciation of the reasons for these differences is useful in any consideration of new training requirements for the Pacific nations.

THE HISTORICAL DEVELOPMENT OF MARITIME TRAINING

Many of the older European countries that were centres of maritime trade, have long histories of technical education, including maritime training. During the last half of the eighteenth and the first half of the nineteenth centuries, countries such as Sweden, Denmark, Norway, the German States, Venice and France had codes of law and training requirements to be complied with by the masters and mates of their merchant ships. The examinations thus tended to develop as an integral part of the training programmes. On the other hand, when the Merchant Shipping Laws were passed in the UK in the middle of last century, introducing marine safety requirements, including mandatory examinations for certificates of competency for masters and mates in merchant ships, the basis for technical education and training did not exist. The State was not involved in education at that time, and mathematics and science did not form part of the curriculum of the endowed grammar schools, which still reflected the Roman philosophy that politics, law and rhetoric were the only requisites for administering the Empire.

In the UK, therefore, an examination system was established within the national statutory marine authority before any courses of training or education were available. The courses that were subsequently developed - in private schools to begin with and then in local education authority colleges - were designed specifically to prepare candidates for the marine authority's examinations for certificates of competency. Before the introduction of sophisticated shipboard equipment, and when on-the-job experience fulfilled the 'training' requirement, the system served its purpose well. However, in the years following the Second World War, the system began to come under strain. There was an increasing need for 'hands-on' training and assessment on modern navigation instruments, and at the same time a greater amount of theory was being incorporated into the syllabuses. This resulted in a conglomeration of 'short courses' being appended to the increasingly lengthy certificate preparatory courses and a gradual shift of the 'fundamental knowledge' subjects from the higher certificate syllabuses, such as Master, to the lower-level ones. The traditional system has become so cumbersome and uneconomical that the transfer of all the written examinations from the statutory marine authority to the local education authority colleges is gradually taking place in the UK.

The European system is quite different. The statutory marine authority in the Federal German Republic, for example, has never found it necessary to conduct its own examinations and grants the Master certificate of competence to candidates who have successfully completed the 3-year diploma course at the Hamburg or Bremen polytechnics and have subsequently acquired the mandatory watchkeeping experience. The USA, when setting up its marine education system, took note of both British and European developments. Comprehensive 'front-ended' courses are provided at the Federal and State Merchant Marine Academies for junior deck and engineering watchkeeping officers. These are followed by examinations set by the coast guard for the higher-level licences.

Those developing countries that already have certificate of competence structures and associated training programmes have generally adopted either the European Continental or the UK model. In the older British Commonwealth countries the traditional UK certificate of competence structure tends to prevail - but generally without the associated educational courses, which in the UK have gradually incorporated more and more of the certificate requirements. One of the major difficulties that these countries - including some in the South Pacific - now face is how to provide these necessary associated courses which, unlike the structure of certificates of competence, must take account of the technological and social needs of the developing country, rather than be modelled directly on the system of a developed country.

MARITIME TRAINING IN THE PACIFIC ISLANDS

Apart from Tahiti, which has a good officer training school based on the French comprehensive maritime training system, the South Pacific countries have very limited maritime training facilities. Only three countries, Fiji, PNG, and the Solomons have capability for officer training for inter-island shipping. Some provision for lower-level work exists in Tonga, Western Samoa, Tuvalu, Vanuatu and Kiribati. A useful summary of maritime training provisions and manpower requirements in the South Pacific is provided in a November 1984 report by Touche Ross & Co, Management Consultants to the SPEC South Pacific Regional Transport Survey. However, it does not address the fundamental issues referred to earlier in this paper.

The South Pacific countries are nevertheless now addressing the training requirements - having recently developed a Code of Uniform Marine Standards, which includes the certificate of competence requirements for seagoing personnel. The Code has been drawn up by consultants appointed by IMO, with financial assistance from the Norwegian Government. Once the Code is formally accepted the provisions will be incorporated into the legislation of the island member countries of the South Pacific Forum.

The Certificate of Competence requirements are based on the traditional system of the UK - and

Australia and New Zealand - with the necessary adjustments to comply with international standards which have recently come into force (and are referred to in the next section). It is understood that the maritime education and training courses are being planned on a regional basis - with colleges in Suva (Fiji), Madang (PNG) and Honiara (Solomons) co-operating to service the needs of the SPEC member countries.

Developing countries in the Pacific region faced with the task of establishing standards of competency and training courses can now benefit from two recent international developments whose potential does not yet appear to be fully appreciated. Yet any consideration of maritime training aid to the developing countries must take account of them.

The first development is the IMO 1978 Convention on Standards of Training Certification and Watchkeeping for Seafarers (STCW), which came into force in April 1984, and which established minimum international standards, in respect of ship-board positions. The second is the establishment of the World Maritime University in 1983, again under the auspices of the IMO, to provide advanced training for specialised maritime personnel in shore-based positions in the developing countries.

THE INTERNATIONAL CONVENTION ON STANDARDS OF TRAINING CERTIFICATION AND WATCHKEEPING FOR SEAFARERS, 1978

It is not the purpose of this paper to describe or analyse in detail the 1978 STCW Convention. However, a number of points arising from it are pertinent to our present considerations.

To start with, it is interesting to consider that the '78 STCW Convention represents the first internationally agreed set of standards on tangible aspects of training and qualifications for seafarers. Yet for many years there have been International Conventions on ships, cargoes, equipment and so on. The fact that it has been much easier to achieve common global standards for such inanimate subjects as loadlines, tonnage, and equipment than for the qualifications of seafarers emphasises the interdependence of the technological and human factors in the case of education and training. This interdependence underlines the relevance of the present workshop's title: in effect that education for new marine technology needs to take account also of social issues.

The STCW Convention was the outcome of the collective deliberations of delegates from the member countries of the IMO. As such, it is something of a compromise, and the ways in which the Convention standards may be achieved is open to different interpretations. It had to be so, because of the vastly different approaches to marine training and education in the various member countries - involving fundamental issues of a non-negotiable nature.

As the existing national systems were too diverse for any one of them to be used as a model, a 'first principles' approach had to be taken to the development of the minimum knowledge standards. The resulting syllabus requirements are thus of particular value to any country setting up a new training system, because - in their simplest interpretation - they represent the minimum requirements, based on a direct consideration of the job specification.

A careful study of the text and syllabuses will reveal that this direct outcome of the 'first principles' consideration is two broad levels of training, or fundamental knowledge requirements. These two levels - set out in Table 3 - provide the basis for the formal training programmes which cover the full Convention requirements, in the simplest and most straightforward format.

Table 3 The levels of fundamental knowledge requirements

DECK OFFICERS	ENGINEER OFFICERS
a syllabus, or set of requirements for Masters and Chief Mates	a syllabus, or set of requirements, for Chief and Second Engineers
a syllabus, or set of requirements for Deck Officers in charge of watch	a syllabus, or set of requirements for Engineer Officers in charge of watch

It is important to appreciate that these two levels of training requirements or syllabuses do not limit the number of grades of certificates of competence which a maritime authority might require, based on prerequisites other than formal training programmes: for example, on watchkeeping experience, and specialist or local knowledge.

The Convention syllabuses reflect a substantial view of the drafting groups that the fundamental knowledge requirements for Chief Mate and Master, and also for Chief and Second Engineers, are essentially the same. The watchkeepers on the other hand - not being concerned with a range of responsibilities extending to the total operation of the ship or its machinery - were seen as needing only the knowledge to keep a safe watch.

The IMO is concerned that the developing countries are able to meet these minimum international standards, and it would, therefore, seem appropriate that those countries which are having difficulty in achieving effective training programmes should aim at the simplest interpretation of the Convention. To adopt training programmes that are in use in developed countries may well involve the imposition of standards in excess of the minimum global requirements.

At the request of the developing countries, model courses to meet STCW Convention requirements are being developed by IMO consultants. This is a task requiring a great deal of care and caution, not only in the interpretation of the Convention, but also in the need to take account of the fact that implementation of the syllabus requirements is often dependent upon particular educational and social provisions - which are different in different countries. In particular, consultants must guard against a natural tendency to interpret the Convention requirements in terms of their own national structure of certificates and training programmes.

CONCLUSION

Development assistance with education and training for marine technology in the Pacific appears to be fragmented and in need of co-ordination. Objectives require clarification, taking account of agreed international standards and of existing education and training facilities. Perhaps most important, development programmes need to take account of the local social scene, as well as of the technological requirements and international obligations.

For the shipping and fishing industries there appears to be a pressing need for training, for both seagoing and shore-based personnel. Such provisions as exist are based primarily on the establishment of certificate of competence syllabuses, with the training courses coming as a secondary - and consequential - consideration. The certificate structures and syllabus standards are generally modelled on those of a developed country and are therefore invariably higher than the internationally agreed minimum requirements. This may well be justifiable in a developed country but equally may not be so in developing countries with quite different social and educational systems. Irrespective of this consideration, it is much easier to determine a certificate of competency structure and standards than to establish a viable training programme. In this regard, a major issue to be addressed is whether the system is to be examination-oriented (i.e. rigid statutory syllabuses and associated preparatory courses) or education-based (flexible programmes requiring overall approval by the regulatory authority).

It is understandable that developing countries should wish to establish their own training facilities; but it is also clear that there are practical limitations on the extent to which South Pacific countries can do so in the foreseeable future. In each case the best compromise can only be achieved after a detailed investigation, and this should have regard to the total requirements of the industry - not just the certificates of competency. Furthermore, there are important international provisions which need to be taken into account. For example, if it were determined that only the training of seagoing personnel should be provided then there would need to be a compelling argument in order to justify the establishment of standards of competence beyond those internationally agreed minimum requirements of the 1978 STCW Convention. Consideration of training for senior shore-based positions should include: in the short term - the post-graduate programmes offered at the World Maritime University (WMU) and associated institutions; and in the longer term - undergraduate maritime courses of professional level either regionally or in major overseas institutions, followed by post-graduate training at the WMU or at a major maritime institution.

Irrespective of the extent of the training to be provided locally, its provision should be considered in the context of the prevailing social and educational structures of the country, or region.

BIBLIOGRAPHY

Agassiz A, 1903 The Coral Reefs of the Maldives, vs 1 and 2 (Cambridge: Harvard)

Alexander P, 1975a Do fisheries experts aid fisheries development?, Maritime Studies and Management, 3(5), (London: Taylor and Francis)

Alexander P, 1975b Innovation in a Cultural Vacuum, Human Organisation 34.

Alexander P, 1982 Sri Lankan Fishermen: Rural Capitalism and Peasant Society Canberra: ANU South Asian Series.

Angle P S, 1983 Goa: An Economic Review (Bombay:Goa Hindu Association Kala Vibhag)

Bavinck M, 1984, Small Fry: The Economy of Petty Fishermen in Northern Sri Lanka. Amsterdam: Free University Press.

Bavinck M and van Dijk F M, 1978 The Transformation of a Fishing Community: The Case of Kadalur, Sri Lanka. Research Report, Amsterdam: Free University.

Bailey K, 1985, Logs as Fish Aggregation Devices in the Equatorial Western Pacific. Paper 13, South Pacific Commission Seventeenth Regional Technical Meeting on Fisheries. Noumea, New Caledonia. 7p.

Batt A N, 1981 Preliminary Assessment of Seawave Energy Potential and Development Prospects for Tongatapu Island, Kingdom of Tonga. Crown Agents, London.

Bayliss-Smith T P and Feachem R M, 1977 Subsistence and Survival (London: Cambridge University Press)

Bayliss-Smith T P, 1978 Batiki in the 1970s: satellite of Suva, In: Bedford R D, et al. (eds), The Small Islands and the Reefs (Paris: UNESCO).

Bayliss-Smith T P, 1980 The Price of Protein : Marine Fisheries in Pacific Subsistence (Unpub. paper Cambridge)

Beckvar N, 1981 Cultivation, spawning and growth of giant clams Tridacna gigas, T derasa and T squamosa in Palau, Caroline Islands, Aquaculture, 24.

Ben-Yami M, 1984 Technology transfer. Parts 1 and 2. World Fishing (September and October issues).

Borgstrom G, (ed), 1965 Fish as Food, V.3, Pt 1 (New York: Academic Press)

Boserup E, 1970 Women's Role in Economic Development (New York: St Martins)

Bour W and Galenon P, 1979 The Development of Tuna Fisheries in the Western Pacific. (Noumea: South Pacific Commission)

Booth I, 1984 Regional Co-operation in South Pacific Fisheries: Legal and Institutional Aspects, in Christopher C Kissling ed. Transport and Communications for Pacific Microstates: Issues in Organisation and Management.

Boy, R L and Smith B R, 1984 Design improvements to Fish Aggregation Device (FAD) mooring systems in general use in Pacific Islands countries. South Pacific Commission Handbook No 24.

Braganca Pereira, 1940 A Ethnografia da India Portugesa V.2 (Panjim:Bastora)

Braley, R D, 1985 Serotinin-induced spawning in giant clams (Bivalvia:Tridacnidae), Aquaculture, 47.

Brodie, J E, 1982 Analysis of deep Ocean Thermal Energy Conversion Site, Coral Coast, Viti Levu, Fiji. INR, USP, Suva.

Brookfield H C, 1972 Intensification and disintensification in Pacific agriculture : a theoretical approach, Pacific Viewpoint, 13(1).

Brookfield H C, 1983 Intensification revisited, Pacific Viewpoint, 25(1).

Brookfield, H C, 1985 Problems in inter-island transport Regional Conference on Sail-Motor Propulsion, Manila.

Brookfield M, 1979 Resource use, economy and society: island at the cross-roads, in H C Brookfield et al (ed), Lakeba: Environmental Change, Population Dynamics and Resource Use.

Carcasson R H, 1977 A Field Guide to the Coral Reef Fishes of the Indian and West Pacific Oceans (London : Collins)

Carrier J G, 1981 Ownership of productive resources on Ponam Island, Manus Province, Journal de Societe des Oceanistes, 72 73.

Carver A, 1980 Australian Fishermen could learn from islanders' tuna techniques. Australian Fisheries 39:7

Catalla R L A, 1957 Report on the Gilbert Islands: some aspects of human ecology. Atoll Research Bulletin No 59.

Clark L, 1984 Fisheries Issues in the Pacific Islands, Honiara, Forum Fisheries Agency Report 84/11

Clarke W C, 1985 The fabric of the world farm: in I. Farrington (ed), Prehistoric Intensive Agriculture in the Tropics (Oxford: British Archaeological Reports No 232).

Clay G S, 1981 Ocean Leasing for Hawaii. Honolulu: Department of Planning and Economic Development, Honolulu.

Collier J and Rosaldo M, 1981 Politics and Gender in Simple Societies. In: Ortner S and Whitehead H (eds) Sexual Meanings (Cambridge: Cambridge University Press)

Constans J, 1979 Marine Sources of Energy. Pergamon, New York.

Couper A D, 1973 Islanders at Sea in Brookfield, H.C. (ed) Pacific in Transition, Edward Arnold.

Couper A D, 1986 New Cargo Handling Techniques: Implications for Employment and Skills in the World Port Industry, ILO, Geneva

Crocombe R (ed), 1971 Land Tenure in the Pacific (Melbourne OUP)

David G, 1985 La Peche Villageoise a Vanuatu (Vanuatu: Mission Orstrom).

Dawson, J K, 1979 Wave Energy. HMSO, London.

Dawson, R F, 1984, Can Australia expect a resurgence of Taiwanese clam boat activity? Australian Fisheries, February.

Dick H W, 1975a,b Prahu shipping in eastern Indonesia (Parts I & II), Bulletin of Indonesian Economic Studies, XI(2&3).

Dick H W, 1978 Inter-island and feeder transport services for developing island countries, United Nations (TD/B/AC.24/2).

Dick H W, 1980a The oil price subsidy, deforestation and equity, Bulletin of Indonesian Economic Studies, XVI(3),

Dick H W, 1980b The rise and fall of economic dualism: the Indonesian inter-island shipping industry, In: R G Garnaut and P T McCawley (eds), Indonesia: Development, Growth and Poverty (C of Pacific Studies, Research School of ANU).

Director of Fisheries, 1955-77, Administration Reports. Colombo: Government Press, Sri Lanka

Dixon R, 1978 Rural Women At Work : Strategies for Development in South Asia (Baltimore : Johns Hopkins University Press)

Dixon R, 1980 Assessing the Impact of Development Projects on Women (Washington : Office of Women in Development)

Emmerson D K, 1979 The case for a maritime perspective on Southeast Asia, unpublished paper from Singapore Seminar, United States Social Science Research Council.

Emmerson D K, 1983 Rethinking Artisanal Fisheries Development: Western Concepts Asian Experience (Washington, D.C.: World Bank).

Evans E B, 1951/6 Marine scientific and technological assistance to developing countries: science for development or technology for malintegrated growth?, Economic Development and Cultural Change, 24.

FAO, 1977 Assessment of Problems and Needs in Marine Small-Scale Fisheries, Sri Lanka. Colombo: FAO report.

FAO, 1981 The Prevention of Losses in Cured Fish, FAO Fisheries Technical Paper No. 219 FIIU/T219 (Rome : FAO)

Far Eastern Economic Review, 1985 Fishing, FEER Yearbook.

Far Eastern Economic Review, 1985 Maldives, FEER Yearbook,

Finsterbusch K, Llewellyn L G and Wolf C P, (eds) 1983 Social Impact Assessment Methods (Beverly Hills: Sage Publications).

Firth R, 1966 (2nd ed.) Malay Fishermen: Their Peasant Economy (Hamden, Connecticut: Archon Books).

Firth R, 1943 Housekeeping Among Malay Peasants (London : LSE)

Firth R, 1975 Malay Fishermen : Their Peasant Economy (New York : Norton)
Fisk E K, 1985 The Economic Independence of Kiribati (Canberra : Australian Development Assistance Bureau)
Foster P, 1972 The Most Abundant Natural Resource of the South Pacific. Search. 3(10).
Fyson J, 1984 Workshop - Artisanal fishing vessels in the Pacific Islands. Sixteenth Regional Technical Meeting on Fisheries. Noumea, New Caledonia.
Geddes W H, 1983 Tabiteuea North (Canberra : Australian National University, Development Studies Centre)
Gentle M and Connon C, 1979 Beche-de-mer of the tropical Pacific; a handbook for fishermen. South Pacific Commission, Noumea, New Caledonia.
Gopalkrishnan C (ed), 1984 The Emerging Marine Economy of the Pacific (Boston : Butterworth)
Government of Kiribati, n.d, National Development Plan 1983-86 (South Tarawa)
Government of Kiribati, 1985 Statistics Bulletin for the Kiribati Aid Donors Meeting, May (Tarawa : Ministry of Finance)
Grimble A, 1952 A Pattern of Islands (London : John Murray)
Grimble A, 1955 Return To The Islands (London : John Murray)
Gulati L, 1984(a) Fisherwomen on the Kerala Coast (Geneva: ILO)
Gulati L, 1984(b) Profiles in Female Poverty (Delhi: Hindustan Publishing Corporation)
Gulbrandsen O, 1984 Ten years boat development in the South Pacific - what can we learn from it? Paper 14, South Pacific Commission, Sixteenth Technical meeting on Fisheries, Noumea, New Caledonia. p26.
Gwyther J and Munro J L, 1981 Spawning induction and rearing of larvae of tridacnid clams (Bivalvia:Tridacnidae), Aquaculture, 24.
Halapua S, 1982 The Fishermen of Tonga, Institute of Pacific Studies, University of the South Pacific, Suva, Fiji
Hamada N, 1985 'The technological development of modern sail-assisted ships', Regional Conference on Sail-Motor Propulsion, Manila.
Hanson A J, 1984 Coastal community development: an international perspective (Halifax, Nova Scotia: D.O.S.P. Publn., Paper prepared for the 26th Annual Meeting, Canadian Commission for UNESCO).
Heslinga G A, Perron F E and Orak O, 1984 Mass culture of giant clams (F Tridacnidae) in Palau, Aquaculture, 39
Hill P, 1970 Studies in Rural Capitalism in West Africa (Cambridge : Cambridge University Press)
Hughes D, 1984 'Indonesian cargo shipping vessels and the problems of technological choice for sea transport in a developing country, PhD thesis (Cardiff: UWIST).

ICLARM 1981 Alternative Energy Sources in Fisheries and Aquaculture, Vol. 4(2) (Metro Manila, Philippines)

Ifeka C, 1985 Hierarchal Women : Towards Rethinking Woman's Role in Development in India (in press)

Ifeka C, 1986 Report on Women and Fish Processing in the South Pacific with special reference to Kiribati and Tuvalu, Australian Development Assistance Bureau, Canberra.

Ifeka C and Chiragakis L, 1985 Christian and Hindu Households in a Changing World : the case of Goa, south-west India. (In press)

IFAD 1985 Report of the Project Identification Mission to the Republic of Maldives Oct. 1985 (Asia Division)

INFOfish, 1983 Improving product quality in the Maldives', INFOfish, 2.

IUCN, 1983, The IUCN Invertebrate Red Data Book (Gland, Switzerland: International Union for the Conservation of Nature and Natural Resources).

Jaquette J, 1984 Women and Modernisation Theory. World Politics 34(2).

James Cook University of North Queensland, 1985, The Culture of the Giant Clam (Tridacna Sp) For Food and Restocking of Tropical Reefs: Progress Report 2, Australian Centre for International Agricultural Research, Canberra.

Jameson J C, 1976 Early life history of giant clams Tridacna crocea (Lamarck), Tridacna maxima (Roding), and Hippopus hippopus (Linnaeus), Pacific Science, 30(3).

Johannes R E, 1978 Traditional marine conservation methods in Oceania and their demise, Ann. Rev. Ecol. Syst., 9,

Johannes R E, 1981 Words of the Lagoon, Fishing and Marine Lore in the Palau District of Micronesia (California: University of California Press).

Johannes R E, 1982 Implications of traditional marine resource use for coastal fisheries developments in Papua New Guinea, In: L Morauta, J Pernetta and W Heaney (eds), Traditional Conservation in Papua New Guinea: Implications for Today (Boroko, P N G: Institute of Applied Social and Economic Research).

Josupeit H, 1983 External assistance to the fisheries sector of developing countries in Asia and the Pacific - A short survey INFOfish 3.

Kearney R E, 1979 Some Problesm of Developing and Managing Fisheries in Small Island States. (Noumea: South Pacific Commission)

Kearney R E, 1981 A Brief Review of the State of the Stocks of Highly Migratory Species of Fish in the Central and Western Pacific. (Noumea: South Pacific Commission)

Kent G, 1980 The Politics of Pacific Island Fisheries (Boulder, Colorado: Westview Press)

King J, 1985 'Ship management and wind assistance', Regional Conference on Sail-Motor Propulsion, Manila.

King M G and Stone R M, 1979 Commercial fisheries in Western Pacific islands: in Utilization and management of inshore marine ecosystems of the tropical Pacific islands. University of the South Pacific/University of Hawaii.

King M G, 1984 The species and depth distribution of deep-water caridean shrimps (Decapoda, Caridea) near some southwest Pacific islands. Crustaceana 47:2.

King M G, 1986 The deepwater shrimp resources of Pacific island countries. FAO Technical Paper (in press).

Knipe E, 1984 Gamrie: An Exploration in Cultural Ecology (Lanham: University Press of America)

Koch G, 1965 Materielle Kultur der Gilbert-Inseln (Berlin : Museum Fur Volkerkunde)

LaBarbera M, 1975 Larval and post-larval development of the giant clams Tridacna maxima and Tridacna squamosa (Bivalvia: Tridacnidae, Malacologia, 15(1).

Lawrence R, 1983 Tamana (Canberra : Australian National University, Development Studies Centre)

Lawson R, 1980 Development and growth constraints in the artisanal fisheries sector in island states, In: R Shand (ed) Island States of the Pacific and Indian Oceans (Canberra : ANU).

Lawson R, 1985 Economics of Fisheries Development (London : Francis Pinter)

Lawson R and Robinson M, 1983 Artisanal fisheries in West Africa, Marine Policy, October: 281.

Lee R and I de Vore (eds) 1968 Man the Hunter (Chicago : Aldine Publications)

Lundsgaarde H P, (ed) 1974 Land Tenure in Oceania (Honolulu: University Press of Hawaii)

McAlister R G, 1985 Application of sail in fisheries development, Regional Conference on Sail-Motor Propulsion, Manila.

McKoy J L, 1980 Biology, Exploitation and Management of Giant Clams (Tridacnidae) in the Kingdom of Tonga, Fisheries Bulletin No. 1, (Nuku'alofa, Tonga: Fisheries Division, Ministry of Agriculture, Forestry and Fisheries).

MacLean J L, 1978 The clam gardens of Manus, Harvest, 4(3)

MacLean R F, 1980 The land-sea interface of small tropical islands : morphodynamics and man, In: H C Brookfield (ed) Population-Environment Relations in Tropical Islands: the Case of Eastern Fiji (Paris : UNESCO),

Maloney C, 1980 People of the Maldive Islands (Bombay : Orient Longman)

Marr J C, 1981 Southeast Asian fishery resources and fisheries, In: Chia Lin Sien and Colin McAndrews, (eds.) South East Asian Seas - Frontiers for Development (Singapore: McGraw Hill).

Marriott S, n.d The South Tarawa Artisanal Fishery (Tarawa: Fisheries Division)
Marriott S, 1984 Rural Fisheries in Kiribati, (Tarawa : Fisheries Division)
Mathur P R, 1971 The Mappila Fisherfolk of Kerala (Trivandrum: Historical Society)
Mees C C, n.d., The Fisheries of Tamana and Aror (Tarawa : Fisheries Division
Mees C C, 1984 A Fisheries Related Market Study of South Tarawa (Tarawa : Fisheries Division)
Mies M, 1982 The Lace Workers of Narsapur (London : Zed Press)
Ministry of Primary Products, 1985, (Suva: Fiji Fisheries Division).
Mitsui T, Ito, F, Sega Y and Nakamoto Y, 1983 "Outline of the 100kW OTEC Pilot Plant in the Republic of Nauru". IEEE Transactions on Power Apparatus and Systems, PAS-102(9).
Morauta L, Pernetta J, Heaney W, (eds) 1982 Traditional Conservation in Papua New Guinea, Institute of Applied Social and Economic Research, Papua New Guinea.
Mukhopadhyay M, 1984 Silver Shackles (Oxford : OXFAM)
Munro J L, 1985a The International Giant Clam Mariculture Project, Annex N(A) In: James Cook University of North Queensland, op. cit. A revised version of ICLARM, mimeo, 1983.
Munro J L, 1985b Economics and social aspects of the development of mariculture systems for giant clams (Tridacnidae: Bivalvia) in the Australasian Region and the West Pacific, International Giant Clam Mariculture Project Discussion Paper No 2 (Townsville:ICLARM, South Pacific Office).
Munro J L, 1985c Ocean nurseries for giant clams : options and problems, International Giant Clam Mariculture Project Discussion Paper No 1 (Townsville:ICLARM, South Pacific Office).
Munro J L and Heslinga G A, 1982 Prospects for the commercial cultivation of giant clams (Bivalvia:Tridacnidae) presented at 35th Annual Meeting of the Gulf and Caribbean Fisheries Institute, Nassau.
Nelson N, 1981 African Women in the Development Process (London : Cass)
Ocean Data Systems, Inc., Large-Scale Distribution of OTEC Thermal Resource, 500-m and 1000-m Charts. Reproduced in Wick and Schmitt.
Pietersz, U., 1978, Development of Offshore and Deepsea Fisheries in Sri Lanka Bulletin of Fisheries Research Station, No 28.

Prescott J R V, 1980 Existing and Potential Maritime Claims in the Southwest Pacific Ocean, In: E M Borgese and N Ginsburg (eds.) Ocean Yearbook 2 (Chicago : Chicago University Press)

Pyrard F, 1964 The Voyage of Francois Pyrard of Laval to the East Indies, the Maldives, the Moluccas and Brazil V.2, Translated and edited by A Gray and H C P Bell (New York: Burt Franklin)

Randall J E, 1955 'Fishes of the Gilbert Islands', Atoll Research Bulletin 47(1).

Re Soeiro e Brito R, 1966 Goa e as Pracas da Norte (Lisbon : Junta de Investigacoes du Ultramar)

Rodke B M, 1984 Wave Energy Utilization Mission, 5-12 November, Unpublished.

Rogers B, 1980 The Domestication of Women (London:Tavistock Publications)

Rosewater J, 1965 The Family Tridacnidae in Indo-Pacific. Indo-Pacific Mollusca, 1(6).

Ross D, 1979 Energy From The Waves : The First Ever Book on a Revolution in Technology. Pergamon, New York.

Schoeffel P, 1984 The Fisheries of the South Pacific : Strategies to Assist the Participation of Women in Fish Marketing, Small-Scale Aquaculture and Fish Processing, Regional Summary, Kiribati (Canberra : Australian Development Assistance Bureau

Schoeffel P, 1985 Women in the Fisheries of the South Pacific. In: H Hughes (ed) Women in Development in the South Pacific, (Canberra : Development Studies Centre)

Sewell B, 1983 Butaritari (Canberra : Australian National University)

Shand R T, (ed) 1980 The Island Stages of the Pacific and Indian Oceans ; Anatomy of Development (Canberra : Australian National University)

Sharma U, 1980 Women, Work, and Property in North-West India (London: Tavistock Publications)

Shepard M P and Clark L, 1984 South Pacific Fisheries Development Assistance Needs: Opportunities for Participation by UNDP, FAO and Other Donors Interested in Supporting South Pacific Fisheries Development. FAO/UNDP Project RAS/73/025

Slatyer T, 1985 The New International Law of Fisheries as it Relates to the South Pacific. Honiara: Forum Fisheries Agency

Stirrart R, 1974 Fish to Market: Traders in Rural Sri Lanka South Asia 7(3).

Stirrart R, 1975 The Social Organization of Fishing in a Sinhalese Village Modern Ceylon Studies 6(2).

Suleman, Wiriadjaja and Schenzie, P, 1985 The Indonesia-German Indosail Project, Regional Conference on Sail-Motor Propulsion, Manila.

Sutherland W M, 1985 Regional Co-operation and Fisheries Management in the South Pacific. LLM thesis, University of Hull, UK

Sutherland W M, 1986 Fisheries Management and Coastal State Jurisdiction in the South Pacific. International Journal of Coastal and Estuarine Law, I

Swantz M, 1985 Women in Development : A Creative Role Denied? (London : Hurst) (Canberra:Australian Development Assistance Bureau).

Thompson P, 1985 Women in the Fishing : The Roots of Power Between the Sexes. Comparative Study of Society and History 27(1).

Tisdell C A and Fairbairn I J, 1983 Development problems and planning in a resource-poor Pacific country: The case of Tuvalu, Public Administration and Development, 3

Tisdell C A and Fairbairn I J, 1984 Subsistence economies and unsustainable development and trade: Some simple theory, Journal of Development Studies, 20.

USP Satellite Network Seminar on Wave Power in the South Pacific, 1980, University of the South Pacific, Suva, Fiji.

Uwate K R, Kunatuba P, Raobati B and Tenakanai C, 1984 A Review of Aquaculture Activities in the Pacific Islands Region (Honolulu: Pacific Islands Development Program, East-West Center).

Van Dyke J and Heftel S, 1981 Tuna Management in the Pacific: An Analysis of the South Pacific Forum Fisheries Agency, University of Hawaii Law Review, No.3.

Van Eys S, 1985 The shrimp industry in the Asia/Pacific INFOfish Marketing Digest 1.

Watters R and Banibati K, 1984 Abemama (Canberra : Australian National University)

Wallman S (ed), 1979 Social Anthropology of Work (London Academic Press)

Whyte S, 1985 Eucheuma seaweed farming in Kiribati. Paper 19 South Pacific Commission, Seventeenth Regional, Technical Meeting on Fisheries. Noumea, New Caledonia p7.

Wick G L and Schmitt W R, 1981 Harvesting Ocean Energy. UNESCO Press, Vendome.

INDEX

Abemama Island 94, 96
Algal blooms 131
Alofi 158
American Samoa 5, 12, 15, 17, 20, 154
Andra Island 81
Aneityum 10, 18, 27
Antarctica 4
  Treaty 4
Appropriate Technology 59, 176
  Institute 175
Aquaculture 53-4
  attractions of 53
  clams 54
  molluscs 54
  mussels 54
  oysters 54
Archipelagic baselines
  regimes 7-11
  states 8-9
Atafu 15
Australia ix, 1, 4, 5, 7-8, 12-14, 53, 75, 77, 83, 118-119, 126
Australian Centre for International Agricultural Research (ACIAR) 54, 55, 79-80
Australian Development Assistance Bureau (ADAB) i, 109, 160, 167, 179
Australian Maritime College (Tasmania) 60, 179
Australian National Mapping Agency 117
Avarua 158

Baitfish 34, 56
Banks Island 18
Baselines
  Australia 7-8
  Archipelagic 8-11
Bauxite 118
Beachseining 66
Billfish 35
Biomass 138
Bismarck Sea 119
Blow holes 134
Boats
  aluminium dinghies 51
  canoes 56, 66
  cutters 148, 172
  loss of 51
  owners 66
  plywood 51
Boigu 13
Bougainville Island 5
Boundaries
  international agreements 12
  physical 4-5
  political 5-6
  see also Claims to Maritime Zones
  see also Maritime Boundaries Agreements, Disputes
Bremen 182
Britain 17
Butaritari Island 94, 95, 96

Canada 26
Canning 29,36
  canned fish 58
Canoes 56
  outrigger 66
Capital Development Fund (UNCDF)
  see United Nations
Cargo handling 145
Caribbean 153
Catamarans 51, 56, 70
Ceva-i-Ra 10, 15
Chinese 93
Christian 107-8
Christmas Island 124
Chromite 123
Ciguatera 56
Circum-Pacific Council for Energy and Mineral Resources 119
Claims to Maritime Zones 12
Clams, giant 54
CNEXO (Tahiti) 54
Coal 129, 137, 140
Cobalt-enriched crusts 121
Coconut crab 55

Index

Code of Uniform Marine Standards 183
Committee for Co-ordination of Joint Prospecting for Mineral Resources in South Pacific Offshore Areas (CCOP/SOPAC) 115, 116-21, 124
Conservation methods 30
Container vessel 145
  containerisation 146-7, 158, 159
  containers 149, 157
Convention on the Law of the Sea 1982 (UNCLOS III)
  see United Nations
Convention on the Territorial Sea and Contiguous Zone, 1958 8
Cook Islands 12, 15, 116, 120, 121, 124, 125, 155, 157
Co-operatives 72
Copper 154
Copra 92, 93, 94, 95, 166
Coral
  black 124
  precious 118
Corallium 124
Corrosion 130, 162, 167
Currents 135

Dauan 13
Delimitation of Marine Waters Act 1978 11
Denmark 181
Deuterium 140
Development Fund (UNDP)
  see United Nations
Diesel 165
  engines 137
Driftnetting 65
Droplining techniques 34
Duff 11

Epi Island 27
Erromango Island 27
European Economic Community 141, 157
Explosives 51
Exports 156

Fakakofo 15
Feeder services 175
Fiji, 1, 4, 5, 7, 10-11, 15, 18-19, 27, 29, 35, 36, 37, 49, 52, 53, 55, 56, 75, 80, 83, 84, 85, 116, 119, 122, 124, 153, 154, 155, 176, 183
  cutters 172
  Fisheries Division, Department of Primary Industry 79
  Marine Spaces Chart 81/3 18
Fish
  aggregation devices (FADs) 28, 34, 37, 43, 58
  flying fish 55
  line fishing 107
  traders 66
  traps 51
Fishermen
  Korean 36
  Taiwan 36
  US 28
Food and Agricultural Organization
  see United Nations
Forum Fisheries Agency 33, 38, 42, 45
  Committee 42
  Convention 39, 40
  State 42
France 12, 14, 15, 16, 17, 126, 181
  French Polynesia 5, 154, 155, territory 14
Fraser Island 14
Freezer cargoes 149
Fuel 166
  costs 173
  economy 165-7
Furneaux Island 8
Futuna Island 4, 5, 12, 15, 18

Gas 140
Geneva Convention on the Territorial Sea and Contiguous Zone 1958 8
  see also United Nations

German States 181
Germany, Federal Republic 122, 182
Gilbertese 92
Gold 123
  detrital 118
Guadalcanal 123
Guam 116, 130, 146, 154
Gulbenkian Foundation 108

Hamburg 182
Handicrafts 94
Handreel 57
Hawaii 57, 155
  Institute of Geophysics 119
Heard Island 14
High seas 20
  enclaves 43
Hong Kong 83, 152
Honiara 41, 147, 184
Hook and line 49, 93
  barbless 50
Houtman Abrolhos Group 8
Hunter Island 10, 15, 16, 17-18
Hydrocarbons 125

Ika Corporation 36
Imports 155-6
India 89, 92, 107, 108
Indonesia 12, 16, 168
Institute of Geophysics of Hawaii 119
Inter-island vessels 147
International Agreements on Maritime Boundaries 12
International Centre for Living Aquatic Resources (ICLARM) 79, 105
International Maritime Organization
  see United Nations
International Transport Workers Federation (ITF) 152
International Union for the Conservation of Nature and Natural Resources (IUCN) 74
Iron 123

Islam 101, 107

Japan 28, 50, 83, 119-20, 157

Kadavu Island 146
Kelp 138-9
Kerala 89, 107
Kerguelen Island 14
Kermadec Islands 20
  Ridge 4
Kiribati 1, 4, 37, 49, 51, 55, 89, 91-2, 94, 96, 101, 106, 108, 116, 120, 121, 125, 151, 157, 158, 183
  Overseas Seamen's Union 152
  Te Matauri Limited 36
Konkan coast 106, 107
Korea 28, 152
  fishermen 36

LASH (Lighter aboard ship) 146
Lau 120, 151
Lautoka 147
Line-fishing 65
  long-line hooks 50
  longliner 36, 37
  long lines 56
Line Islands 121
Livestock 149
Logs 157
Lome Convention 141

Macquarie Islands 5, 8
Magnetite 123
  sand 123
Mahimahi 34
Malabar coast 106
Malaita Island 81
Malakida Island 27
Maldives 89, 92, 100, 102, 107
Manganese nodules 115, 118, 120
  economics of 122
  occurrences 120-1
Manihiki 15
Manus 81

Basin 119
Mariculture 74
conditions for 74
giant clams
distribution of 76
growth 182
management of 80-1
status of 75
technology for cultivation 78-9
utilization 77
value 83-4
socio-economic aspects 85-6
Marine Spaces Act 1977 10
spaces (Amendment) Act 1978 10
(Territorial Seas) (Rotuma and its Dependencies) Order 1981 11
Maritime Boundaries Agreements 12
Australia and France 14
Australia and Papua New Guinea 13
France and Tonga 14
Indonesia and Papua New Guinea 16
United States, Cook Islands and Tokelau 15
Maritime Boundaries Disputes 16
Matthew and Hunter Islands 17
Minerva Reef 18
Pocklington Reef 17
Western Samoa and American Samoa 20
Maritime enclaves and corridors 20, 43
Matahiva lagoon 124
Matthew Island, 10, 15, 16, 17-18
Maupiti 9
Medang (PNG) 184
Memorandum of Understanding 117
Merchant companies 147
Merchant Marine Academies 182
Metalliferous sediments 118, 122
Methane 139
Micronesia 30, 47, 77
Federated States of 77
Mariculture Demonstration Center (MMDC) 78, 79, 80, 82
Middle East 102
Minerals, detrital 123
mineralization, deep sea 119
Minerva Reefs 17, 18-20
Republic of 18
Molluscs 54
Mopplahs 107
Motorisation 170
Mullet 53
Muslim 107
Mussels 54

National Fisheries Development Limited 36
National Seas Act 1977 10
Native Land and Fisheries Commission 86
Nauru 124, 130, 154
Nelson Polytechnic, New Zealand) 60
Nets
gill 51, 93
monofilament 55
monofilament nylon netting 51
nylon 71
sennet (coconut fibre) 56
New Britain Trench 119
New Caledonia 4, 5, 7, 12, 14, 15, 17, 124, 151, 154
New Georgia 11
New Guinea
see Papua New Guinea
New Hebrides 17, 18
New Zealand 4, 5, 7, 12, 15, 20, 116, 118, 119, 126, 157, 158
geological survey 117
Nelson Polytechnic 60
Nickel 154
Niue 157, 158

Norfolk 5
Norway 181
Noumea 146, 147
Nuclear 129
Nuffield Foundation ix
Nukumanu Island 10
Nukunonu 15

Ocean Island 124
Ocean thermal energy conversion (OTEC) 129, 131
  corrosion 130
  design of 129-30
Oil 140, 163
  research 119, 126
  seeps 118, 125
Okinawa 75
Ontong Java 9, 11, 77
Organisation of Petroleum Exporting Countries (OPEC) 128, 168
Outrigger canoe 66
Ovalau 29
Oysters 54

Pacific Forum Line 154, 158
Pacific Maritime Standards Code 150
Pago Pago 36, 146
Palau 36, 50, 78, 80
Papua New Guinea 1, 4, 5, 7, 8, 10, 12, 13-14, 16, 17, 20, 35, 49, 56, 116, 119, 122, 124, 125, 140, 147, 153, 154, 155, 157, 183
Pearl-shell lures 50, 56
Penrhyn 15
  Basin 120
People's Republic of China (PRC) 152
Petroleum 119, 155
Pharmaceutical 55
Philippines 77, 79, 80, 83, 152
Phosphates 123, 154
Phosphorite 123-4
Pitcairn Island 5
Poaching 77
Pocklington Reef 16, 17
Pole-and-line 28, 29, 34-5, 37, 44, 66
Polynesian 47, 77
Port 157
  technology 145
Prawns 57
Pukapuka 15
Purse seiners 28, 29, 36-37, 57, 59

Queensland 13, 14

Rakahanga 15
Ranching 81
Rarotonga 158
Redundancy 147
Reef tenure 96
Regional Register of Foreign Fishing Vessels 41
Remittances 94
Rennel Island 11, 118
Research School of Pacific Studies ix, 1
Rewa 146
Riparian rights 56
Rock lobsters 53
RoRo 145
  ferries 148
Rotating hooks 50
Rotuma Group 10
  Island 10
  archipelago 11

Saibai 13
Sails 137
  assisted technology 175-6
  power 166, 168, 173
  technology 137, 177
Salinity Gradients 138
Salter Duck 132
Samoa
  see American
  see Western
Sand and gravel 118, 125
Santa Cruz 11
Santo 36
Savaii 134
Savo Island 81
Scotland 26
SCUBA (Self-contained underwater breathing

apparatus) 53
Sea Transport 145
Seafarers 151
Seaweed 55
farming 95
Sennet(coconut fibre)nets 56
Sharks 53
Shell shops 84
Shipping 137, 145, 148, 153, 160
Ships
"Hakurei Maru No.2" 120
"Kana Keoki" 119
"Machias" 117-118
"Moana Wave" 119
"Natsushima" 119
"Princess Ashika" 149
"SP Lee" 119
Shrimps 57
Snapper 56
Society Islands 9
Solar ponds 139
Solomon Islands 4, 5, 7, 9, 10, 11, 17, 35, 36, 49, 56, 77, 80, 81, 83, 85, 116, 118, 119, 122, 123, 124, 153, 154, 157, 183
arc 119
South Pacific Bureau for Economic Co-operation 41, 141, 153, 184
South Pacific Commission 41
Deep Sea Fisheries Programme of 34, 56
South Pacific Forum 19, 38, 39, 44, 130
Sri Lanka 63, 66, 69, 102
Steam 166
Strikes 147
Sugar 146, 147, 155
Sulphide deposits 122
Suva 146-7, 158, 184
Swains Island 20
Sweden 181

Tabu (taboo) 52, 56
Tahiti 36, 183
CNEXO 54
Taiwan 36, 77, 83
Taiyo Fishing Company 36
Tamana 95
Tamil fishing communities 71
Tana 18, 27
Tarawa 55, 92, 93, 94, 95, 97, 98, 100
Tasmania 7, 120
Tauu Island 10
Teatfish 53
Thorium 140
Tides 134
ranges 132, 134
Tilapia 75
Timber 154
Titanium 123
Tokelau, 5, 12, 15, 20
Tonga 1, 4, 5, 12, 14, 18-20, 36, 44, 51-2, 116, 118, 119, 120, 122, 124, 134, 154, 155, 183
Territorial Sea and Exclusive Economic Zone Act 1978 11, 19
Toredo worm 162
Torres
Islands 18
Strait 5, 8, 13
Treaty 8, 13
Tourists 59, 125, 134
Toxins 51
Trade 153-4
Training 56-7, 60, 117, 152, 160, 167, 179-81
Transportation 125
Trans-shipment 158
Trimarans 51
Trobriand Trough 119
Trolling 65
Truck 149
Trust Territory of the Pacific Islands 20
Tsunamis 1
Tuna 28, 34-37, 47, 50, 56, 99, 102
bait 34, 37, 50
cannery 29, 36, 58
catches 47
fish aggregation device (FAD) 28, 34, 37, 43, 58
longline 36, 37, 50

pole-and-line 28, 29, 34, 37, 44
prices 28
purse seine 28, 29, 36, 37, 57, 59
vessels 28, 56
Tug-and-barge systems 151
Tutuila 20
Tuvalu, 1, 4, 5, 12, 36, 116, 120, 121, 124, 125, 130, 157, 158, 183

Unemployed 147
United Kingdom 17, 181
United Nations 126
Capital Development Fund (UNCDF) 51
Convention on the Law of the Sea 1982 (UNCLOS III) 8, 9, 11, 12, 17, 19, 38, 43, 45, 126
Development Programme (UNDP) 36, 41, 116, 117
Economic and Social Commission for Asia and the Pacific (ESCAP) 116
Educational, Scientific and Cultural Organisation (UNESCO) 24
Food and Agricultural Organisation (FAO) 24, 34, 41, 51, 58, 65, 102
International Maritime Organisation (IMO) 179, 183, 186, Convention on Standards of Training Certification and Watchkeeping for Seafarers (STCW) 150, 184, 186, 187
United States of America 12, 15, 28, 36, 37, 83, 118, 181, 18
Universities
Australian national ix, 1
Guam 78
Haiwaii 119
James Cook 78-9
New Guinea 79
New South Wales 78
Philippines 79
Silliman 79
South Pacific 60, 117
Wellington (Victoria) 117
World Maritime 184, 187
Upwelling 130
Uranium 140

Van Camp 36
Vanuatu 7, 10, 12, 15, 16, 17-18, 26-27, 116, 118, 119, 123, 151, 154, 183
Venice 181
Viti Levu 130, 132

Wallis Island 4, 5, 12, 15
Waves 131
Energy Utilization Mission 134
Western Samoa 5, 17, 20, 56, 116, 125, 132, 154, 183
Whalers 52
Winds 136, 166
Woodlark Island 119
World Maritime University 184, 187